Intellectual Development

ABOUT THE AUTHOR

PANNEER SELVAM is born in Salem - Valappady of Tamil Nadu. He started his career as school teacher in New Delhi in the year 1991. He joins as lecturer in DIET, perundurai of Erode in 2000. Bharathiyar University were gave the Philosophy in Doctorates in Language and Education. He is the seventh diploma holder from National University of Educational Planning and Administration (NUEPA), New Delhi in 2002. In 2005, the Tamil Nadu government was given the 'Excellence Award' for his unrivalled teaching activities and some organization also. He has published more than hundreds of Research Papers and books in the field of Education. At present he is working in the department of Education, Bharathidasan University, Tamil Nadu.

ABOUT THE BOOK

Society is significant medium where certain quality of life and certain types of activity and occupation are provided with the aim of securing child's development based on the social needs. Since is a stem of growth characteristics of teacher trainees should adapt to the society which we live and to which he is expected to adjust and contribute, the social maturity receives importance at the present context. The conduct of many individual in the society tells about the trainees social maturity through which he can respond right according to the teaching situation.

At the present age of competitive world, every human being meets a lot of problems in his daily activities. The root of most of human psychological problems is more socially based that psychologically based. It is in social situation a lack of competence as well as social maturity. So, every human needed knowledge about teaching competence and social maturity for leading a very healthy life in this world.

Intellectual Development

Dr. S.K. Panneer Selvam
Assistant Professor, Department of Education
Bharathidasan University, T.N.,India

AMIGA PRESS INC.

AMIGA PRESS INC.
H.O:- 28-A, Indra Park, St.No-9
Near-Chander Nagar, Krishna Nagar
Delhi: - 110051 (India)
Tel: - 011-22504028, +91-98736-57000
Email: - amigapress@gmail.com
info@amigapress.co.in
amigaeditorial@gmail.com
amigapub@gmail.com

Website: - www.amigapress.co.in

This edition is published by Amiga Press Inc.

ISBN: 978-93-84533-60-1

First Published 2020

Printed and bound in India by Replika Press Pvt. Ltd.

Contents

❑❑❑

1

Attitude of Teacher Educators towards Blended Learning

Education is probably the single most important function of human civilization, not merely the formal education system but the broader question of educating human beings around the world. Recent breakthroughs in communication technology have given us immense possibilities in this regard. According to Don Berg, education is a process of cognitive cartography, mapping our experiences and finding a variety of reliable routes to optimal states when we find ourselves in non-optimal states. A quality education is a learning and personal development programme characterized by processes wherein students are fully engaged resulting in value added student outcomes.

The central task of education is to implant a will and facility for learning; it should produce not learned but learning people. The truly human society is a learning society, where grandparents, parents, and children are students together. No one has yet realized the wealth of sympathy, the kindness and generosity hidden in the soul of a child. The effort of every true education should be to unlock that treasure. The only purpose of education is to teach a student how to live the life by developing the mind and equipping to deal with reality.

The aim of education should be to teach us rather how to think, than what to think rather to improve our minds, so as to enable us to think for ourselves, than to load the memory with the thoughts of other men. The one real object of education is to leave a man in the condition of continually asking questions. The central job of educational institutions is to maximize the capacity of each student.

NEW WAYS OF LEARNING WITH TECHNOLOGY

In this information age, it is inevitable to witness technology use in educational settings. Teachers working in educational environments show great efforts to provide students with information by using effective technology based methods. Parallel to these efforts, students become more qualified. In this way, students are supposed to be Internet literate or computer literate to obtain the information they need. Students can reach the necessary information not in traditional classrooms – used since Aristotle – but in their houses and even on holiday. In other words, with the use of educational technologies, learning becomes constant. Thus, most schools in developed or developing countries try to adapt their education systems to communication technologies. Therefore, educational technologies are used effectively by instructors in educational settings and will continue to be used in future as well since the moment information and communication technologies were used for the first time, there have been great developments in this field.

Major advances in the fields of cognitive psychology and neuroscience have significantly impacted the educational landscape. The convergence of these disciplines with technology is increasing at a fast pace, and it is affecting academia and their professional practice in many ways. The emergence of the Internet as a mainstream communication medium has resulted in the development of new educational opportunities, such as instruction delivered via asynchronous learning networks, synchronous online seminars, blogs, wikis, podcasts, etc. Internet-based tools can facilitate communication, interaction and collaborative learning in ways that were not possible before (The Node, 2001). Paradigms such as just-in-time learning, constructivism, student-centered learning and collaborative approaches have emerged and are being supported by technological advancements such as simulations, and virtual reality. As a result, the higher education landscape is changing from the de-emphasis on the delivery of instruction and the concurrent emphasis on the facilitation of student learning, to the use of technology to expand access and participation in education, and to the recognition of the importance of collaborative learning through communities of learners. These developments have created both opportunities and areas of serious concerns around supporting pedagogies in the digital age.

BLENDED LEARNING

Blended learning or hybrid learning describes a learning environment that either combines teaching methods, delivery methods, media formats or a mixture of all these. It also refers to the integrated learning activities such as a mixture of online and face-to-face learning. In other words, Blended learning is a mixture of e-learning and traditional types of learning. It is mentioned as the integrated combination of traditional learning with web-based online approaches, the combination of media and tools deployed in an e-learning environment and the combination of a number of pedagogical approaches. Elaborated Blended learning as a set of learning strategies or dimensions that mixes various event-based activities, including traditional instructor-led training, synchronous online conferencing or training and asynchronous self-paced study. Among the benefits of blended learning reported by recent research were provide students with more control over learning.

Like many advances in educational practice, blended learning is defined and implemented in multiple ways. As more and more schools use this model, many different meanings have evolved. for INACOL, the International Association for K-12 Online Learning, defines blended learning as "combining online delivery of educational content with the best features of classroom interaction and live instruction to personalize learning, allow thoughtful reflection, and differentiate instruction from student-to-student across a diverse group of learners." In a similar vein, the Sloan Consortium, an institutional and professional. leadership organization dedicated to integrating online education into mainstream education, describes blended learning as part online and part traditional face-to-face instruction. San Diego State University also offers an interesting perspective on blended learning. In the university online Encyclopedia of Educational Technology, the article Blended Learning Solutions notes, "blended learning combines the engaging benefits of traditional instructor-led training with the advantages brought by a variety of technologies to create an optimum program". The article also underscores that many "ingredients" can comprise a blended learning model, including instructor-delivered content, e-learning, webinars, conference calls, live or online sessions with instructors, and other media and events. Blended learning is broadly defined as an instructional practice that combines teaching methods from both face-to-face instruction and online learning. Blended learning has increased the possible ways learners can acquire knowledge, with learning occurring across different mediums and various times.

THE CONCEPT OF BLENDED LEARNING

Sharma and Barrett, Starting with an overview of the existing definitions of blended learning and building upon such methodological aspects as a combination of online and in-person learning, a mixture of face-to-face and distance learning as well as the incorporation of various ICT technologies and e-learning platforms, Sharma and Barrett generalize their understanding of blended learning as the learning processes where learners meet with a teacher for a face-to-face instruction. The term blended learning is applicable to a variety of teaching and learning situations and pertinent to a broad range of combinations with regard to face-to-face and computer - mediated teaching and learning.

CHARACTERISTICS OF BLENDED LEARNING

- High priority attached to student learning and pedagogical needs when considering and applying blended learning approaches.
- Strategic and systematic use of technology in association with a quality face-to-face environment to support student learning.
- Enhancement and ultimate transformation of existing learning and teaching processes.
- Flexibility in terms of implementation at the program and course levels.
- Accommodation of diversity in student learning experiences.
- Encouragement and nurturing of innovation among students and staff.
- Enhanced interaction between students, staff, peers and the community.
- Increased capacity for student-managed learning.
- Learning that takes place at students' discretion in terms of time and place.
- Enriched opportunities for work-integrated learning activities.
- Enhanced research–teaching linkages.
- Creation of collaborative distributed learning environments.
- A professional team approach to course design, delivery and evaluation.
- Targeted professional development, including resources to support blended learning curriculum design and requisite technical skills acquisition.

MODELS OF BLENDED LEARNING

Model 1: Face-to-Face Driver

The programs that fit in the face-to-face-driver category all retain face-to-face teachers to deliver most of their curricula. The physical teacher deploys online learning on a case-by-case basis to supplement or remediate, often in the back of the classroom or in a technology lab.

Model 2: Rotation

The common feature in the rotation model is that, within a given course, students rotate on a fixed schedule between learning online in a one-to-one, self-paced environment and sitting in a classroom with a traditional face-to-face teacher. It is the model most in between the traditional face-to-face classroom and online learning because it involves a split between the two and, in some cases, between remote and onsite. The face-to-face teacher usually oversees the online work.

Model 3: Flex

Programs with a flex model feature an online platform that delivers most of the curricula. Teachers provide on-site support on a flexible and adaptive as-needed basis through in-person tutoring sessions and small group sessions. Many dropout- recovery and credit-recovery blended programs fit into this model.

Model 4: Online Lab

The online-lab model characterizes programs that rely on an online platform to deliver the entire course but in a brick-and-mortar lab environment. Usually these programs provide online teachers. Paraprofessionals supervise, but offer little content expertise. Often students that participate in an online-lab program also take traditional courses and have typical block schedules.

Model 5: Self-Blend

The nearly ubiquitous version of blended learning among American high schools is the self-blend model, which encompasses any time students choose to take one or more courses online to supplement their traditional school's catalog. The online learning is always remote, which distinguishes it from the online-lab model, but the traditional learning is in a brick-and-mortar school. All supplemental online schools that offer courses to individual students for facilitate self-blending.

Model 6: Online Driver

The online-driver model involves an online platform and teacher that deliver all curricula. Students work remotely for the most part. Face-to-face check-ins are sometimes optional and other times required. Some of these programs offer brick and-mortar components as well, such as extracurricular activities.

COMPARISON OF TRADITIONAL AND BLENDED LEARNING ENVIRONMENTS

TABLE. 1.1: Comparison of Traditional and Blended Learning Environments

Traditional Learning Environments	Blended Learning Environments
Instructivist	Shift in focus to the constructivist pedagogical philosophy
Behaviourist	Shift in focus to the cognitivist learning theory Teacher-centered instruction Student-centered learning
Single-sense stimulation	Multi-sense stimulation; Access and exchange information in a variety of ways
Single-path progression	Multi-path progression
Single medium	Multimedia
Isolated work	Collaborative work
Information delivery	Information exchange
Passive learning	Active/exploratory/inquiry-based learning
Factual, knowledge-based learning	Critical thinking and informed decision-making
Reactive response	Proactive/planned action
Isolated, artificial context	Authentic, real-world context

CRITERIA FOR DEVELOPING BLENDED LEARNING

Components are the elements that can be pieced together and integrated into a blended solution. Criteria are the principles and policies, which shape the choice of components in a blended solution. Six criteria's:

Learning
Maintenance
Resources
Learners
Scalability
Sustainability

Learning

A considerable amount of work has been produced by cognitive psychologists over the last 50 years. These include Bloom, Gagne, Mager, Belbin, Bruner, Biggs and Collins, Pedler, Merriam and Caffarella. In practice the schemas produced by these authors are very similar, resulting in the following general categories: Knowledge, Procedural skills,Interpersonal skills, psychomotor skills, Attitudes and Aspirational learning. Procedural skills involve following processes or routines from memory, manuals or computers. Knowledge of a range of procedures is required and learners appreciate the significance of the parts in relation to the whole. It may be expected to apply demonstrate, calculate, complete, solve, modify, relate, classify or find. Mental skills involve the application of methods and theories in new situations; solve problems using required skills or knowledge. Problem solving is demonstrated by coming up with effective solutions. Interpersonal skills have been increasingly recognized as a distinct skill set in themselves, along with emotional intelligence. These are skills in listening, questioning, presenting, interviewing, counseling, appraising and so on. Writing skills, telephone skills and electronic communication skills using email etc are also included.

Learners

To understand blended learning we must focus on learners. Learners blend anyway. They'll learn through lots of different learning encounters. In learning a language the leaner is likely to take some classes, use online resources, CD-ROMs, audio cassettes, audio CDs, videos watch TV, listen to radio programmes in that language, use books, access dictionaries, get a pen-pal, speak to native speakers, even go to that country for practice. Blended learning was always the norm-for learners.

- The learner population has to be profiled, including
- Number of learners
- Geographic dispersion of learners
- Available time by learners
- Learner's motivation to learn
- Novices versus experts
- Academic versus non-academic

Maintenance

Different types of content need different levels of maintenance. Non-volatile factual content such as basic science may need little or no updating. Middle ground content such as management skills may need a modest amount updates. However, induction, product knowledge, legislative issues and many other topics will need major updates.

Scalability

Scalability is the ability of a delivery mechanism to cope with large members, on-demand at little incremental cost. Scalability is usually achieved through technology. A hand written letter can be scaled through word-processing, photocopying, printing and ultimately, the most scalable of all, email, where huge members can be delivered instantly, on demand and at a tiny incremental cost. The classroom is only scalable in the sense of having more people in the room at any one time. A good example, would be a conference with thousands of people seeing a keynote speech by an experts..

Sustainability

The sustainability of your blend will make the difference between short and long-term success. Cultural resistance is usually the major obstacle to change and if you exist in a culture where change difficult, newer components may be difficult to implement. At one level sustainability will depend on cultural issues and change management may be needed. On another level, sustainability will depend on the ability of your blend to support an ongoing learning culture within the organization.

Resources

Whatever may be the intentions in blended learning, if you don't have the human, organizational, technical and fiscal resources, you're bound to fail. The type of blend you want may be different from the blend you can deliver.

CHALLENGES TO BLENDED LEARNING

The common challenges and mistakes are:

- Administrative challenges (e.g., absence of a visionary leadership, lack of awareness, policies, plans, goals, support and implementation plans related to blended learning).
- Lack of faculty preparedness and quality assurance systems in place.
- Technical barriers: lack of appropriate infrastructure and inadequate technical support to students and tutors.
- Lack of expertise in technology; Professional development is an important part of successful educational technology implementation.
- Lack of skills in time and workload management.
- Lack of understanding of the term 'blended learning' itself, and their lack of expertise in deciding the optimal blended learning approach appropriate in their own context.
- Lack of alignment of blended learning philosophy with institutional goals and priorities.
- Resistance to organizational change.
- Tutors' concerns about losing control over the course; Lack of certain critical skills among some students.

BLENDED LEARNING IN SCHOOL EDUCATION

Blended Learning in School Education provides a vision and a roadmap for School students to understand the content in blending face-to-face and online learning for engaging and meaningful learning experiences as like play way method. Blended Learning provides an organizing framework to guide the exploration and understanding of the principles and practices needed to effect the much needed transformational changes in School education. It also provides practical examples in childhood itself and organizational support structures required to fuse a range of face-to-face and online learning to meet the quality challenges and serve disciplinary goals effectively and efficiently for their future Higher Education.

The Teachers in School Education using creativity in the classroom to create interest among the students. Creativity makes a huge difference. Creativity is vital for a classroom to be successful. There is a common misconception that the word "creative" has to do mostly with the arts. But being artistic is only a small part of creativity. While any classroom environment would benefit from a teacher blessed with the gift of artistic talent, creativity is many other things.

BLENDED LEARNING IN HIGHER EDUCATION

Today's world is moving at a very rapid pace. The teacher's role, the student's role and the acquired knowledge are essential components in assessing the effectiveness of blended learning. A former Vice Chancellor of Information Technology suggests that instead, blended learning should be viewed as an opportunity to redesign the way that courses are developed, scheduled and delivered in higher education through a combination of physical and virtual instruction, "bricks and clicks".

Learning and learner

There are two key players in the process of learning: the student and the teacher. In secondary schools in Singapore, students study additional subjects such as Geography, History, Literature, Home Economics, the Sciences, Citizenship Education and other specialized subjects available in certain schools. Degree education, Diploma education, masters and PhD research education are components of a tertiary education which holds high stakes in country's economic resource and development.

The interest of students' will be more aroused through the use of Information technology in the classroom because it has already been integrated as a part of their everyday lives through the technological appliances such as Mobile Phones, TV, Computers, the medium of the internet and prominent social networking and media sites. Suiting technology to education goals and standards in Higher Education. Having a vision for the use of technology to support curriculum.

Information and Communication Technology

Teaching higher educational students to assess their transfer of theoretical knowledge from online and face to face teaching is an interesting task. Here students are more effective in transferring their theoretical knowledge from online teaching towards a multimedia project than from face to face teaching

(Demirer and Sahin, 2013). Online teaching is a boon to today's educators as they could spend class hours to interact and discuss with their students without much hassle. Flipping the classroom is one approach to try to maximize the face to face interaction among the students and teachers.

The historical ideal of higher education has been to learn in collaborative communities of inquiry. The key is to redesign in an active and collaborative learning experiences that enable students to take responsibility for their learning and validate their understanding through discourse and debate with their peers. Blended Learning in Higher Education provides a vision and a roadmap for higher education students to understand the possibilities of organically blending face-to-face and online learning for engaging and meaningful learning experiences. Blended Learning provides an organizing framework to guide the exploration and understanding of the principles and practices needed to effect the much needed transformational changes in higher education. It also provides practical examples and organizational support structures required to fuse a range of face-to-face and online learning to meet the quality challenges and serve disciplinary goals effectively and efficiently.

The transformation of teaching and learning in higher education is inevitable with the use of Web-based communications technology (Newman, Couturier & Scurry, 2004). Fundamental redesign based on blended approaches to teaching and learning represent the means of address the challenges associated with providing a quality of learning experience. Although the catalyst for change in teaching and learning has been technology, it is the need to enhance quality standards that is drawing attention to the potential of blended approaches. Technology is an enabling tool. Because blended learning is an approach and design that merges the best of traditional and Web-based learning experiences to create and sustain vital communities of inquiry, many higher education institutions are quietly positioning themselves to harness its transformational potential.

Blended learning for Higher Education Learners will be:

- Highly interactive with practice exercises and activities.
- Less expensive, more flexible and more effective.
- Meeting the learner's expectations for utilizing technology in learning skills.
- Developing independent learning skills.
- Offering increased flexibility and convenience.
- Providing better success to those with learning difficulty.
- Enhancing technical savvy.

BLENDED LEARNING IN TEACHER EDUCATION

Blended learning develops individuals learning skills, meets their requirements for using technology, affords flexibility and convenience, provides access to those with job, family, distance barriers and reduces the educational cost for the students by the teacher. Blended Learning in Teacher Education approach combines face to face classroom methods. A thoughtfully designed integration of live and online methods in the post digital materials and methods in the post digital materials have served in a supplementary role helping to support face to face instruction for students of all ages and levels of learning. The best aspects of online instruction students in advance interactive experiences. Meanwhile the online portion of the course can provide students with multimedia rich content at any time of day anywhere the students has internet access from computer labs.

The Blended Learning approach used consists of face to face instruction. A Blended Learning should describe a planned and deliberate educational activity that integrate students-centered learning classroom based teaching and learning based on individual learners and their specific needs.

Blended learning Teacher

The effective educator within the blended learning environment there are factors beyond that of the traditional school setting. Through blended learning models the role of the teacher has shifted as with the role of the learner. Content can be accessed independently; investigation and depth of understanding can be found divergent of the teachers influence. Both teachers and students must begin to understand how they play these new roles in learning prior to it becoming effective in the learning environment. The best way to expedite this transition is the development of process focused learning..To develop the independence and define the new roles of the teacher and student we have developed a instructional process flowchart. This allows the teacher to focus their attention of the micro groupings of students within the classroom to build and refine the skills that will be used throughout the lessons development.

The teacher, rather than the giver of knowledge has shifted to become the learner, being taught not only the objectives of the lesson but also the meta-cognitive components of the individualized learning process the student went through to reach the outcomes that they present. The student has been pushed to the highest order of thinking skills and has developed a true depth of understanding in the learning process, all as the teacher has played the role of educational support-the cheerleader of learning for each individual student.

When blended learning occurs ssin classrooms where technology is limited, students may learn mostly through face-to-face lessons, but use computers or other devices to complete group assignments or submit completed work to their teachers.

SIGNIFICANCE OF THE PRESENT STUDY

Blended Learning is an engaging multidisciplinary approach to teaching and learning that encourages learners to leverage the technology they use in their daily lives to solve real-world problems. Challenge Based innovative Learning is collaborative and hands-on, asking students to work with peers, teachers, and experts in their communities and around the world to ask good questions, develop deep subject area knowledge, identify and solve challenges, take action, and share their experience.

The present Teacher trainees are future teachers. In future, they are going to implement blended learning approach in the classroom climate. So, the investigator undertook the present study on attitude of teacher educators towards blended learning.

CONCLUTION

The first chapter deals with introduction and importance of blended learning. The conceptual frame work of the present study given in the next chapter.

❐

2

Conceptual Frame Work

NEED AND IMPORTANCE OF EDUCATION

Education is vital to the human resources development and empowerment in the stages of growth of a nation. In any education system, higher education encompassing management, engineering, medicines etc., plays a major role in imparting knowledge, values, and developing skills and, in the process, increase the growth and productivity of the nation. While the Government is committed to providing primary education and certain facilities for higher education, given the higher cost involved in the establishment of higher education institutes, we are witnessing the entry of private sector to run educational institutions. On the need for education, Mahatma Gandhi said that education not only molds the new generation, but reflects a society's fundamental assumptions about itself and the individuals which compose it. While discussing the importance of education, schools have become the most important means of transforming wealth of knowledge and skills from one generation to another. However, the role of institutions becomes more challenging in the modern world with innovations and technological developments. Investment in education and educational institutions should be viewed as an investment for economic prosperity.

PRINCIPLES OF BLENDED LEARNING APPROACH

Learning technologies can contribute to the creation of a dynamic teaching and learning environment, supporting interaction among distributed communities and increase student access to resources, experiences and expertise. In this context, learning technologies will be used to enhance student opportunities and provide flexibility and learner choice, therefore blended approaches that combine face-to-face and technology supported learning will be emphasized. Our use of technologies will support student and staff interaction. The University will identify preferred learning technologies such as video streaming, podcasting and social networking tools which will be supported through staff development and training and appropriately resourced technical support. All learning technologies will be selected on the basis of their capacity to support effective teaching and student learning, and their adoption and use will be guided by our commitment to student learning.

1. Assist students in learning how to use technologies effectively.
2. Create learning experiences that would otherwise be difficult to provide.
3. Enhance the nature and scope of learning experiences.
4. Enrich the campus experience for students.
5. Facilitate leading practice and innovative approaches to learning and teaching.
6. Increase access to resources that support learning.
7. Provide flexibility of provision to support a diverse student population.
8. Meet student expectations about appropriate uses of technologies to support learning and Engagement.
10. Provide increased flexibility for staff and students.
11. Support collaboration and communication between staff and students, and among students.

BLENDED LEARNING

Blended learning refers to a mixing of different learning environment. The phrase has many specific meanings based upon the context in which it is used. Blended learning gives learners and teachers a potential environment to learn and teach more effectively. A blended learning program uses a combination of e – learning and classroom instruction.

Whether a course should be proposed as a face – to – face interaction, an online course or a blended course depends on the analysis of the components at stake, the nature and location of the audience, and the resources available. Depending on the cross – analysis of these 3 parameters, the course designer will opt for one of the 3 options. In his course scenario he / she will then have to decide which parts are online, which parts are offline? A basic example of this is a course of English as a second language where the instructor reaches the conclusion that all audio – based activities (listening comprehension, oral expression) will take place in the classroom where all text – based activities will take place online (reading comprehension, essays writing).

Blended learning increases the options for greater quality and quantity of human interaction in a learning environment. Blended learning offers the opportunity "to be both together and apart." A community of learners can interact at anytime and anywhere because of the benefits that computer – mediated education tools provide. Blended learning provides a 'good' mix of technologies and interactions, resulting in a socially supported, constructive, learning experience; this is especially significant given the profound effect it could have on distance learning.

FORMAT OF BLENDED LEARNING

When choosing to explore blended learning as a course format, there are several dimensions to course planning and development that should be considered:

Technology

Just like online courses, hybrid/blended courses are dependent on several technologies to function. These can include;

- Learning management system
- Digital libraries
- Mobile technologies
- Streaming audio and/or video media
- Reusable learning objects and materials

Integration

Online materials are central to a blended course's success, and the students' work online must be relevant to the in – class activities. Aycock, Garnham, & Kaleta (2002) at the university of Wisconsin's blended learning effort revealed the importance of integration:

"The project's participants emphasized this point repeatedly. When asked, 'What would I do differently?' they were united in their response: 'I'd devote more attention to integrating what was going on in the classroom with the online work.' This was true even though the project's faculty development sessions repeatedly emphasized the importance of connecting in – class material with out – of – class assignments. One instructor responded emphatically, 'Integrate online with face – to – face and online learning too much." Students can be critical of blended instruction if they felt the face – to –face and time – out – of –class components of the course were not well integrated.

Organization

For the most part, the blended format will be new to students, and they will benefit greatly from a clear rationale for its use. Instructors may need to explain the model and why it was chosen. A carefully constructed syllabus can provide much of the information about course structure for students; information like when and where the face – to –face meetings will be held, when and how assignments should be submitted, and what exactly will occur during the class meeting times are all critical aspects of course that may not be obvious to those students new to blended learning.

Interaction

Research indicates that student satisfaction with the blended format is highly dependent on the level of interaction with instructors and other students. Instructors can address interaction issues by providing time during the face to face sessions for discussion, in addition to using available online discussion tools such as ANGLE discussion forums.

Student Expectations

Blended learning students require a greater ability to regulate their work and manage their own time. This is because they have fewer in – class meeting, and thus may realize that they are falling behind in the course. Many blended instructors report significant problems with students not taking responsibility for their courses and with students' poor time management skills.

In addition, some instructors have found that students occasionally assume that online and blended courses are inherently "easier" than traditional face – to –face courses. This can create problems when the rigors of the course surpass the expectations of some students. Again, a well – constructed syllabus can provide the essential details on what expected of students, thereby mitigating possible confusion on the part of students.

ROLE OF INSTRUCTOR BLENDED LEARNING

The instructor can combine two or more methods of teaching method. A typical example of blended learning methodology would be a combination of technology – based materials and face – to –face sessions to present content. An instructor can being a course with a well – structured introductory lesson in the classroom, and then proceed with follow – up materials online. Blended learning can also be applied to the integration of e –learning with a learning management system using computers in a physical classroom, along with face – to –face instruction guidance is suggested early in the process, to be used more sparingly as learners gain expertise

The role of the instructor is critical as this requires a transformation process to that of learning facilitator. Quite often, with the increase of baby boomers going back to school and pursuing higher education the skills require for technology use are limited. Instructors then find themselves more in the role of assisting students with computer skills and applications, helping them access the internet, and encouraging them to be independent learners. Blended learning takes time for both instructor and learner to adapt to this relatively new instructional concept.

BLENDED LEARNING: A GROWING NEED

Take a snapshot of a day in the life of America's schools and the picture will show students and educators grappling with a host of challenges and presented with a kaleidoscope of remarkable new learning opportunities. From unprecedented budget pressures and over-burdened teachers to the need for more effective, more personalized learning to accommodate each student's individual learning style, schools are facing complex issues. The opportunities are enormous as well. Whether it is tapping the vast stores of digital information now available or using new technology tools to learn, teachers and students alike have the opportunity to move the learning experience forward in new ways. Today's digital native students expect their learning environment to include technology because it is an intrinsic part of their lives. The publication Learning in the 21st Century: 2009 Trends Update1 offers these important data points:

Students want control of their own learning. When asked why learning through an online class might make school more interesting, 47 percent of students in grades 9-12, 39 percent of students in grade 6-8 and 25 percent of students in grades 3-5 responded that they wanted to learn online to control their own learning experience. Students do not expect online courses to be easier. They do however, expect the online learning environment to facilitate their success because they can review materials when they want and are more comfortable asking teachers for help. Online teachers see great benefits to student online learning. 76 percent of educators believe that online learning benefits students by putting them in control of their own learning.

Blended learning, which typically extends classroom instruction online, is giving schools new approaches and strategies for addressing the challenges they face and for taking advantage of the exciting new learning opportunities that are now available. More and more schools and districts of all sizes are introducing blended learning into their instructional programs and they are discovering that this model is effective, affordable, and responds to students' and teachers' growing interest in technology based learning experiences.

WHY A BLENDED LEARNING IS EFFECTIVE?

Two of the reasons for employing a blended approach that are given above are improved learning effectiveness and cost effectiveness, but how effective really is blended learning? And in what ways is it effective? According to Dewar and Whittington (2004: 5) there is a good deal less literature on the effectiveness of blended learning than there is defining it and suggesting how to implement it. They state that 'There is some anecdotal evidence about how well participants liked blended learning and many articles outlining the costs saving associated with integrating technology. There is also a growing literature base about the learning outcomes achieved through using various types of technology. The biggest challenge is finding studies that specifically address blended learning, as opposed to the use of technology alone.'

In the context of higher education, Dziuban et al. (2004: 5) found that their blended learning courses had 'the potential to increase student learning outcomes while lowering attrition rates in comparison with equivalent fully online courses' and that blended learning results 'in success and attrition rates were comparable to the face-to-face modality for all ethnicities.' A study conducted by Harker and Koutsantoni (2005: 197) also found that 'the blended learning mode was much more effective in student retention' than the distance learning mode on their English for Academic Purposes (EAP) programme, 'whilst students' achievement levels were similar in both groups' as were their satisfaction rates.

A number of studies investigate learners' attitudes towards blended learning. Leakey and Ranchoux (2006: 367) found that 'the students in large measure found the blended experience a positive and motivating one and tended towards preferring this approach to the traditional classroom based learning.' Brett's (1996) results showed 'strongly favorable attitudes; that learners believed they could learn effectively from multimedia and that it delivered a high quality independent learning experience.'

Lin (2003: 1) also found that the majority of Taiwanese learners 'had a positive attitude towards the use of multimedia resources in their language programme, appreciating, in particular, opportunities to practice and extend their language abilities by surfing the internet, to take laboratory-based listening tests via a test analyzer, and to record and save their own writing and to make use of multimedia resources for developing their reading skills'. In response to the question 'Is the TELL [technology-enhanced language learning] course an effective curricular design for achieving second language development?' Adair-Hauck et al. (1999: 293) found that 'after carefully monitoring and assessing language skills in listening, speaking, writing and cultural knowledge, we recognize that the TELL course was indeed effective in helping our students learn French. Its strength in this particular instructional context appeared to be in writing and its weakness in speaking.' Contrary to their findings regarding speaking, Banados's (2006: 542-543) results indicated 'a remarkable improvement in speaking skills' in addition to 'important improvements in all the skills, especially in listening, pronunciation, vocabulary and grammar' in a study carried out with students on an English programme in a Chilean University. Little more appears to have been published on the effectiveness of blended learning since Dewar and Whittington (2004) noted the lack of literature on the subject.

A number of studies have been conducted on learners' attitudes, concluding that they are positive towards the integration of multimedia. At tertiary level evidence indicates that blended learning may improve student retention rates. However, there is little evidence available to suggest that blended learning is pedagogically effective even though 'improved pedagogy' is often cited as a reason for blending. This leaves questioning if this is a primary consideration for many of the educational providers for adopting a blended approach especially at tertiary level and may be increasingly so in the learning sector, or if flexibility and cost, to provide a competitive edge in a global market, are the real drivers for change. Clearly more studies to investigate the pedagogical effectiveness of blended learning in teaching are required that provide us with empirical rather than impressionistic evidence in its favor. However, Salaberry (2001: 52) cautions that 'a healthy dose of scepticism about the pedagogical effectiveness of many current technological tools appears to be well justified if one considers the perhaps overly enthusiastic reaction to previous technological breakthroughs' such as language labs, cassette recorders, and computer-assisted instruction.

According to Dewar and Whittington (2004) differences have been identified as to why the corporate sector and academic sector introduced blended learning solutions. For the corporate sector the results from an online survey reported by Sparrow in Dewar and Whittington (2004: 5) list the following reasons: ability to match learning styles (80 per cent); individually tailored solutions (70 per cent); improve the learning rate (62 per cent); exploit the investments they have already made in re-usable training resources (59 per cent); shortage of time to use purely classroom events (57 per cent). They do not elaborate on the content of this list, nor provide evidence that any of the reasons given are actually valid and not purely assumptions, for example improving the learning rate. There are commonalities between the above list and that of Singh and Reed (2001). They identified four benefits to using a blended learning solution a couple of years before the above study was conducted, which were: improved learning effectiveness; extending the reach; optimizing development cost and time; optimizing business results (reduces travel costs and learning objectives are obtained quicker). Sharma and Barrett (2007) also refer to the cost-saving element of blended learning with reference to the business world, as work time is not sacrificed for training and furthermore travel costs are negated. In addition to cost savings they also emphasize the 'convenience' of blended learning courses as students can study when they want, at the speed they want. It would appear that cost saving was an important driver for change in the move towards blended learning in the business world and we will see the same is also true in the academic sector.

With regard to the academic sector both Dewar and Whittington (2004) and Graham (2004) cite Osguthorpe and Graham's (2003) six suggested reasons: pedagogical richness; access to knowledge; social interaction; personal agency (i.e. learner control and choice); cost effectiveness; and ease of revision. Interestingly the term 'pedagogical richness' is used rather than 'pedagogical effectiveness'. Presumably what is meant by the phrase is the variety of different pedagogical approaches that can be incorporated in a blend, rather than if they are effective or not.

Marsh et al.(2003) also mention the use of a blended learning solution to reduce costs in higher education, as well as improving the teaching of large groups. Likewise, MacDonald (2006: 22) refers to ever expanding classroom numbers as well as 'changes in student demography ...a growth in part-time study' as reasons for incorporating 'online media'. Sharpe et al. (2006) found from their review of blended e-learning in the tertiary sector that 'although the rationales for blended e-learning were highly contextualized and specific to each institution they included: flexibility of provision, supporting diversity, enhancing the campus experience, operating in a global context and efficiency'.

Nicolson et al. (2011) reiterate Sharpe et al.'s (2006) findings regarding flexibility as they claim that, in a UK context in particular, there is a demand for flexible learning opportunities that has been driven by social, cultural, economic and political changes. Graham (2004:7) and Graham et al., as quoted in Stracke (2007:59), have condensed these lists down to three main reasons in higher education which are: improved pedagogy; increased access/flexibility; and increased cost effectiveness. Improved pedagogy is often cited as a reason for implementing a blended learning approach yet most authors do not expand on the subject. Indeed the phrase 'pedagogy before technology' (Beetham and Sharpe, 2007:3) has been used by some reflective practitioners to stress the need to adopt technology for pedagogical reasons and because it adds value to the teaching rather than simply as an add-on.

Improved pedagogy is also claimed with reference to blended learning in although once again little appears to have been written on the subject apart from such general statements as: 'blended learning seeks to combine the best of the taught element of a course with the benefits of technology, so that, the argument goes, better learning outcomes can be achieved' (Sharma, 2007). In a different publication Sharma and Barrett (2007:7) are slightly more explicit and say 'we will assume that you have decided to incorporate technology into a language course for a pedagogical reason, and by doing so, you are adding value to the teaching'.

BENEFITS OF BLENDED LEARNING

Learning requires some soot of experience to the place in learning environment which may be quite different for each learner in that we have to conceder different in Banathy (1968).The some of the importance's of Blended Learning are

- Great potential for improving the teaching – learning process.
- Learning system that combine face – to – face instruction with computer mediated instruction.
- Ability to recollect, recall and apply the skill at appropriate time and place.
- Develops classroom interaction depends heavily on instructional strategies.
- Combines different learning methods, something as supplement classroom discussion, face – to – face learning and just as reading, writing, speaking and listening can be used together in one lesson.
- Represents a grater change in basic technique as traditional classroom methods and independent study to create new, a hybrid methodology.
- Helps to make a strong match to the values of Teacher – Education.
- Enhances and personalizes interactions between teacher and student and student and student in an innovative way.
- Helps a student learns at least in past through delivery of content and interaction via digital and online media and some other sources.
- Develops learning skills, needs their requirements for using technology, affords flexibility and convenience, provides access to those with job, family, distance barriers and reduces educational cost for students.
- Helps the students to study the scheduled class sessions in an assigned independent study via online.
- Incorporate online opportunities and online learning process for learners.
- Affective integration of different modes of delivery, modes of teaching and styles in various aspects.

- Improve the quality of the individualized learning experiences for all learners.
- Lead to increase personalization with individual pacing and will free up to make interactions with their teachers more effective and meaningful.
- Acquire knowledge with learning occurring across different medium and various time.
- Increase access and flexibility for learners, increase level of active learning and achieve better student experiences and outcomes.
- Relate to media used for social networking and communication.
- Online learning resources with classroom training or mixing the use of a self-faced work book with one-to-one coaching.
- Emerged as an alternative to the instructor led training.
- Blended learning enables the teachers and students to understanding the subject matter vividly. Worldwide there has been a strong push to get educational technology into the hands of teachers and students – yet it remains a reality that most teachers across the world continue to struggle with their day to day challenges in classrooms and remain completely un – impacted by technology even today. The primary reason for this is that most technology integration initiatives developed for schools ignore to look at the specific pain areas and real life challenges that teachers experience in classrooms. There is much talk nowadays about the need for blended learning in day today life. The development of vision, character, and competence in our young people is necessary to allow our nation to continue its role of world leader into the 21st century. Therefore, the study of blended learning provides a better platform to develop our young generation. Hence, the present study is a high need and importance of the hour.

NEED AND IMPORTANCE OF THE STUDY

Blended learning enables the teachers and students to understand the subject matter vividly. Worldwide there has been a strong push to get educational technology into the hands of teachers and students – yet it remains a reality that most teachers across the world continue to struggle with their day to day challenges in classrooms and remain completely un-impacted by technology even today. The primary reason for this is that most technology integration initiatives developed for schools ignore to look at the specific pain areas and real life challenges that teachers experience in classrooms. There is much talk nowadays about the need for blended learning in day today life. The development of vision, character, and competence in our young people is necessary to allow our nation to continue its role of world leader into the 21st century.

Therefore, the study of blended learning provides a better platform to develop our young generation. Hence, the present study is a high need and importance of the hour.

CONCLUTION

Based on the above observation, the blended learning approach plays a vital role in quality teaching and learning. So, the investigator selected the present topic on attitude of teacher educators towards blended learning.

3

Review of Related Literature

Research in education is no better than the information upon which it is based. Review of the related literature allows the researcher to acquaint himself with current knowledge in the field in which he is going to conduct the research. It helps the researcher to know about the tools and instruments which provide to be useful and professing in the previous studies.

To put in the words of J.Francies Rummel "Research is an endeavor to discover and help knowledge. It is an intellectual process that has developed our hundreds of years every changing in purpose and form and always searching for truth (Aggarwal, 1966). The review of related literature helps to sharpen and define understanding of existing knowledge in the problem area and provides and background for the existing knowledge. The literature in any field forms the foundation upon which all future work will be built. Since the researcher is a specialist rather than a generalist (Best 1986).

PURPOSE OF REVIEW OF RELATED STUDIES

Review of the related literature, besides, allowing the researcher to acquaint himself with current knowledge in the field or area in which he is going to conduct his research, serves the following specific purposes.

- The review of related literature enables the researcher to define the limits of his field. It helps the researcher to delimit and define his problem.

- By reviewing the related literature the researcher can avoid unfruitful and useless problem areas.
- Through the review of related literature, the researcher can avoid unintentional duplication of well-established findings.
- The review of related literature gives the researcher an understanding of the research methodology which refers to the way the study is to be conducted. It helps the researcher to know about the tools and instruments which proved to be useful and promising in the previous studies. The advantage of the related literature is also to provide insight into the Statistical methods through which validity of results is to be established.
- The final and important specific reason for reviewing the related literature is to know about the recommendations of previous researchers listed in their studies for further research.

STUDIES RELATED WITH BLENDED LEARNING

Lidia Bilbatua and Alfredo Herrero de Haro (2014) investigated the Teachers' attitudes towards Computer-Assisted Language Learning in Australia and Spain. This study focuses on teachers' attitudes towards CALL (Computer-Assisted Language Learning) in order to gain a better understanding of what issues, advantages, and disadvantages teachers come across when incorporating CALL into their teaching. Furthermore, a group of teachers from Australia and Spain has been interviewed to compare how views on CALL vary across professionals in these two countries. As some authors have previously proved, the more IT literate teachers are, the more likely they are to use CALL in their teaching.

Chun Meng Tang, Lee Yen Chaw (2014) studied the attitude of students towards different learning aspects could influence their readiness for blended learning. Analyses revealed three key findings. First, the use of technology in education was not a hindrance to the students. Second, blended learning adaptability, which was modeled as a second-order formative construct and formed by four first-order reflective constructs—attitude towards online learning, study management, online interaction, and learning flexibility—had a positive relationship with student readiness for blended learning. Third, attitude towards classroom learning had a negative relationship with student readiness for blended learning. An understanding of student attitude towards different learning aspects can be critical in the assessment of student readiness for blended learning, which is a prerequisite for successful implementation of blended learning.

Shirin Ghahari and Ahmad Ameri-Golestan (2014) investigated the impact of blended and classroom teaching methods on Iranian EFL learners'writing. To this end, a group of 29 upper intermediate and advanced EFL learners were randomly placed in two groups: an experimental group, namely Blended Learning and a control group, namely Classroom Learning after taking part in a placement test. Participants of the Blended Learning group received traditional teaching methods of writing plus learning through the web. Participants of the Classroom Learning group, however, were taught based on the traditional teaching methods of writing and received the materials, instructions, and feedback merely through traditional methods. In order to collect the data, participant's first piece of writing was regarded as the pretest and their last one was the posttest. The results of the independent-samples t-tests showed that participants of the Blended Learning group significantly outperformed the ones in the Classroom Learning group in their writing performances. In conclusion, the results of the study revealed that employing a blended teaching method can create a more desirable condition to enhance the EFL learners'writing performance and that doing research in this field can be a promising area for those interested.

Mohammad A. Alseweed (2014) investigated the effects of the traditional learning, blended learning and virtual classes learning on university students' achievement and attitudes. 34 male students studying at the English Language Program, Qassim University were divided randomly into three groups, (blended learning, traditional learning, or virtual classes learning). Results indicate that there are significant differences among the instructional approaches in the achievement test scores in favor of blended learning. In addition, the results show significant differences in students' attitudes in favor of blended learning.

Dr inż. Colin F. Hales and Dr Barbara Fura (2014) undertook a study on attitude of students' towards a wider use of ICT in the education process (e-learning/blended learning). The analyses were conducted against the backdrop of the students' subjective assessment of their general computer aptitude as well as their access to and use of ICT. Results prove that students' opinions on the wider use of ICT in the learning process were influenced by a subjective assessment of their general computer skills. That level was in turn determined by factors including study specialization as well as socio-demographic characteristics of the respondents, such as gender, place of residence and age. Access to a computer/Internet had some influence upon familiarity with given applications and online activities. Research results confirm the presumption that students with a higher appraisal of their competence were more positively inclined towards a wider use of ICT than those with lower levels of competence.

Mukaddes Erdem and Pınar Nuhoğlu Kibar (2014) determined the students' opinions on blended learning and its implementation. The other purpose was to explore the students' opinions on Facebook integration into blended learning environment. The participants of this study were 40 undergraduate students in their fourth semester of the program. Participants had no prior experience in Blended Learning Environment, but they were well informed about online distance education. A combination of qualitative and quantitative approaches was used in this study. Quantitative data were collected through a scale called as "Students' Views on the Use and Implementation of Blended Learning" and qualitative data were collected through open-ended questions. Based on the result of the study, students have also positive opinions on the blended learning method. The findings from this study indicate that Facebook may be an appropriate tool for communication and interaction whereas, the online environment may be appropriate for sharing content, homework / projects.

Vijay Jaiswal (2014) conducted a Case study to find out the current status of e-learning in higher education. Thus, in order to study this objective 2919 teachers (839 teachers from professional courses and 2080 teachers from non-professional courses) and 7717 students (4512 students from professional courses and 3205 from non-professional courses at UG & PG levels) were selected as a sample from the eleven state universities of U.P. for the present study. It was found that below average number of professional courses' teachers in higher education are using e-learning mode whereas only a few non-professional courses' teachers are using e-learning mode. There are three modes of e-learning viz. online mode, hybrid/blended mode and e-enhancement mode but only e-enhancement mode is being presently used by the professional and non-professional courses' teachers in Indian higher education.

Nallusamy, T (2014) examined the level of Attitude towards Blended learning among student-teachers. This study belongs to survey method. The size of the sample in the study was 200 student – teachers who were selected through random sampling technique. The study concludes that the student-teachers are having more level of Attitude towards Blended learning.

Saminathan, G (2014) discussed the Student attitude towards Audio-Visual Aids used by the teacher in Coimbatore District. Samples of 100 respondents selected randomly were studied and this study belongs to survey method. The result of study concludes that the Student have positive attitude towards Audio- Visual Aids used by the teacher

Angadi, Dr. G. R (2014) concluded that male and female as well as science and arts teachers' of B.Ed colleges have significant difference in their attitudes towards Information and Communication Technology (ICT) whereas this attitude of senior teachers has not been found significant difference between the senior and junior teachers' of B.Ed colleges. It also has found that the knowledge of ICT will be highly helpful in the development of educational institutions.

Rama Chandra Dhir (2014) studied the e-learning: attitude of graduating students case study of kendrpara (auto)college E-learning teaching technology improves students learning where faculty members associated with e-learning methods can teach well in order to achieve desired course goals as well as objectives of education more effectively. It not only designs the course materials but also manages the course content both online and class room teaching learning process as a result of which it will make teaching more rewarding and exciting for academics.

Neelam Dhamija (2014) investigated the attitude of undergraduate students towards the use of e-learning. For this purpose, 300 undergraduate students of Kurukshetra district were randomly selected. Attitude Scale for e-learning was developed and administered on them. To find out the significance of difference between different groups, t-test was applied. The overall results indicate that maximum undergraduate students have a positive attitude towards e-learning. No significant difference was found in the attitude of Arts and Science, Arts and Commerce as well as Science and Commerce undergraduate students towards the use of e-learning. However, significant difference was seen in the attitude of Male and Female and Urban and Rural undergraduate students towards the use of e-learning.

Mohammad A. Alseweed (2013) investigated the effects of the traditional learning, blended learning and virtual classes learning on university students' achievement and attitudes. 34 male University students studying at the English Language Program, University were divided randomly into three groups, (blended learning, traditional learning, or virtual classes learning). Results indicate that there are significant differences among the instructional approaches in the achievement test scores in favor of blended learning. In addition, the results show significant differences in students' attitudes in favor of blended learning.

Thiyagu, K (2013) studied the B.Ed., Trainees perceptions towards Blended learning in teaching learning of mathematics. Survey method is employed for this study. The investigator has chosen 150 mathematics optional B.Ed., Trainees for this study. Finally the investigator concludes (a) 16% of B.Ed., mathematics Trainees have low level, 67.3% of average level and 16.7% of them have high level of perception to towards Blended learning. The mean of the perception towards Blended learning is 148.46 and standard deviation is 15.92. It is inferred that more number of B.Ed., Trainees have moderate level of perception towards Blended learning. (b) There is no significance difference in perception towards Blended learning among the B.Ed., Trainees with respect to their gender.

Vijay Jaiswal (2013) the present Case study was conducted to find out the current status of e-learning in higher education. Thus, in order to study this objective 2919 teachers (839 teachers from professional courses and 2080 teachers from non-professional courses) and 7717 students (4512 students from professional courses and 3205 from non-professional courses at UG & PG levels) were selected as a sample from the eleven state universities of U.P. for the present study. It was found that below average number of professional courses' teachers in higher education are using e-learning mode whereas only a few non-professional courses' teachers are using e-learning mode. There are three modes of e-learning viz. online mode, hybrid/blended mode and e-enhancement mode but only e-enhancement mode is being presently used by the professional and non-professional courses' teachers in Indian higher education.

Parthasarathy.M., Ananthasayanam.R and Ravi.R (2013) conducted a study on Usage of Internet Applications among B.Ed Students in Tamilnadu by nature. This was administered as a descriptive research. This study exposes the minimum usage of internet Applications among B.Ed Students.

Gopal, B.V and Anandan, K (2013) conducted a study on Attitude towards e-learning in classroom instruction among the B.Ed student at college of education. Result showed that there is significant difference of the Attitude of B.Ed students towards e-learning with respect to their discipline of the between the score subject-wise.

Punam Bansal, Dr (2013) indicated the Higher education in India is facing the greatest challenge of expanding intake capacity substantially from 13 percent to 20 percent as envisaged in 11th Five Year Plan(2007-2012).The other challenges that knowledge based societies re likely to face are learners from diverse backgrounds and their needs ,time availability, flexibility in course content and innovative use of Information and Communication technology. Blended Learning is a mixed educational paradigm and offers promise faor addressing these challenges. It offers great flexibility and great effectiveness as it can choose the best medium for every objective. It will expand access to an institution's educational offerings and increase enrolments and reduce operating costs. Blended learning is shifting information transfer paradigm from teaching to learning. Since blended approach combines face-to-face and computer based learning opportunities, teachers are able to use variety of instructional techniques. Computer-based technologies can be used to selectively present case studies, tutorials, self-testing exercises, simulations, or other online work in place of some lecture or lab material. The traditional Indian education is undergoing slow transformation. Hence new educational models based on constructivism may be used in parallel with traditional learning by introducing a blended learning approach in higher education. However, the challenge is to make the blend not only effective but also efficient. The present paper is an attempt to look into challenges posed by technology and corresponding strategies to make blended learning effective in higher education institutions in India.

Mohammad Ataur Rahman (2013) examined how teacher educators' perceive the attitude towards use of computer technology in Teachers' Training Colleges. This study investigated teacher educators' computer attitudes by using the valid and reliable instruments of Loyd and Gressard's (1984) Computer Attitude Scale (CAS). The data was collected through questionnaires from 75 teacher educators of teachers' training college and eventually received 46 responses. The results revealed that the teacher educators' possessed their high attitude towards computer. It also determined that there is no significant difference between male and female in terms of their attitudes toward computer technology.

Nannette P. Napier, Sonal Dekhane, Stella Smith (2013) described the conversion of an introductory computing course to the blended learning model at a small, public liberal arts college. Blended learning significantly reduces face-to-face instruction by incorporating rich, online learning experiences. To assess the impact of blended learning on students, survey data was collected at the midpoint and end of semester, and student performance on the final exam was compared in traditional and blended learning sections. To capture faculty perspectives on teaching blended learning courses, written reflections and discussions from faculty teaching blended learning sections were analyzed. Results indicate that student performance in the traditional and blended learning sections of the course were comparable and that students reported high levels of interaction with their instructor. Faculty teaching the course share insights on transitioning to the blended learning format.

Farouq H. Aziz Al-Rahman (2013) examined students' suggestions for improving the quality of Blended Learning courses. The sample consists of 160 male students. The participants completed a 33-item questionnaire. The results indicate the clear advantages of this new experience in broadening students' reading opportunities and enriching their English vocabulary. Moreover, the component on advantages clearly demonstrates how Blended Learning provides an environment for more effective employment of indirect language learning strategies such as meta-cognitive strategies (arranging and planning learning), affective strategies, and social strategies. The limitations and problems of Blended Learning highlighted by the respondents are followed by a number of practical suggestions for addressing these drawbacks, including solving technical problems, providing proper training to students, increasing the number of labs, and recognizing excellent performance of both instructors and students. Translating these suggestions into an action plan and a road map will enhance the effectiveness of using Blended Learning to create supportive learning opportunities for language learners.

Philip Rotich (2013) compared the graduate student attitudes towards different instructional approaches within online, blended, and face-to-face courses in a public institution of higher learning. The participants completed an online survey questionnaire that was designed by the researcher using learning theories in education: behavioral, cognitive, constructivism, and humanistic approaches towards teaching and learning. There were 210 total responses from graduate students enrolled during 2013 spring semester. There were more female (71.4%) than male (28.6%) students who responded. Previous studies have compared face-to-face (F2F) and online methods of instructions and have shown mixed results. Whereas some studies have shown F2F instructional methods as favorable to students, others found no differences between F2F and online methods. This study was guided by 4 research questions. Analysis of variance (ANOVA) and t test statistical procedures were used to analyze the data. The findings of this study showed significant differences in students' preference in instructional methods and in instructional approaches (behavioral, humanistic, cognitive, and constructivist). The study found that full-time graduate students tended to prefer F2F instructional methods, while part-time students preferred online methods. Additionally younger students (< 35 years) reported stronger preference for F2F methods of instruction than older students (> 36 years) in cognitive and constructivist instructional approaches with no significant differences by age for behavioral and humanistic instructional approaches.

Wing AU, Dr., Greg C. R. Dr and Yates (2013) examined university students' online learning attitude changes and the factors which could predict their attitude changes. The paper aimed to investigate 120 Australian university students' attitudes towards online learning in a blended course. The factors, such as prior attitudes, prior experiences, and motivation, were examined with the participants' online learning attitudes by the end of the course. Two phases in the study included the pre- and post-test and course participation (developed from the data of the students' weekly reports and online forum transcripts) in Phase One and interviews in Phase Two. It was found that the students became more positive toward online learning by the end of the course. The predictors for their online learning attitudes by the end of the course were their prior online learning attitudes and motivation in learning.

Mukaddes Erdem, Pınar Nuhoglu Kibar (2013) determined the students' opinions on blended learning and its implementation. The other purpose was to explore the students' opinions on Facebook integration into blended learning environment. The participants of this study were 40 undergraduate students in their fourth semester of the program. Participants had no prior experience in Blended Learning Environment, but they were well informed about online distance education. A combination of qualitative and quantitative approaches was used in this study. Quantitative data were collected through a scale called as "Students' Views on the Use and Implementation of Blended Learning" and qualitative data were collected through open-ended questions. Based on the result of the study, it appears that students have quite positive opinions on blended learning and its implementation. The highest score given to face-to-face environment throughout the process of implementing blended learning. However, students have also positive opinions on the blended learning method. The findings from this study indicate that Facebook may be an appropriate tool for communication and interaction whereas, the online environment may be appropriate for sharing content, homework / projects.

Yurdal Dikmenli and Ülkü Eser Ünaldi (2013) studied the elucidation of the effect of the virtual classroom application and blended learning medium upon the academic achievement of the students and their attitudes against the geography curse compared to the face to face expository (traditional) method. The study was carried out according to pre-test - post-test experimental design with control group. The group was constituted by 73, 9th year students. The experimental groups have been subjected to the blended learning approach throughout the study. The topic was also given to the first experimental group with the face to face expository method where the teacher explained the subject while the second experimental group was subjected to virtual classroom application. The course was given to the control group with the traditional face to face learning method. The data of the study were collected by the use of by the use of the geography achievement test (Kr-20=0.77) and the attitude scale towards the geography course (α=0,918) . The data collected were one factor variance and co variance analyses. The results showed that the blended teaching media and virtual classroom practices had a statistically significant contribution on the achievement of the students in geography and their attitudes towards the geography course compared to the face to face expository method. However since the attitudes of the students towards the geography course in both control and experimental groups at the beginning and the end of the experiment were high the methods used did not made a significant contribution to it.

Gulden ILIN (2013) explored the probable consequences of a blended Teaching English to Young Learners (TEYLs) course comprised of Moodle applications and face to face instruction in the English Language Teaching (ELT) context. Contrary to previous face to face only procedure, the course was divided into two segments: traditional classroom instruction where lectures and discussions on how to teach English to young learners were held and the Module application where students uploaded their micro-teaching sessions and discussed and criticized one another's work online. The procedure was designed in a manner that time to be devoted to microteaching sessions in the classroom was expected to be saved and left room for classroom discussions. To gather data, a student readiness scale, a questionnaire eliciting student teachers' views about the experience and, to bring more depth to the study, semi- structured interviews were used. The results reveal that a blended young learner course has various positive contributions other than time management for the instructor as well as on behalf of the course attendants.

Lily Wong (2012) investigated to measure students' attitudes towards e-learning . A mixed methodology using both quantitative and qualitative measures was adopted for this research. The results of this research indicate that despite having 3 new online options readily available via WebCT, strong support of traditional approaches to teaching was evident. Students ranked the delivery of face-to-face lectures as the most effective in assisting their learning and potentially affecting their assessment outcomes, closely followed by face-to-face tutorials. Of the online options, the viewing of online lectures rated the highest, whilst the viewing of recorded tutorials was rated lowest. These results may be reflective of their preference for active involvement through student interaction rather than passive viewing of online recordings to better engage in the learning process.

Yu-Cheng Shih and Pei-Ren Huang and Yung-Chi Hsu and Sherry, Y (2012) studied the integrative approach to investigate the causes and consequences of disorientation problems so that a complete understanding can be obtained. Unlike previous empirical studies, which use statistical techniques, this study attempts to expose unexpected relationships with a data mining approach. The results indicate that the causes of disorientation problems are associated with learners' computer experience, the frequencies and time of using each navigation tool. On the other hand, the consequences of disorientation problems are concerned with learning effort and learning performance. Based on the findings, a framework is proposed to provide guidelines for the development of Web-based learning systems that are able to reduce learners' disorientation problems.

Ramayaha,T (2012) studied the advent of the Internet, more and more public universities in Malaysia are putting in effort to introduce e-learning in their respective universities. Using a structured questionnaire derived from the literature, data was collected from 250 undergraduate students from a public university in Penang, Malaysia. Data was analyzed using AMOS version 16. The results of the structural equation model indicated that service quality ($\beta = 0.20$, $p < 0.01$), information quality ($\beta = 0.37$, $p < 0.01$) and system quality ($\beta = 0.20$, $p < 0.01$) were positively related to user satisfaction explaining a total of 45% variance. The second regression analysis was to examine the impact of user satisfaction on continuance intention. The results showed that satisfaction ($\beta = 0.31$, $p < 0.01$), system quality ($\beta = 0.18$, $p < 0.01$) and service quality ($\beta = 0.30$, $p < 0.01$) were positively related to continuance intention explaining 44% of the variance. Implications from these findings to e-learning system developers and implementers were further elaborated.

Simon Stebbings and Phil Blyth and Jenny McDonald (2012) aimed to develop a blended learning course for teaching rheumatology within the existing musculoskeletal course. We developed a multimedia online learning resource structured to support class based problem-based learning (PBL) sessions, and enhance student engagement and promote clinical reasoning. We also aimed to align teaching over three geographically separate campuses, promote more student-centered approaches to learning and meet the challenge of the limited teaching time available for undergraduate learning in the field of rheumatology. Our redesigned course was evaluated longitudinally over eighteen months through student focus groups, Blackboard and Moodle electronic access data, and course evaluation questionnaires. Online materials integrated into the new curriculum and combined with in-class PBL and clinical sessions, proved popular with students. Students accessed the newly developed online materials far more frequently than the previously available unstructured content, which they felt to be of limited value or relevance to their studies. Furthermore the blended learning approach allowed delivery of common content across three separate campuses.

Lambropoulos, Niki; Faulkner, Xristine; Culwin, Fintan (2012) undertook a study on supporting social awareness in collaborative E-Learning. The results indicate the importance of social awareness in effective e-learning; the quality of active participation can be increased by the use of associated tools. The e-tutor's role is still to facilitate and to support such engagement towards collaborative learning.

Gibson, Moline Teddy and Dyck Brenda (2012) studied the free service teachers need both awareness of and skill with the latest technologies in order to use these tools effectively in the teaching. It's more direct experience in the subject – specific pedagogy courses is necessary to develop a deep understanding about how a technology – rich environment can help to develop subject – specific knowledge. This study reported here examined the influences of two technologies – infused social studies pedagogy courses on student's perceptions about why, when, and how most effectively to infused technology in the teaching of social studies and their feelings of preparedness to use those technologies.

Hakvendi – Can Meral and Dana, Thomas M (2012) conducted a study on exemplary science teachers' use of technology. This study focused to examine exemplary science teachers' level of computer use their knowledge or skills in using specific computer applications for science instruction. The major finding of this study indicated revealed that students use of technology in their science classroom is highly correlated with the frequently of their science teachers use of computer applications or tools.

Nikolaos Vernadakis and R Efthimis Kioumourtzoglou (2012) Blended learning with the concerns and dissatisfaction with e-learning, educators are searching for alternative instructional delivery solutions to relieve the above problems. The blended e-learning system has been presented as a promising alternative learning approach. While blended learning has been recognized as having a number of advantages, insufficient learning satisfaction is still an obstacle to its successful adoption. Therefore, the purpose of this study was to evaluate students' satisfaction with blended learning course delivery compared to a traditional face-to-face class format in a general multimedia course in physical education. Forty six (n=46) undergraduate students, between the ages of 20-22 years old, were randomly assigned into two teaching method groups: Classroom Lecture Instruction (CLI) and Blended Lecture Instruction (BLI). For the data collection at the end of this study, students completed an online satisfaction questionnaire. Independent sample t-test analysis was conducted to measure students' satisfaction towards the CLI and BLI methods. Results indicated that a blended course delivery is preferred over the traditional lecture format. These finding suggest that students' satisfaction could increase when the instructor provides learning environments not only in a traditional classroom, but in an asynchronous online system as well.

Umit Yapici and Hasan Akbayin (2012) determined the effect of the blended learning model on high school students' biology achievement and on their attitudes towards the Internet. Among the experimental models, the pretest-posttest control group model was used in the study. The study was carried out with 107 students (47 of whom were in the experimental group, and 60 of whom were in the control group) attending Nevzat Ayaz Anatolian High School in Diyarbakır in Spring Term of the academic year of 2009-2010. In the experimental group, the courses were taught based on the blended learning model via a website (www.e-biyoloji.net), while in the control group, the courses were taught based on traditional teaching methods. An Internet Attitude Scale

=0,97) and an achievement test of 40 questions (KR-20=0.88) were used as the data collection tools. For the analysis of the data, mean scores, independent t-test and paired samples t-test were used. The research results revealed that the blended learning model contributed more to the students' biology achievement than traditional teaching methods did and that the students' attitudes towards the Internet developed statistically significantly.

Henry Julie Etienne, Vandeput Etienne (2012) study on development of the Internet led to an explosion of learning/teaching strategies and opened the way to distance learning (DL). People dreamt of full distance learning systems. But those dreams were rapidly replaced by more rational blended learning scenarios (1). This evolution was quite normal if we admit that DL creates new constraints (loneliness, lack of motivation...) by removing other important ones (physical distance, scheduling...). In addition, DL doesn't allow, as face-to-face learning, a great variety of interaction techniques and a communication that makes use of almost all the human senses. So what we suggest is to evolve from a blended learning to a « coached » learning to exploit any resource: human, material, organizational or educational resources, on the condition to act for the learner's good. Main constraints impossible to overcome in a blended learning context will possibly be avoided thanks to a coached learning. Two important concepts should be taken into account to succeed: the coach and the community of practice (CoP) (2). A coach is quite different from a tutor. First of all, he works in face-to-face with the learner, while the tutor acts at a distance. Then, he is not necessarily an expert even though he is intended to « know the score ». His role is to stimulate, to prompt, to encourage, to suggest trails... The coach must be able to imagine a customized educational system to each of his coaches. In such a context, the coach's practice is emerging, complex and, as a consequence, far to be reified. A Cop is a convenient support to provide coaches with a mean to share and capitalize about this practice. Sharing strategies and collaboration may bring a larger flexibility to the learning structure. Flexibility must also be reflected in the organizational autonomy of the learner. Learning activities must constantly stimulate the learners to become motivated to learn and interact. Even if the coach is a powerful instigator, learners are regularly alone in front of their screen. In this context, we were interested in all the elements that contribute to maintaining motivation: psycho pedagogy (3), ergonomics of human-machine interfaces (4,5) and didactics of the discipline. The « visaTICE » project (6) sets up a « coached » learning and takes into account all the motivational aspects described above. Through this project, we can develop learning strategies where the constraints appear as obstacles to avoid and not to overcome.

Vladlena Bensona, Deborah Andersona and Ann Oomsb (2012) adoption of blended learning is a complex process for higher education institutions and academic staff. Although the move towards blended learning is generally investigated at institutional level, factors determining its success and minimizing resistance of faculty often emerge at delivery level. This paper explores adoption of blended learning practices in a Business School at a university in the United Kingdom. Based on the interviews with a purposive sample of 16 academic staff members delivering 36 business modules, this case study explores the concept of blended learning from the academic staff's perspective. A typology of three distinct approaches to blended learning – 'Technology is all', 'Bolt-ons' and 'Purely pedagogic' – emerged from the data extending understanding of blended learning practices. A team of three researchers conducted the study. Two of the researchers were academic staff members from the Business School and one researcher was an academic staff member from another faculty within the same university.

Ibrahim Umit Yapici and Hasan Akbayin (2012) determined the high school students' views on blended learning. The study was carried out in biology course for the lesson unit of "Classification of Living Things and Biodiversity" with 47 9th grade students attending Nevzat Ayaz Anatolian High School in the second term of the academic year of 2011- 2012. The lessons were taught in a way appropriate to the blended learning model both via the Internet and on face-to-face basis. As the online dimension of the blended learning model, Moodle, a Learning Management System (LMS), was used. The interviews held with the students revealed that the blended learning model provided students with various opportunities such as getting prepared for the lessons, reviewing the lessons as many times as wanted, reaching the subject-related materials without being dependent on time and place, testing oneself and communicating with the teacher and other students out of the school. The interviews also revealed that there were various problems though such as lack of Internet connection at home and problems experienced while playing the videos.

Ram maher (2012) conducted a study on "e-learning for professional development of teacher". This study highlights the idea that technological changes results to the changes in teacher professional development. It was proved to be achievement and their level of achievement and their proficiency in teaching learning process. Only the e-learning environment makes the student retro-active participating in the learning process, as opposed to being passive in the traditional classroom environment.

Selvan.A and Paul Devanesan (2012) conducted a study on Utilization of online programs by teachers in teaching learning processes at secondary level. In this study aimed at identifying among others the online programs used by teachers in the teaching learning processes and the importance given to them, the investigators found that the teachers had high level of awareness about using online programs white the female teachers utilized the online programs better.

Rengarajan,P and Senthilnathan,S. (2012) the study deals with the Teacher- Educators Attitude towards e-learning. As the study is descriptive by nature, normative study technique has been adopted and chose the random sampling technique. The study had shown that there is wide scope for improving the Teacher- Educators Attitude towards e-learning. This study presents a positive Attitude in the minds of the Teacher- Educators towards e-learning.

Vamadevappa, H.V(2012) gave his comments in his article in Edutracks about Developing Internet research skills among university students. Internet research skill can help the university students find the information needed for their university score and improve their grades. Internet research skill can be developed among university students in three stages namely site seeing, discovering stage and judging stage. In this thematic paper on Internet research skills, his suggested a number of useful Internet research tools and websites. Internet has become an indispensable tool as a cell phone in today's computer age. The university students are trained in this Internet research skill they can take up qualitative research work, they can contribute their research work through the web pages and they can earn better grades in their P.G courses and research degrees.

Sivakumar, D (2012) conducted a study on "Awareness of internet usage among the school teacher". This study mainly focused on the purpose of educational technology is to improve the effectiveness of teaching learning processes. The major finding of this study this school system at the secondary level there is a need for the teachers to attain computer proficiency.

Ronald, A (2012) conducted a study on "How to create thriller PowerPoint in the classroom". PowerPoint presentation in academia has a reputation for being less then engaging in this era of learner-centered teaching. The next generation also presents a formidable challenge to using PowerPoint that research will be briefly reviewed. Since the use of multimedia as instructional tools has been largely ignored by the major sources on PowerPoint, this study presents so specific practical applications enabling faculty members to improve the effectiveness of their PowerPoint presentation and to grab and maintain students attention and foster deep learning.

Shinde, S. P and Deshmukh,V. P (2012) conducted a study on online teaching methods in secondary schools, which reported that it improves practices in both virtual and face-to-face settings. The research also points out the teacher's experiences in delivering instruction online where they can also teach face-to-face courses.

Nirmal,M and Udayarekha, M (2012) conducted a study on students towards the use of the internet for learning and career orientations – a study. This study mainly focused the attitude towards using internet as an instrument for enhancing their learning and career orientation under five dimensions. The major finding of this study indicated in students use internet for knowledge development, seeking career guidance and increase professional development. social relational and using internet for entertainment purpose.

Vilma,B and Svetlana, R (2011) The study deals with the application of ICT and the use of blended teaching and learning within the curriculum of general English at the levels A1-B2 in tertiary education. The research presented in the paper focuses on analyzing the language teachers' experience in computer assisted language teaching as well as their practices and attitudes towards the blended learning courses created at the Centre of Foreign Languages. Therefore, the authors of the present paper take it as their aim to ease the above indicated task of the teachers by scrutinizing and casting light on their relevant doubts, needs and end eavours. The research is based mainly on qualitative methodology including the methods of an informal interview and a questionnaire. Research shows that the English language teachers display a generally positive attitude towards blended learning.

Vandana Mehra, Dr (2012) studied the student's attitude towards e-learning can in many ways help managers better prepare in light of e-learning for the future. This article describes the process of the development of an instrument to measure university students' attitude towards e-learning. The scale was administered to 200 University students. The 83-item attitude towards e-learning scale was developed on six domains as Perceived usefulness Intention to adopt e-learning, Ease of e-learning use Technical and pedagogical support, E-learning stressors, Pressure to use e-learning.

Keisham Shitaljit Singh, Dr (2012) concluded that male and female as well as science and arts teachers' training college teachers have significant difference in their attitudes towards Information and Communication Technology (ICT) whereas this attitude of senior teachers has not been found significant difference between the senior and junior teachers' training college teachers. It also has found that the knowledge of ICT will be highly helpful in the development of educational institutions.

Mohammad Ataur Rahman (2011) examined how teacher educators perceive the attitude towards use of computer technology in Teachers' Training Colleges in Bangladesh. This study investigated teacher educators' computer attitudes by using the valid and reliable instruments of Loyd and Gressard's (1984) Computer Attitude Scale (CAS). The data was collected through questionnaires from 75 teacher educators of teachers' training college in the

Rajshahi division in Bangladesh and eventually received 46 responses. The results revealed that the teacher educators' possessed their high attitude towards computer. It also determined that there is no significant difference between male and female in terms of their attitudes toward computer technology.

Satya Sundar Sethy (2011) discussed the nature and status of distance education in the age of globalization, i.e. how best it fits for the present educational scenario. In this connection, we will discuss how Blended Learning (hence after, BL) is one among the other learning strategies mostly helpful for the learners. Keeping this view in mind, this paper is divided into three sections. The first section aims to discuss the nature of distance education in the age of globalization. The second section devotes a discussion on why we need blended learning in ODL system and in which way it plays a vital role for maximizing the benefit of the learners, tutors, and the institutions. The third section explains the pros and cons of blended learning to evaluate how successfully it can be implemented in the ODL system. The paper concludes with an established view that blended learning is a globalized approach to the distance education.

Samma Reddy,P and yunmdra, G (2011) assessed ICT literacy among high school students. This study mainly focused on to increase the ICT literacy among the school students. The major findings of this study indicated the ICT literacy of boy's students are significantly better than girls students.

Iolanda Garcia, Universitat Oberta de Catalunya (2011) clarified issues relating to the types of activities that technologies support in everyday and academic life for both groups of students. The initial hypothesis is that the use of technology to support learning is related with the type of actions and tasks being carried out on a daily basis and therefore it is also influenced by the academic learning context, in this case the university model (online or face-to-face/blended). The results obtained cannot favour the idea of online learning environments being superior to blended learning environments in terms of development of students' digital competence, as more research should be carried out into the educational model used in the different universities. However they do lead us to suggest the need to consider that technology-rich learning environments foster students' digital competencies.

Pinelopi Zaka (2011) investigated how blended teaching and learning was implemented in a New Zealand secondary school. An ecological perspective was taken to clarify the complexity of blended teaching and learning implementation by researching the roles of students, teachers, school leaders and other educational stakeholders, in and beyond the school. An ecological framework was developed that gives rise to several recommendations for individuals and groups within the three levels of the school's multilevel ecology: the classroom, the school, and the wider ecosystem in which the school is located.

Dana Adas & Wafa Abu Shmais (2011) investigating An-Najah National University students' perceptions towards Blended Learning environment using traditional methods in addition to OCC (Online Course Container) which is both a synchronous and asynchronous tool for computer assisted communication used to aid EFL learners improve their four language skills. The study included (92) students enrolled in a general English course (10103) offered at the language Center at the university. A questionnaire was designed to measure the students' attitudes towards BL (Blended Learning) using (OCC) in terms of: the process, ease of use, and content. Interviews were also conducted to validate the study and elicit more feedback. The study concludes that in general the students' attitudes towards BL were positive in terms of the three domains. Moreover, it reflects the students' internet and IT skills and interests due to internet availability and accessibility.

Vilma Bijeikienė, Svetlana Rašinskienė, Lina Zutkienė (2011) analyzed the English language teachers' attitudes to the application of ICT and blended learning in general. The study is based on the methodology of a small scale mainly qualitative analysis including the methods of a survey conducted using informal interviews and questionnaires. The present research shows that the English language teachers display a generally positive attitude towards blended learning.

Vladlena Bensona, Deborah Andersona and Ann Oomsb (2011) studied the Educators' perceptions, attitudes and practices: blended learning in business and management education. It is case-study methodology was used to investigate academic staff perceptions and attitudes towards blended learning and current blended learning practices. The challenge for institutions implementing blended learning strategies is to build on positive staff attitudes, provide appropriate resources and help staff develop blends of teaching practices and use of technologies that deliver the best outcomes in particular teaching and learning contexts.

Ahmad Al-Saai, Aisha Al-Kaabi, Sarah Al-Muftah (2011) investigated the effect of a blended e-learning environment on students' achievement and attitudes toward using e-learning at the university level. A sample of 43 female students was randomly assigned to receive one of two instructional treatments (blended e-learning approach & traditional face-to-face teaching approach). Results showed insignificant difference between the instructional treatments in gain scores of the achievement test. However, the results in the attitudes scale showed a significant difference in gain scores in favor of blended e-learning approach.

Yasemin Kırkgoz (2011) conducted a blended learning study on implementing video recorded Speaking tasks in task-based classroom instruction. This study investigates designing and implementing a speaking course in which face-to-face instruction informed by the principles of Task-Based Learning is blended with the use of technology, the video, for the first-year student teachers of English in Turkish higher education. The study consisted of three hours of task-based classroom instruction, complemented with one hour of additional class time, which was devoted to viewing and evaluating students' video recorded speaking tasks, assigned as homework. Analysis of quantitative and qualitative data revealed that students made noticeable improvement in their oral communication skills, and they were positive in their perceptions of integrating technology in the lesson. The study also indicated that the use of video camera, as a technological tool, had a positive impact on students' viewing and critically evaluating their speaking tasks. Attention is drawn to a number of potential advantages of integrating technology into face-to-face instruction, and it is suggested that video cameras represent a language learning resource worthy of further investigation.

Julie Willems (2011) what are the differences in learning styles between students and educators who teach and/or design their e-learning environments? Are there variations in the learning styles of students at different levels of study? How may we use this learning styles data to inform the design in e-learning environments? This paper details mixed-methods research with three cohorts teaching and learning in e-learning environments in higher education: novice undergraduate e-learners, graduate e-learners, and educators teaching in, or designing for, e-learning environments (Willems, 2010). Quantitative findings from the Index of Learning Styles (ILS) (Felder & Silverman, 1988; Felder & Soloman, 1991, 1994) reflect an alignment of the results between both the graduate e-learner and e-educator cohorts across all four domains of the ILS, suggesting homogeneity of results between these two cohorts. By contrast, there was a statistically significant difference between the results of the graduate and educator cohorts with those of the undergraduate e-learners on two domains: sensing-intuitive($p=0.015$) and the global-sequential ($p=0.007$), suggesting divergent learning style preferences. Qualitative data was also gathered to gain insights on participants' responses to their learning style results.

Tutkun and Omer.F (2011) conducted a study on internet Access, use and sharing levels among students during the teaching - learning process. The purpose this study was to determine the awareness among students and levels regarding student's access, use and knowledge sharing during the teaching - learning process. This study was obtained teaching – learning process highly, developed students interest in the level of accessing knowledge via the internet, but differ on the subject of use and knowledge sharing.

Marta Zuvic-Butorac and Nena Roncevic and Damir Nemcanin (2011) studied the process of implementing blended learning, by using e-learning tools as a support for traditional classroom teaching, started at the University of Rijeka at the beginning of 2008, following general strategic principles adapted to local environment. The process has been constantly supported and assessed for quality, but up to now only from the institutional, teachers' and support services' perspective. Assuming that continuous and careful monitoring of learner's satisfaction is important for the success, feasibility and viability of e-learning, we conducted the research on students' perspective. As the student's perception regarding e-learning is one of the most important steps in developing and implementing a successful e-learning environment, we conducted the study of student's perception and e-learning acceptance, with three specific items addressed in the study: 1) student's perception of quality of already delivered e-courses, 2) level of importance for the specific elements of e-learning encountered, and 3) student's general attitude towards e-learning and their needs with respect to quality of course materials, communication and support of the learning process. The study outcomes generally suggest the need to enhance teachers' competencies for online teaching, particularly in acquiring successful tutoring methods and learners' support methods, and together with continuous and careful monitoring of learner's satisfaction we hope to ensure the success, feasibility and viability of online learning, as supporting educational tool in our university study programs.

Abdul Karim, Abdulhameed Rakan Alenezi and Abdul Malek (2010) undertaken an Empirical Investigation Into The Role Of Enjoyment, Computer Anxiety, Computer Self-Efficacy And Internet Experience In Influencing The Students' Intention To Use E-Learning. The current study has extended Technology Acceptance Model (TAM) to investigate the role of Enjoyment, computer anxiety, computer self-efficacy and Internet experience in influencing the students' intention to use E-learning in Saudi's universities. 402 governmental universities' students were participated to test the proposed hypotheses and to determine whether the proposed variables have an effect on the students' intention to use E-learning system. The results of stepwise regression indicated that computer anxiety, computer self-efficacy and Enjoyment were significantly influence the students' intention to use E-learning while the Internet experience was insignificantly influence them. Furthermore, the importance of Attitude in mediating the relationship between perceived usefulness, perceived ease of use and the students' behavioral intention was confirmed.

Maria Giannousi and Nicholas Vernadakis and Maria Michalopoulos (2010) studied that new information and communication technologies (ICTs) have provided educators and learners with an innovative learning environment to generate new paths in the learning process. In this context, new educational concepts such as blended learning are being introduced. This style of learning is usually defined as the integration of traditional classroom methods with online activities. The purpose of this study was to examine the relationship between students' perceived course interaction and their satisfaction in a blended learning environment in undergraduate education. Study participants consisted of thirty-one undergraduate students. Ten of the participants were male and twenty-one were female. The participants ranged in age from 18 to 21 years old. At the end of this study, students completed a questionnaire with three sections. The first section included the students' demographic/personal data. The second section evaluated students' perceived e-learner satisfaction from the blended learning course and the third, students' perceived interaction with others. The correlation analyses identified a significant positive correlation between students' perceived course interaction and their satisfaction.

Stella Mary (2010) described the conversion of an introductory computing course to the blended learning model at a small, public liberal arts college. Blended learning significantly reduces face-to-face instruction by incorporating rich, online learning experiences. To assess the impact of blended learning on students, survey data was collected at the midpoint and end of semester, and student performance on the final exam was compared in traditional and blended learning sections. To capture faculty perspectives on teaching blended learning courses, written reflections and discussions from faculty teaching blended learning sections were analyzed. Results indicate that student performance in the traditional and blended learning sections of the course were comparable and that students reported high levels of interaction with their instructor. Faculty teaching the course share insights on transitioning to the blended learning format.

Angel Rathnabai,S and Viswanathappa,G (2010) studied the ICT Mediation in Learning Mathematics. This study mainly focused on VIII standard students and it attempts to compare the effectiveness of computer-assisted instruction in teaching mathematics to VIII standard students. This study reveals that CAI can be used effectively to facilitate teaching and learning.

Shaik Fehameeda and Humiera Jawad (2009) conducted a Experimental study on The Effectiveness of CAI Program in high school Biology. In the study, the researcher wanted to find out the effectiveness of computer-assisted instruction program. For this the researcher analyzed both qualitative and quantitative data. The major findings of this study indicated the posttest scores on achievement test are significantly higher than pretest scores which means that the CAI program is effective.

Heomisook (2009) conducted a study on design considerations for today's online learners: A study of personalized, Relationship- Based social Awareness information. This study examined online learners' preferences in personalized, relationship-based social awareness information sharing in course management systems. The results indicated that today's online learners are opening minded in sharing social awareness information and their trust of course management systems is sign.

Wan Fatimah Bt Wan Ahmad, Afza Bt Shafie, Josefina Barnachea Janier (2009) studied the influence of blended learning approach on students' perceptions towards learning application of integration. A total of thirty engineering students were involved in the study. A set of questionnaire was given to evaluate the students' attitudes and learning perceptions. From the findings, conclusion has been drawn regarding the role of blended learning to support teaching and learning. The result shows that students demonstrate positive perceptions using the blended learning approach.

Ian Robertson (2009) based on a small scale study of postgraduate learners in a teacher training program who have used a wiki to support problem based and group based learning in a blended learning model, this paper concludes that the design and functionality of wikis is consistent with characteristics that promote adoption. Whilst respondents have recommendations for improvement, these are more in the nature of 'wanting more' rather than being critical of what currently exists. They also make recommendations about the role of the teacher that have the potential to improve the learners' experience. Using research on factors that support the adoption of technology for teaching it is concluded that the use of the wiki in Facilitating learning in the workplace is consistent with promoting awareness, providing participants with an opportunity to assess the technology for further use, and to be able to make a decision about potential use on their own practice as teachers.

Özgen Korkmaz and Ufuk Karakuş (2009) conducted a study on impact of blended learning model on student attitudes towards Geography course and their critical thinking dispositions and skills. An experimental pattern with pretest-posttest control group was used in the study. The study group consists of a total of 57 students – 28 in the experiment group and 29 in the control group – at Kırşehir High School. The experiment group was subject to hybrid learning through the Geography web page, while the traditional learning model was used for the control group. The data were collected through literature review, the Geography Attitude Scale, and the California Critical Thinking Disposition Inventory with Cronbach Alpha values of 0.92 and 0.88, respectively. The data were then subjected to percentage, arithmetic mean, t-test, ANOVA, Scheffé and Pearson correlation tests and the results were interpreted ($p<0.05$). As a results: Blended learning model contributed more to student attitudes toward geography course when compared to the traditional learning model; blended learning model contributed more to student critical dispositions and levels when compared to the traditional learning model; and there was a positive correlation between student attitudes toward geography course and their critical thinking dispositions and levels.

Lord, G., & Lomicka, L (2008) Blended learning in teacher education: An investigation of classroom community across media. Contemporary Issues in Technology and Teacher Education, 8(2), 158-174. 158 The study described in this paper investigates how graduate students in language and linguistic specializations develop and perceive community and how these perceptions or developments differ according to medium (chat, discussion board, or face-to-face class and group discussions). In this investigation, the factors relating to different perceptions of community were also considered. The goal of the study was to explore and analyze the incorporation of technological tools into blended learning in order to assist other teachers in the creation of collaborative cross-institutional situations. Their experiences in these situations assisted them in modeling such communities for their students so their students will potentially benefit from a well-developed and well-understood sense of community, both with onsite peers and with peers at a distance.

Paul Ginns and Robert Ellis (2008) quality in blended learning: Exploring the relationships between on-line and face-to-face teaching and learning. This study draws on a large body of seminal research showing that the approaches students take to learning, and the subsequent quality of their learning, is closely related to their perceptions of their learning experience. Recent research has demonstrated these findings also hold for non-standard modes of delivery such as distance education using on-line strategies. However, there is currently little research about how predominately campus-based students' experiences of the on-line part of their course are associated with their experience of the course as a whole. The present study extends previous research into the domain of blended learning, by exploring the relations between student perceptions of the e-Learning environment, approaches to study, and student grades.

Elke Mader, Philipp Budka and Elisabeth Anderl (2008) conducted a study on Blended Learning Strategies for Methodology Education in an Austrian Social Science Setting. In a changing European educational landscape, e-learning strategies become important tools to cross national and disciplinary boundaries. This paper introduces the first strategic e-learning project at the Department of Social and Cultural Anthropology of the University of Vienna. Furthermore, it discusses selected results of an evaluation of blended learning scenarios and models designed within the project. An adapted model for modes of interaction is deployed to develop and analyze these blended learning scenarios. Results indicate that holistic learning strategies are necessary to integrate all actors within this specific educational setting.

Hong Kian-Sam and Julia Ai Cheng Lee (2008) Blended learning, using e-learning tools to supplement existing on campus learning, often incorporates asynchronous computer conferencing as a means of augmenting knowledge construction among students. This case study reports findings about levels of knowledge construction amongst adult postgraduate students in six asynchronous computer conferences in a blended learning environment. The aim is to document and understand the kinds of task related postings in asynchronous computer conferencing that foster knowledge construction. The tool for analysis is an adaptation of the model by Veerman and Veldhuis-Diermanse (2001). Data were collected from Quick place, thee-learning system at Universiti Malaysia Sarawak, with 22 adult postgraduate students enrolled in the Masters of Science in Human Resource Development who were attending a 14-week course on Cognition and Learning. The results showed that the students were active in constructing knowledge but limited to seeking and giving opinions among peers and knowledge telling. The prevalence of low level knowledge construction points to the need for the e-learning facilitator to encourage the students to go beyond regurgitating facts of what they have learned. More guidance should be given to the students to refrain from mere knowledge telling. Results suggest that there are blended learning benefits for these students as they are given improved opportunities to learn outside the classroom.

Scheuermann, Friedrich and Angela Guimarães Pereira (2008) towards a Research Agenda on Computer-Based Assessment. Luxembourg Retrieved 2008-07-15. Cite uses deprecated , An e-assessment system designed to focus on more sophisticated forms of knowledge requires some sort of interactive activity and a system for inviting students to reason or solve problems around that activity. One influential program of research is known as Evidence Centered Design, or ECD. ECD involves the use of Bayesian Inference Nets to create a sophisticated model of student cognition [citation needed], and a set of activities or problems that students work on that allow the system to estimate the individuals understanding of the particular domain.

Scheuermann, Friedrich, Julius Björnsson (2008) studied transition to Computer-Based Assessment - New Approaches to Skills Assessment and Implications for Large-scale Testing. Luxembourg, Luxembourg. Retrieved 2009-04-02. Computer-Based Assessment refers to assessment which is built around the use of a computer; the use of a computer is always intrinsic to this type of assessment. This can relate to assessment of IT practical skills or more commonly the on screen presentation of knowledge tests. The defining factor is that the computer is marking or assessing the responses provided from candidates online assessment refers to assessment activity which requires the use of the internet. In reality, few high stakes assessment sessions are actually conducted online in real-time, but the transfer of data prior to and after the assessment session is conducted via the internet. There are many examples of practice and diagnostic tests being run real time over the internet.

Rajasekar and Vayapuri Raja (2008) conducted a study on higher secondary teacher computer anxiety. This study mainly focused on higher secondary teachers, who attended the computer classes and who did not attend computer classes. The major findings of this study indicated the gender, locality and subject taught by the teacher do not differ significantly in respect of their computer anxiety.

Arun (2008) conducted a study on "Assessment of the ICT skill of the M.Ed., scholars of Calicut university region" and revealed that the majority of the M.Ed., scholars accesses the internet for downloading academic material for self – development.

Annie Marie Merlene (2008) emphasized that most of the teachers of the teachers of today happen to belong to the Television – generation and being 'Television – Shaped learners', will have to learn new methods of ICT, to keep pace, and to be at par with the present day 'Internet-shaped, Neo-millennial learners'.

Deepa Frankly Mahalakshmi (2008) explained e-learning is essentially the network enabled transfer of skills and knowledge concluded that e-learning creates an interactive classroom environment.

Pushparaj (2008) conducted a study on "use of e-journals by the graduate students of plant science in trichy". Which concluded that most of the student uses the e-journals for their studies?

Venketaraman, S and Nellaiyappan, N.O (2008) conducted a study on Computer assisted Instruction (CAI) and some of its technical issues. This study showed that CAI is ins decided effective in bringing about learning. The packages when used in the self learning / group learning mode can be never replace good teacher. They can only enhance their effectiveness.

Franklin and Teresa (2008) conducted a study on "Mathematics educators and students engage in mobile learning". This paper presents a case study in which ipod touch was used to help middle school students learn about algebraic equations and in particular, the concept of slope, absolute value, and elimination. The development of math movies for use on the ipod touch provided students with mobile means of informal math learning beyond the hours of the classroom, while the study explored the use of mobile devices in an eighth grade math classroom, the lessons learned are invaluable to those seeking to implement mobile technologies to support teaching and learning with typical software such as movie, PowerPoint. The public continuing crisis in math education in our high schools and the convergence of technologies for teaching and learning.

Manivannan,M (2006) conducted a study on "Attitude of teacher and disabled graduated towards the computer application in teaching learning process". The findings were computer technology should not be a remote access to person with disabilities. A lot of advancement has come to make educations reachable, accessible and interesting to be. These advanced technologies are to be made easy for the person with disabilities to enhance their learning and doing fast and perfect. Let us try to bring up with disabilities together with us in all education and employment opportunities so us provide them better like in the society.

Narayanasamy, M and Thankasamy, S (2001) conducted a study on computer users among teacher educators in teacher training institution in Tamil Nadu. This study focused on increase the computer usage in teacher training students. The major finding of this study indicated in the majority of the teachers in DIET's show very positive attitude towards computer use them.

CONCLUSION

The investigator has reviewed studies related with attitude of teacher educators towards blended learning. They are recorded under their respective headings. In the review chapter, most of them have deal with various aspects of attitude, blended learning and teacher educators. This chapter is helpful to find out research problem and formulating objective, hypotheses method of study. Review is helpful to formulating the methodology. According, the method and procedure of this present study is given in next chapter.

❐

4

Plan and Procedure

Methodology is defined as the study of methods by which we gain knowledge. It deals with the cognitive processes imposed on research by the problems arising from the nature of its subject matter. Methods comprise the procedures used for generating, collecting and evaluating data. The main purpose of the study was to know about the attitude of teacher educators towards Blended learning. In this chapter the researcher has given the objectives, hypothesis, and sample of the study. And the validity and reliability of the Questionnaire constructed by the researcher was also given in this chapter.

STATEMENT OF THE PROBLEM

Problem of the study is stated as *ATTITUDE OF TEACHER EDUCATORS TOWARDS BLENDED LEARNING.*

OPERATIONAL DEFINITION OF THE KEY TERMS

Attitude

Attitudes are generally positive or negative views of a person, place, thing, or event this is often referred to as the attitude object. People can also be conflicted or ambivalent toward an object, meaning that they simultaneously possess both positive and negative attitudes toward the item in question. In this study, attitude means a positive or negative point of view of teacher educators towards blended learning.

Teacher Educators

The teacher who are working in college of education.

Blended learning

Blended learning has increased the possible ways learners can acquire knowledge, with learning occurring across different mediums and various times. In this study blended learning is a mixture of e-learning and traditional types of learning.

OBJECTIVES OF THE STUDY

1. To find out the attitude of teacher educators towards blended learning.
2. To find out the significant difference in attitude of teacher educators towards blended learning with respect to gender.
3. To find out the significant difference in attitude of teacher educators towards blended learning with respect to age.
4. To find out the significant difference in attitude of teacher educators towards blended learning with respect to locality.
5. To find out the significant difference in attitude of teacher educators towards blended learning with respect to marital status.
6. To find out the significant difference in attitude of teacher educators towards blended learning with respect to educational qualification.
7. To find out the significant difference in attitude of teacher educators towards blended learning with respect to teaching experience.
8. To find out the significant difference in attitude of teacher educators towards blended learning with respect to locality of Institution.
9. To find out the significant difference in attitude of teacher educators towards blended learning with respect to optional subject teaching.
10. To find out the significant difference in attitude of teacher educators towards blended learning with respect to guidance provides to students.

HYPOTHESES OF THE STUDY

1. There will be a significant mean score difference in attitude of teacher educators towards blended learning with respect to gender.
2. There will be a significant mean score difference in attitude of teacher educators towards blended learning with respect to age.
3. There will be a significant mean score difference in attitude of teacher educators towards blended learning with respect to locality.
4. There will be a significant mean score difference in attitude of teacher educators towards blended learning with respect to marital status.

5. There will be a significant mean score difference in attitude of teacher educators towards blended learning with respect to educational qualification.
6. There will be a significant mean score difference in attitude of teacher educators towards blended learning with respect to teaching experience.
7. There will be a significant mean score difference in attitude of teacher educators towards blended learning with respect to locality of Institution.
8. There will be a significant mean score difference in attitude of teacher educators towards blended learning with respect to optional subject teaching.
9. There will be a significant mean score difference in attitude of teacher educators towards blended learning with respect to guidance provides to students.

VARIABLE USED IN THE STUDY

1. Dependent Variable:
   Attitude towards Blended Learning.
2. Independent Variable

In this study, the following variables are considered as independent variables:

1. Gender
2. Age
3. Locality
4. Marital status
5. Educational Qualification
6. Teaching Experience
7. Locality of Institution
8. Optional Subject Teaching
9. Guidance Provides to Students

METHODOLOGY OF THE PRESENT STUDY

Research methodology is the description, explanation and justification of various methods of conducting research. Research studies adopting different methods, however do not as a rule, differ significantly in their procedures, selection, formation and definition of the problem, survey of related information, collection, analysis and interpretation of new data and reporting of the work done are steps of procedure common to all type of method of research. Here, the investigator used survey method for the present investigation. It is the most commonly used descriptive method in educational research. It is concerned with the present and attempts to determine the status of the phenomena under investigation. The various types of survey and different techniques used in survey have their respective significance and value. In survey, practical remedies to solve and resolve problems can be put forward and these remedies will normally be efficacious because they are the outcome of scientific study and analysis.

RESEARCH TOOL

For the present study, the researcher developed an own questionnaire to find out the Attitude of Teacher Educators towards Blended Learning with 40 items. On the basis of expert's opinions 10 items were omitted. The final scale consists of 30 items on the basis of two factors such as Personal and Teaching-Learning.

Scoring procedure

Strongly Agree – 4
Agree – 3
Disagree – 2
Strongly Disagree – 1

Higher the score indicates the higher the level of attitude towards blended learning.

PILOT STUDY

The pilot study was conducted from 40 teacher educators working in college of education. In order to establish the reliability of the tool, split half method was employed.

RELIABILITY OF THE TOOL

Reliability of the tool was established by using Spearman- Brown formula.

$$r_{tt} = 2r_{hh}/1+r_{hh}$$

Where,

r_{tt} = reliability coefficient of the full test

r_{hh} = reliability coefficient of the half test

Hence, the reliability of the tool was found to be 0.73.

VALIDITY OF THE TOOL

This tool was given to experts in the field of Education. On the basis of the suggestions, few of the items were altered.

POPULATION AND SAMPLE OF THE PRESENT STUDY

The population of the study was secondary teacher educators in the around of Salem district. The researcher has selected 240 teacher educators as sample by using random sampling technique. The details of the sample were presented in the following table

TABLE. 4.1: Break-up of sample

Variables	Sub Variables	No. of Sample
Gender	Male	103
	Female	137
Age	Below 30	96
	30 & Above	144
Locality	Urban	116
	Rural	124
Marital Status	Married	178
	Unmarried	62
Educational Qualification	P.G	132
	M. Phil & Ph.D	108
Teaching Experience	Below 5 years	97
	5 years & Above	143
Locality of Institution	Urban	83
	Rural	157
Optional Subject teaching	Science	144
	Language & Social Science	96
Guidance provide to students	Yes	43
	No	197

ADMINISTRATION OF THE TOOL

The final tool was administered to 240 Teacher Educators from Salem district. Directions were given to the samples before administering the tool. And the subjects were requested to give their views and opinions in the proper places. They were assuring that the information given by them would kept confidential. After administering the tool, the responses were evaluated and scored on the basis of the scoring procedures.

DATA ANALYSIS

After the collection of pertinent data through the use of appropriate tools and techniques, the next step is the process of analysis and interpretation in the research. The collected data were analyzed by using appropriate statistical techniques that are Mean, SD- Standard Deviation and t- test.

CONCLUSION

This chapter outlines the design of the present study, the procedure followed and the nature of the sample. It describes the hypotheses to be tested, the tools to be used and the methods of administration and scoring. The method of investigation designed was found to be quite appropriate and effective for the study. The data analysis and interpretation are presented in the next chapter. ❐

5

Analysis and Interpretation

Analysis and Interpretation are central step in the research process. The goal of analysis is to summarize the collected data in such way that they provide answers to the questions that triggered the research. After collection data, it has to be processed and analyzed in accordance with the outline laid down for the purpose at the time of developing the research plan. The term analysis refers to the computation of certain measures along with searching for patterns of relationship that exists among data groups. Analysis is not complete without interpretation; and interpretation cannot proceed without analysis. Both are, thus, interdependent. In fact, interpretation can be conceived of as a part of analysis. It is the task of interpretation to find out a link or a position of the study in the whole analytical framework. It connects the findings with the established theories. Although, chronologically, analysis and interpretation occupy the last stage of the research process. Interpretation leads to the establishment of explanatory concepts that can serve as a guide for future research studies.

STATISTICS USED IN THE PRESENT STUDY

The role of statistics in research is to function as a tool in designing research, analyzing its data and drawing conclusions there from. Descriptive statistics concern the development of certain indices from the raw data, whereas inferential statistics concern with the process of generalization. The statistics that were used in the study to analyze the data were mean, standard deviation (Descriptive statistics), and t-test (inferential statistics).

ATTITUDE OF TEACHER EDUCATORS TOWARDS BLENDED LEARNING

TABLE. 5.1: Attitude Towards Blended Learning

Variables	Sub Variables	N	Mean
Gender	Male	103	101.76
	Female	137	103.15
Age	Below 30	96	101.82
	30 & Above	144	103.28
Locality	Urban	116	103.59
	Rural	124	101.95
Marital Status	Married	178	103.06
	Unmarried	62	101.32
Educational Qualification	P.G	132	101.59
	M. Phil & Ph.D	108	103.34
Teaching Experience	Below 5 years	97	101.22
	5 years & Above	143	103.41
Location of Institution	Urban	83	103.27
	Rural	157	101.83
Optional Subject Teaching	Science	144	102.96
	Language & Social Science	96	101.53
Guidance Provide to Students	Yes	43	100.91
	No	197	103.22

According to the above table 5.1, the mean score is greater than 100. It is revealed that the teacher educators attitude towards blended learning is on higher level.

HYPOTHESES TESTING

Hypothesis -1

There will be a significant mean score difference in attitude of teacher educators towards blended learning with respect to gender.

TABLE. 5.2: Mean Score Difference in Blended Learning among Teacher Educators with Respect to Gender

Factors	Variables	N	Mean	S.D	t-Value	Level of Significance at 0.05 Level
Personal	Male	103	43.84	3.97	1.63	NS*
	Female	137	44.69	3.91		
Teaching-Learning	Male	103	57.91	5.3	0.78	NS
	Female	137	58.46	5.38		
Total	**Male**	**103**	**101.76**	**7.2**	**1.52**	**NS**
	Female	**137**	**103.15**	**6.8**		

N.S – Denotes Not Significant.

According to the table 5.2, the calculated t- value is less than the table value at 0.05 level. So, there is no significant difference in attitude towards blended learning among teacher educators with respect to the gender. So the hypothesis No.1 is rejected. Further, the male and female teacher educators are does not differ in attitude towards blended learning.

Hypothesis-2

There will be a significant mean score difference in attitude of teacher educators towards blended learning with respect to age.

TABLE. 5.3: Mean Score Difference in Blended Learning among Teacher Educators with Respect to Age

Factors	Variables	N	Mean	S.D	t-Value	Level of Significance at 0.05 Level
Personal	Below 30	96	44.14	3.83	0.78	NS
	30 & Above	144	44.54	4		
Teaching-Learning	Below 30	96	57.69	5.12	1.53	NS
	30 & Above	144	58.74	5.3		
Total	**Below 30**	**96**	**101.82**	**7.68**	**1.42**	**NS**
	30 & Above	**144**	**103.28**	**7.84**		

From the table 5.3, the calculated t- value is less than the table value at 0.05 level. So, there is no significant difference in attitude of teacher educators towards blended learning with respect to age. So the hypothesis No.2 is rejected. It is also reveals that the age factor does not influence the attitude towards blended learning.

Hypothesis -3

There will be a significant mean score difference in attitude of teacher educators towards blended learning with respect to locality.

TABLE. 5.4: Mean Score Difference in Blended Learning among Teacher Educators with Respect to Locality

Factors	Variables	N	Mean	S.D	t-Value	Level of Significance at 0.05 Level
Personal	Urban	116	46.47	4.03	1.97	Significant
	Rural	124	44.19	3.87		
Teaching-Learning	Urban	116	59.13	5.03	1.98	Significant
	Rural	124	57.77	5.63		
Total	**Urban**	**116**	**103.59**	**6.58**	**1.96**	**Significant**
	Rural	**124**	**101.95**	**6.4**		

According to table 5.4, the calculated t- value is greater than the table value at 0.05 level. So, there is a significant difference in attitude of teacher educators towards blended learning with respect to the Locality. So the hypothesis No.3 is accepted. Further, the teacher educators belong to urban area are better than their counterpart.

Hypothesis-4

There will be a significant mean score difference in attitude of teacher educators towards blended learning with respect to marital status.

TABLE. 5.5: Mean Score Difference in Blended Learning among Teacher Educators with Respect to Marital Status

Factors	Variables	N	Mean	S.D	t-Value	Level of Significance at 0.05 Level
Personal	Married	178	44.58	3.93	1.63	NS
	Unmarried	62	43.65	3.73		
Teaching-Learning	Married	178	58.48	5.26	1.02	NS
	Unmarried	62	57.68	5.34		
Total	**Married**	**178**	**103.06**	**7.79**	**1.50**	**NS**
	Unmarried	**62**	**101.32**	**7.87**		

It is seen from the table 5.5, the calculated t- value is less than the table value at 0.05 level. So, there is no significant difference in attitude of teacher educators towards blended learning with respect to the marital status. So the hypothesis No.4 is rejected. The variable marital status does not influence in this study.

Hypothesis-5

There will be a significant mean score difference in attitude of teacher educators towards blended learning with respect to educational qualification.

TABLE. 5.6: Mean Score Difference in Blended Learning among Teacher Educators with Respect to Educational Qualification

Factors	Variables	N	Mean	S.D	t-Value	Level of Significance at 0.05 Level
Personal	P.G	132	44.36	3.81	1.55	NS
	M. Phil & Ph.D	108	45.11	3.56		
Teaching-Learning	P.G	132	57.23	5.32	1.51	NS
	M. Phil & Ph.D	108	58.23	4.87		
Total	**P.G**	**132**	**101.59**	**7.22**	**1.96**	**NS**
	M. Phil & Ph.D	**108**	**103.34**	**6.4**		

According to the above table 5.6, the calculated t- value is less than the table value at 0.05 level. So, there is no significant difference in attitude of teacher educators towards blended learning with respect to educational qualification. So, the hypothesis No.5 is rejected. Further, the P.G and M. Phil and Ph.D holders are homogeneous in attitude towards blended learning.

Hypothesis-6

There will be a significant mean score difference in attitude of teacher educators towards blended learning with respect to teaching experience.

TABLE. 5.7: Mean score Difference in Blended Learning among Teacher Educators with Respect to Teaching Experience

Factors	Variables	N	Mean	S.D	t-Value	Level of Significance at 0.05 Level
Personal	Below 5 years	97	44.02	4.11	1.99	Significant
	5 years & Above	143	44.72	3.86		
Teaching-Learning	Below 5 years	97	57.2	5.15	2.61	Significant
	5 years & Above	143	58.97	5.18		
Total	**Below 5 years**	**97**	**101.22**	**7.75**	**2.14**	**Significant**
	5 years & Above	**143**	**103.41**	**7.8**		

According to the above table 5.7, the calculated t- value is greater than the table value at 0.05 level. So, there is significant difference in attitude of teacher educators towards blended learning with respect to teaching experience. So the hypothesis No.6 is accepted. Further, the 5 years and above experienced teacher are superior in attitude towards blended learning.

Hypothesis-7

There will be a significant mean score difference in attitude of teacher educators towards blended learning with respect to locality of institution.

TABLE. 5.8: Mean Score Difference in Blended Learning among Teacher Educators with Respect to Location of Institution

Factors	Variables	N	Mean	S.D	t-Value	Level of Significance at 0.05 Level
Personal	Urban	83	45.05	3.9	1.2	NS
	Rural	157	44.41	3.89		
Teaching-Learning	Urban	83	58.22	5.33	1.05	NS
	Rural	157	57.41	5.74		
Total	**Urban**	**83**	**103.27**	**7.65**	**1.36**	**NS**
	Rural	**157**	**101.83**	**7.79**		

According to the above table 5.8, the calculated t- value is less than the table value at 0.05 level. So, there is no significant difference in attitude of teacher educators towards blended learning with respect to the locality of institution. So, the hypothesis No.7 is rejected. Further, the urban and rural teacher educators are homogeneous in attitude towards blended learning.

Hypothesis-8

There will be a significant mean score difference in attitude of teacher educators towards blended learning with respect to optional subject teaching.

TABLE. 5.9: Mean score difference in blended learning among teacher educators with respect to optional subjects teaching

Factors	Variables	N	Mean	S.D	t-Value	Level of Significance at 0.05 Level
Personal	Science	144	44.57	3.79	1.54	NS
	Language & Social Science	96	43.8	3.77		

Teaching-Learning	Science	144	58.39	5.34	0.90	NS
	Language & Social Science	96	57.73	5.82		
Total	**Science**	**144**	**102.96**	**7.08**	**1.50**	**NS**
	Language & Social Science	**96**	**101.53**	**7.41**		

According to the above table 5.9, the calculated t- value is less than the table value at 0.05 level. So, there is no significant difference in attitude of teacher educators towards blended learning with respect to the Optional Subject teaching. So the hypothesis No.8 is rejected. Further, the science and language and social science teacher educators are homogeneous in attitude towards blended learning.

Hypothesis-9

There will be a significant mean score difference in attitude of teacher educators towards blended learning with respect to guidance provides to students.

TABLE. 5.10: Mean Score Difference in Blended Learning among Teacher Educators with Respect to Guidance Provide to Students

Factors	**Variables**	**N**	**Mean**	**S.D**	**t-Value**	**Level of Significance at 0.05 Level**
Personal	Yes	43	43.86	3.43	1.40	NS
	No	197	44.78	3.96		
Teaching-Learning	Yes	43	57.05	5.1	1.60	NS
	No	197	58.45	5.21		
Total	**Yes**	**43**	**100.91**	**7.3**	**1.82**	**NS**
	No	**197**	**103.22**	**7.58**		

According to the above table 5.10, the calculated t- value is less than the table value at 0.05 level. So, there is no significant difference in attitude of teacher educators towards blended learning with respect to guidance provide to students. So, the hypothesis No.9 is rejected. Further, the selected independent variable does not influence in this study.

SUGGESTION GIVEN BY TEACHER EDUCATORS TOWARDS BLENDED LEARNING

TABLE. 5.11: Suggestion given by Teacher Educators towards Blended Learning

S. No.	Suggestion	Strength	Persentage
1	It helps to improve the learning.	38	15.83
2	Save the time and energy	21	8.75
3	Easily to understand	22	9.17
4	Blended learning helpful to avoid academic stress	14	5.83
5	Learning in a joyful way	41	17.08
6	Easily understand the difficult concept through blended learning	59	24.58
7	Blended learning helpful to prepare for examination	12	5
8	Blended learning enhance the self confident in the learning	45	18.75
9	Blended learning improve the quality of education	52	21.67
10	Useful to avoid exam anxiety	9	3.75
11	Blended learning creates more interest among learners	51	21.25
12	It is very useful for life	13	5.41
13	Blended learning supports practical knowledge	34	14.17
14	Increases the communication skill among learners	29	12.08
15	It is useful for higher studies	19	7.91
16	Blended learning is useful for self-learning	12	5
17	It is a effective learning.	30	12.5

According to table – 5.11, 24.48% of teacher educators suggested that blended learning is uesful to understand the difficlut concepts. Remaining teacher educators also faour to blended learning techniques.

CONCLUSION

In this chapter, analysis and interpretations of the results was done. The next chapter deals with major findings, suggestions, educational implications and conclusion.

❒

6

Findings and Conclusion

A detailed presentation of the findings of the study, with supporting data is the next step in writing the research report. After a brief statement of the problem and a description of the procedures used in the investigation, the findings and conclusion are presented. This is the most important section of a project work because it gives a shape to the whole study. In this chapter some recommendations for further researches, findings of the study and educational implications of the study were given by the researcher.

STATEMENT OF THE PROBLEM

Problem of the study is stated as *ATTITUDE OF TEACHER EDUCATORS TOWARDS BLENDED LEARNING.*

OBJECTIVES OF THE STUDY

1. To find out the attitude of teacher educators towards blended learning.
2. To find out the significant difference in attitude of teacher educators towards blended learning with respect to gender.
3. To find out the significant difference in attitude of teacher educators towards blended learning with respect to age.
4. To find out the significant difference in attitude of teacher educators towards blended learning with respect to locality.

5. To find out the significant difference in attitude of teacher educators towards blended learning with respect to marital status.
6. To find out the significant difference in attitude of teacher educators towards blended learning with respect to educational qualification.
7. To find out the significant difference in attitude of teacher educators towards blended learning with respect to teaching experience.
8. To find out the significant difference in attitude of teacher educators towards blended learning with respect to locality of Institution.
9. To find out the significant difference in attitude of teacher educators towards blended learning with respect to optional subject teaching.
10. To find out the significant difference in attitude of teacher educators towards blended learning with respect to guidance provides to students.

HYPOTHESES OF THE STUDY

1. There will be a significant mean score difference in attitude of teacher educators towards blended learning with respect to gender.
2. There will be a significant mean score difference in attitude of teacher educators towards blended learning with respect to age.
3. There will be a significant mean score difference in attitude of teacher educators towards blended learning with respect to locality.
4. There will be a significant mean score difference in attitude of teacher educators towards blended learning with respect to marital status.
5. There will be a significant mean score difference in attitude of teacher educators towards blended learning with respect to educational qualification.
6. There will be a significant mean score difference in attitude of teacher educators towards blended learning with respect to teaching experience.
7. There will be a significant mean score difference in attitude of teacher educators towards blended learning with respect to locality of Institution.
8. There will be a significant mean score difference in attitude of teacher educators towards blended learning with respect to optional subject teaching.
9. There will be a significant mean score difference in attitude of teacher educators towards blended learning with respect to guidance provides to students.

FINDINGS OF THE STUDY

1. According to the table 5.2, the calculated t- value is less than the table value at 0.05 level. So, there is no significant difference in attitude towards blended learning among teacher educators with respect to the gender. So the hypothesis No.1 is rejected. Further, the male and female teacher educators are does not differ in attitude towards blended learning.

2. From the table 5.3, the calculated t- value is less than the table value at 0.05 level. So, there is no significant difference in attitude of teacher educators towards blended learning with respect to age. So the hypothesis No.2 is rejected. It is also reveals that the age factor does not influence the attitude towards blended learning.
3. According to table 5.4, the calculated t- value is greater than the table value at 0.05 level. So, there is a significant difference in attitude of teacher educators towards blended learning with respect to the Locality. So the hypothesis No.3 is accepted. Further, the teacher educators belongs to urban area are better than their counterpart.
4. It is seen from the table 5.5, the calculated t- value is less than the table value at 0.05 level. So, there is no significant difference in attitude of teacher educators towards blended learning with respect to the marital status. So the hypothesis No.4 is rejected. The variable marital status does not influence in this study.
5. According to the above table 5.6, the calculated t- value is less than the table value at 0.05 level. So, there is no significant difference in attitude of teacher educators towards blended learning with respect to educational qualification. So, the hypothesis No.5 is rejected. Further, the P.G and M. Phil and Ph.D holders are homogeneous in attitude towards blended learning.
6. According to the above table 5.7, the calculated t- value is greater than the table value at 0.05 level. So, there is significant difference in attitude of teacher educators towards blended learning with respect to teaching experience. So the hypothesis No.6 is accepted. Further, the 5 years and above experienced teacher are superior in attitude towards blended learning.
7. According to the above table 5.8, the calculated t- value is less than the table value at 0.05 level. So, there is no significant difference in attitude of teacher educators towards blended learning with respect to the locality of institution. So, the hypothesis No.7 is rejected. Further, the urban and rural teacher educators are homogeneous in attitude towards blended learning.
8. According to the above table 5.9, the calculated t- value is less than the table value at 0.05 level. So, there is no significant difference in attitude of teacher educators towards blended learning with respect to the Optional Subject teaching. So the hypothesis No.8 is rejected. Further, the science and language and social science teacher educators are homogeneous in attitude towards blended learning.
9. According to the above table 5.10, the calculated t- value is less than the

table value at 0.05 level. So, there is no significant difference in attitude of teacher educators towards blended learning with respect to guidance provide to students. So, the hypothesis No.9 is rejected. Further, the selected independent variable does not influence in this study.

EDUCATIONAL IMPLICATIONS

1. This study will help to develop positive attitude towards blended learning among teacher educators.
2. This study will help to implement virtual learning concept.
3. This study will helpful to the future researchers in developing a new research in understanding a difficult concept in a simpler way through the blended learning.
4. This research work will help to know the importance of blended learning and its practical knowledge in all levels of education.

RECOMMENDATIONS

1. Developing teachers' confidence in using blended learning.
2. Teacher educational institutions should ready to organize programme on blended learning.
3. Teachers need to be fully aware of the technology as a stepping stone to academic achievement of learners.

SUGGESTIONS FOR FURTHER RESEARCH

1. This kind of study may take up by other researchers by taking large number of samples and variables.
2. Similar study may take up by future researchers on analysis of attitude of teacher trainees towards blended learning.
3. This study may undertaken by future research scholars in the attitude of college teachers towards Blended learning.
4. Future researchers may take up a comparative study on conventional learning and Blended learning.

CONCLUSION

In this study, the researcher studied the attitude of teacher educators towards blended learning. The findings reveal that the teacher educators are better in attitude towards blended learning. The urban located teachers are superior to the rural teachers. Further, 5 and above 5 years experienced teachers are greater in attitude towards blended learning. Other selected variables are does not influence in this study.

❐

7

Self Acceptance and Locus of Control

Education is a lifelong process that begins at birth and continues throughout our life. Knowledge or information is nothing but the experiences based on the sense of perception. The bodily faculties that give an ability to gain experience in this universe are called senses, viz. the senses of sight, hearing, smell, taste and touch. It is during this educational life many of the adolescents face different problem. To lead a secure life everyone needs to adjust with the present environment and have the ability to control effectively. In order to arrive at such a level of positive interaction the individual needs to possess a positive self acceptance of himself during their educational period requires their ability of accepting himself as he is in order to live effectively and dynamically with the environment.

Adolescence is a period when the students need proper motivation to reach the goals set in the academic field. Thus motivation is closely related to locus of control. The focus on the two types of locus of control would enable the adolescence to develop the right mode of thinking leads to positive self-acceptance.

Adolescence is generally regarded as a period of great stress and strain. It is so because of the nature of the physical and mental development during the period. Adolescence is normally a period between 13 and 19 or 20 years of age. Some psychologists are of the view that it starts from twelfth year and stretches upto 21 or 23 years of age. Mostly the students between the age 14 to 16 or 17 are called teenagers and the educational system categories them as High school students ranging from VIII, IX and X standard. Some adolescents talk amongst themselves about their need of earning money. One will say 'he have no love for school'. The other will reply 'he deeply love school'. It indicates that their tastes, interests and aptitudes vary. The main problem of adolescents are overzealous, idealists and fame-hungry, impatient behavior, adverse effect of elders policy of double standard. But posing the factors of their failure on others especially on fate is high among the High school students.

DEFINITION OF SELF ACCEPTANCE

According to Wayne Dyer, "Self Acceptance means liking the entire physical you, and eliminating those cultural impositions to be proper or to merely tolerate your body when it behaves other than in a cosmetic fashion".

According to Jersild (1963), the sum total of a person's view of what he wishes he were or think he ought to be, as distinguished from what he is generally is called self acceptance. The adolescent's self acceptance has many facts, It includes aspirations he is vigorously striving to attain, or hopes dimly some day to relays.

According to Roger (1951), self-acceptance comprises what the person would like to be or holds out as a goal for individual development and achievement.

Garrison et al, (1967) says the term self acceptance has been shown to be valuable in determining the relationship between how the child sees himself and what he thinks he should be like. The self acceptance begins when the child identifies with as parental figure. During middle childhood and early adolescence it moves through a stage of romantics and glamour and culminates in the late adolescence as a composite of desirable characteristics which may be symbolized by an attractive, real and visible young adult or perhaps even an imaginary person.

Hilgar (1971) expressed that the self consists of all the ideas, perceptions and values that characterize 'I' and 'me' It includes the awareness of ' what I am and what can do'.

Garrison et al (1967) says that the person who accepts himself is guided by his own standard. He has insight and understanding in relation to his ability, worth and in relation to others. In order to be able to accept himself, a person must have a Self Concept which is realistic and which is not too different from his ideal of what he should be the Self Accepting person is familiar with his weakness. He recognizes those that he cannot change, those he must accept and live with. Such a person approves himself with his deficiencies and self acceptance promotes self evaluations. Such a person can be critical about him and has sense of responsibility for his actions. He don't blame others or destiny for his condition. Nor does he strive to put up a show in order to win the approval of others.

Sheerer (1949) in his study on the acceptance in the following manner.

(a) To perceive one's self as a person of worth, worthy of respect rather than condemnation

(b) To perceive one's standards as being based upon his own experience rather than the attitudes or desires of others.

(c) To perceive one's own feelings, motives and personal experience without distraction of the sensory data. It is found that if an individual thinks well of himself, he is likely to think well of others and a person who is highly Self Accepting also accepts others ideas and guidance.

THE CONCEPT OF SELF-ACCEPTANCE

Self-Acceptance is love and happy with whom you are now. Some call it self-esteem, others self-love, but whatever you call it, you'll know when you are accepting yourself cause it feels great. Its an agreement with yourself to appreciate, validate, accept and support who you are this very moment, even those parts you'd like to eventually change.

Self Acceptance is one of the influencing factors of personality to determine the quality of one's behavior. Self-Acceptance is the fullest description of oneself of which a person is capable of at one time.

No one, not even the greatest in any field, in the wildest imagination possible is born with a Self Acceptance. Self Acceptance is something that is developed through countless learning experiences as the child interacts with others and with his environment, as he discovers himself, a he becomes aware of what he is capable of doing and what he cannot do.

PROCESS OF ACCEPTANCE

Acceptance exists at the care of your being. It is your default status. In order to reach this base level of acceptance, you need only remove the items lying on top. To do this you must first identify all the things you do not accept about yourself. Then one by one eliminate them by examining and questioning your beliefs around the issue.

1. Know yourself and your beliefs.
2. Take a good hard look at your honesty level.
3. Know you are doing the best you can.

4. Relax your value judgments.
5. Examine guilt.
6. Understand your motivations.
7. Ask yourself questions about what you don't accept.

SELF ACCEPTANCE AND ADOLESCENTS

Adolescence is the period when one thinks about one's own identity physical, intellectual, emotional and moral aspects that influence the development of one's self.

It is more difficult for girls to formulate a clear and accepting view of their feminine identity than it is for boys, to accept their masculinity. In their upbringing there is more incentive for boys to prefer to be boys than for girls to prefer to be girls. Boys have more privileges they are less strictly supervised, they are not judged as severely as girls for misconduct, they move in to a man's world very smoothly.

The masculine gender looks forward to an occupation and financial independence as a necessity in life than the feminine gender. As girls reach and advance through adolescence, the major occupation many of them look forward to his marriage and motherhood. It has been found that with increasing age boys become more secure in their masculine role whereas the girls become less firmly identified with their feminine role. This paves the way for the masculine and feminine gender to develop a positive self-acceptance.

MOTIVATION BEHIND THE ACCEPTANCE

Acceptancc is a concept that sounds positive and also provides opportunities for positive development within an individual, but generally acceptance of self becomes difficult as adolescence do not look at them with a positive approach. The necessity for motivation becomes a driving force behind the concept of self acceptance.

The high school level of the student population requires a positive self acceptance to improve their achievement motivation. Motivation directs the Self Acceptance of the students. The Locus of Control, level of aspiration and their strength of need freely influence it. Internal locus of control may not improve their Self Acceptance but on the other hand. External locus of control has a direct influence on their self acceptance. Self acceptance plays a key role on academic achievement.

LOCUS OF CONTROL

Originally developed within the framework of Rotter's (1954) Social learning theory, the Locus of Control construct refers to the degree to which an individual believes the occurrence of reinforcement is contingent on his or her own behavior. The factors involved with reinforcement expectancy are labeled "external" and "Internal" control. In short, internal locus of control refers to the perception of positive or negative events as being a consequence of one's own actions and thereby under one's own personal control. In contrast, external locus of control believes that her behavior is guided by fate, luck. A locus of control orientation is a belief about whether the outcome of our actions is contingent on what we do (internal control orientation) or on events outside our personal control (external control orientation) (Zimloardo, 1985).

Thus the locus of control is conceptualized as referring to a undimensional continuum ranging from external to internal.

INTERNAL LOCUS OF CONTROL

Individual believes that his/her behavior is guided by his/her personal decisions and efforts.

EXTERNAL LOCUS IF CONTROL

Individual believes that his/her behavior is guided by fate, luck, or other external circumstances.

The locus of control is a concept in psychology, originally developed by Julian Rotter in the 1950's.The Locus of Control represents how a person's decision-making ability is influenced, essentially those who make choices primarily on their own are considered to have internal locus of control. People with external locus of control are generally more apt to be stressed and suffered due to depression as they are more aware of work situations since those who make decisions based more on what others think are said to have external locus of control. Women tend to have more external locus of control than men. Having an internal locus of control can also be referred to as "Personal control" or "Self - determination".

HISTORY OF LOCUS OF CONTROL

The locus of control construct originated from social learning theory, though the groundwork for his theory was laid by Fritz Heider (1958). According to social learning theory, the potential for any given behavior to occur is function of the individual's expectancy that the behavior will be effective in securing a desired end or reinforcement.

Social learning theory attempts to explain the person's selection of specific responses from a larger repertoire in predicting behavior in social settings. Although social learning theory evolved from association and instrumental conditioning theories, it encompasses a wide range of behavior determinants including personality, motivation and situational context. Within this frame work, Rotter developed the concept of Locus of control.

Heider's speculations were refined and formalized also by Weiner, Frieze, Reed, Rest and Rosenbaum (1971). Weiner described the elements in the kinds of explanations individuals use to account for their performance. The internal versus external dimension of behaviors is known as locus of control orientation.

Internals believe that the reinforcements they receive are primarily a result of their own behavior, ability, effort or characteristics. Individuals at the external end of the locus of control continuum attribute the control of their reinforcements to force outside themselves, such as luck, chance, fate or powerful others.

Individuals may learn to attribute to themselves greater control over their own behavior and view themselves as agents who can affect the world, rather than as passive objects being victimized by environmental commands. This fact is one of the focal issues of the Bandura's (1977) self-efficiency theory. Self-efficiency is one's perceived capacity to meet some challenge or perform a particular response.

According to Rose (1981), teachers with a generalized expectancy of internal control perceive classroom events as being a consequence of their own actions and under their personal control. Teachers with an expectancy of external control perceive little contingency between their actions in the class room and student behavioral outcomes. The degree of contingency expected by individuals between their behavior and its effect has been conceptualized by Rotter as the personality dimension Internal - External (I-E) Locus of Control.

According to Brown Autry and Langenback (1985), the Locus of Control construct is an element of attribution theory. Attribution theory is associated with the investigation of the perception of causality, the judgment of why a particular incident occurred.

THE CONCEPT OF LOCUS OF CONTROL

The essence of the Locus of Control concept is that each of us located the controlling elements in our lives either inside or outside ourselves. The person who believes that he can decide for himself what he will do or be that he is the 'captain of the soul'. Locates his control internally and the person who believes that what happens to him is largely a matter of luck or who depends on the decisions of other is locating his control externally. The Locus of Control construct originated from Rotter's (1966) social learning theory. So the concept of Locus of control is rather a recent origin. Many of the Psychologists are interested in this idea and a number of studies are going on in this new field.

DEFINITIONS OF LOCUS OF CONTROL

According to Roddin Considerable attention has been devoted to this construct since the 1980s, because many mental and physical outcome variables have been identified that depend largely on the extent to which the individuals actually are and even more importantly - perceive themselves to be in control of their lives and of the resources needed to make meaningful decisions about their life circumstances (Rodin et al.,) It has been argued that as adults age they experience an increasing number of life events over which they have little or no control.

TYPES OF LOCUS OF CONTROL

A number of researches have been conducted to find out whether Locus of Control is a too broad term. They have suggested that it might be better to breakdown the concepts internal and external into component parts. Levenson (1973) for instance, maintains that externals may be of two different sorts, people who believe the world as disordered (that things happen by chance) and people who believe the world as ordered but luck decides the fate or result.

Researchers have developed a test that distinguishes between the internals who take responsibility primarily for his success and the internals who blame himself for his failures. These two types have been shown to follow different developmental courses and to have differences in the classroom situation.

INTERNAL LOCUS OF CONTROL

If one person perceives that an event or achievement is contingent on his own behaviors or his own relatively permanent characteristics, he is termed to have internal control.

Here he assumes that he is the master of his fate and the captain of his soul. He thinks he can do what he wants to do and achieve results by his own efforts. Such people have internal locus of control.

CHARACTERISTICS OF INTERNAL LOCUS OF CONTROL

1. Internals are more likely to seek information
2. They are more sensitive and alert
3. Internals pay more attention to relevant cues, when there are uncertainties in the situation.
4. They show more incidental learning
5. They are more responsive to information requirements.
6. Internals pursue goals by paying careful attention to demands of the taste.
7. They set realistic goals and take responsibility for their actions.

EXTERNAL LOCUS OF CONTROL

When the subject as following some action of his own, but not being entirely perceives reinforcement contingent on his action, then it is typically perceived as the result of luck, fate, etc. When the events are interpreted or attributed in this way by an individual, this signifies the belief in external control.

If one believes that his ability and his skill would not make much difference because luck and other people will govern the outcome of his efforts. He is said to have external locus of control.

CHARACTERISTICS OF EXTERNAL LOCUS OF CONTROL

1. Externals are more suspicions to social influences and social demands.
2. They pursue goals by relying more on behavior-oriented outcomes towards the social agent in the situation.
3. They are not ready to take the responsibility of their actions.

LOCUS OF CONTROL Vs EDUCATION

It has often been said that obtaining a good education is the key to being successful in the world. Many things may contribute to school achievement and one variable that is over looked is locus of control. In the context of education, locus of control refers to the types of attributions are makes for reaching success and/or failure in school tasks. If someone believes that his or her successes and failures are due to the factors within their own control such as effort or ability, then that person is said to have an internal locus of control. On the other hand if someone believes that his or her successes and failure are due to factors outside of their own control, such as fate, luck, then person is said to have an external locus of control.

MODIFICATION OF STUDENTS LOCUS OF CONTROL

Attribution training, which concentrates on strengthening the students' internal locus of control (Deshler, Schumacher & Lenz, 1984), may be helpful in increasing motivation. Attribution training has been shown to increase internal locus of control and improve task persistence (Shelton, Anastopoulos & Linden, 1985). Usually the implementation of attribution training utilizes some form of self instructional set of statements. Students are trained to say positive things to themselves, first out loud, then in a whisper, then silently to themselves. This type of training is easy to implement & requires no special materials. For some students, attribution training can have a considerable impact on their overall efforts at school. When students are struggling or not putting forth much effort, it would be wise to consider locus of control as a possible contributor to the problem. A teacher's effort to motivate a student may prove futile, the child has external locus of control. Teaching children from a young age that hard work can pay off would be beneficial. If they were taught to believe in their own ability to control their lives and the reinforcements in their lives, they would be more likely to succeed in school.

DEVELOPMENT OF LOCUS OF CONTROL

Generally, the development of locus of control stems from family, culture and past experiences leading to rewards. Most internals have been shown to come from families that focused on effort, education, and responsibility. On the other hand, most externals come from families of a low socioeconomic status where there is a lack of life control.

NEED AND SIGNIFICANCE OF THE STUDY

The study of self acceptance and locus of control among high school students is very important. This study may help us to diagnose the psychological problem faced by the students. Mostly the students are lack in their personality. Self acceptance is one of the main variables of personality which is taken for this study. And every person especially the students need some type of motivation to reinforce their attitude. Hence locus of control is one of the main variables of motivation which is also considered for this study. Our present society shows positive signs of self-empowerment. Our adolescent population have also empowered themselves to meet the exclusive challenges in the Society.

Viewing the state of their self acceptance the adolescent needs to be encouraged in the educational field, to think for themselves, act rationally and reach the goals they have set. The adolescents of our present time need to face problems and demand which needs to be tackled effectively. The school and the family provide the support and Guidance for there. The individual himself should learn to acquire self-confidence and self-acceptance.

Adolescence is the most crucial and significant period of an individual's life. It represents the culmination of childhood and an initiation of the adult who is to be. In this stage, human personality develops new dimensions. It is the period to learn new things. It is the period of anxiety and worries. Adolescents are tightly ambitions. They will develop so many desires and ambitions to be filled. Despite their best planning and efforts they may not get the desired success. At times they find themselves in a state of utter confusion and bewilderment. All the paths for face repeated failures that lead them to distances. The main significant of Self Acceptance is once you truly accept yourself, you will waste no energy or time on self deception or deceiving others and you will develop clarity as to just what needs improving.

As everyone know, generally in an educational setting knowledge flows from the teacher to the student. This type of environment could cause students to withdrawn. It is suggested that students take more of an active control in the learning process. It is also important to take into consideration whether each student has an external or internal locus of control.

STATEMENT OF THE PROBLEM

Self Acceptance and Locus of control among High School students in Tiruvallur District.

DEFINITION OF THE TERMS

(a) **Self Acceptance**

Self acceptance is one of the influencing factors of personality as it governs the individual's reaction towards people and situations and determines the quality of one's behavior.

Self-Acceptance as measured through this inventory in an assessment of factors such as sense of personal worth and satisfaction with self.

(b) **Locus of Control**

Locus of control refers to an individual's generalized expectations concerning where control over subsequent event resides. In other words, who or what is responsible for what happens.

OPERATIONAL DEFINITIONS

(a) **Self Acceptation**

Self Acceptance scores are obtained by administering self acceptance inventory constructed and standardized by Kakkar, Patiala, 1984.

(b) **Locus Control**

Locus of control scores are obtained by administering Locus of control Scale constructed and standardized by Stephen Nowicki, Strickland in 1973.

OBJECTIVES OF THE STUDY

1. To study the level of self acceptance among High School students.
2. To Study the level locus of control among High School students
3. To find out the significant difference between boys and girls of High School students in their self Acceptance.
4. To find out the significant difference between boys and girls of High School students in their locus of control.
5. To find out the significant difference between different ages among High School students in their self acceptance.
6. To find out the significant difference between different ages among High School students in their locus of control.

7. To find out the significant difference between the high School students studying in different management in their self acceptance.
8. To find out the significant difference between the high School students studying in different management in their locus of control.
9. To find out the significant difference between joint and nuclear family of High School students in their self Acceptance.
10. To find out the significant difference between joint and nuclear family of High School students in their locus of control.
11. To find out the significant difference between rural and urban area High School students in their self acceptance.
12. To find out the significant difference between rural and urban area High School students in their locus of control.
13. To find out the significant difference between English and Tamil Medium of High School students in their self acceptance.
14. To find out the significant difference between English and Tamil Medium of High School students in their locus of control.
15. To find out the Significant Relationship of Self Acceptance and Locus of Control among High School students.

LIMITATIONS OF THE STUDY

- The sample is restricted to 300 students
- The study is restricted to High School students
- The study is limited to 5 Schools of Tiruvallur District.

CONCLUSION

The first chapter highlights the overview of the problem and the statement of the problem, need and significance of the study, objectives and limitations of the study. A review of related literature is dealt in the chapter that follows. ❐

8

Review of Related Literature

The purpose of present investigation is to study the effect of Locus of control and Self Acceptance. A large number of studies have been carried out in the field of Locus of control. The research literature is reviewed under the following captions.

(a) Study related to Self Acceptance
(b) Study related to Locus of Control

STUDIES RELATED TO SELF ACCEPTANCE

STUDIES ABROAD

Fuster's (1964) A Study on the relationship between Self Acceptance and acceptance of others among College Students.

According to Fuster, Self Acceptance implies the formation of a realistic Self concept which includes one's strength and weakness. Self Acceptance flows from that inner craving of waiting to be that person which is truly one. A fine feeling of being in this world for a puropose which is fully within his reach and which is achieving gradually as the years roll by Self Acceptance should be developed in Children because it makes a person like comfortably with himself. Self Accepted Child adopts a realistic approach to life situation. Such a Child can develop a positive attitude towards life.

BAKER (1977) studied the influence of psychological education to enhance Self-understanding and Self Acceptance in College Students.

The result shows that there is no demonstrated effect of the course on the participants Self Acceptance because these Students were the kind of people who improve without participating in this course. Baker's Study also emphasizes the need for psychological education to improve Self Acceptance in Adolescents.

HURLEY (1990) Studied the "Constructive thinking and elevated ratings of Self in interpersonal groups".

First they conducted the constructive thinking inventory (CTI) for one hundred and three university students. Results shows that constructive thinking and rating one's self above peers, especially, for acceptance of Self consistently correlated positively, suggesting an underlying sense of independence, From this study it is clear that constructive thinking can be inculcated in Children by proper Self Acceptance programme.

Fraley-Stephen-E. (1992) From Self-Blame to Self-Acceptance: Freeing Myself in a Prison Undergraduate Program.

A prison inmate who is a graduate psychology student reflects on how the study of social and behavioral sciences contributed to his moral and ethical growth.

Starn (1993) Studied learning disabilities of male adolescents. Thirty Seven 9th and 10th grade males from two suburban Midwestern School systems were administered the California psychological inventory (CPI) Self Acceptance taken as one of the variable. The data do not provide evidence that adolescents with learning disabilities experience greater dependence and greater isolation and loneliness than their non-learning disabled peers. Correlation showed that there is a significant relation between Self Acceptance and their disabilities.

Statman-Daniel (1993) Studied Self-Assessment, Self-Esteem, and Self-Acceptance. Discusses students self-esteem is best improved through self-acceptance rather than by comparisons with others. Argues that some comparisons are essential to the concept of self and therefore are important to self-esteem. Concludes that some students may have low self-esteem because they accurately assess their abilities with others.

Randolph, Elizabeth (1993) Developed Self-Awareness and Self-Acceptance in Emotionally Handicapped Students through the Bibliotherapeutic Process.

This practicum involved the development, implementation, and evaluation of a program which used a bibliotherapeutic approach to develop specific behaviors with three second graders and seven fifth graders, all in a resource program for students with emotional handicaps. A needs assessment survey of mainstream teachers identified needs in the following areas: responsibility, cooperation, conflict resolution, and truthfulness. Although projected goals were not met, individual students made gains in each area. Students experienced attitude changes, improved self-concepts, and more realistic awareness of objective areas. Items in the appendix include the student contract, target behavior survey, the data collection chart, and critical thinking questions.

Mills-Brett-D. (1993) studied the Rehabilitation Counselling for Athletes Prior to Retirement: A Preventative Approach Using Self-Acceptance To Enhance Performance before and after Retirement.

This study suggests that collegiate and professional athletes preparing to retire should be provided with pre retirement and postretirement rehabilitation counseling. The counseling should involve a preventative approach centered around self-acceptance, to enhance the athlete's performance before and after retirement. The development of self-acceptance in an athlete helps him or her to experience less competitive cognitive anxiety. Questions are presented that athletes can ask themselves to examine their level of self-acceptance and that coaches can ask themselves to determine their enhancement of athletes' self-acceptance. Counselors are encouraged to provide empathy and support, break the problem into manageable parts and develop a plan to tackle those parts, and determine the athlete's internal and external strengths and resources.

Yuan,-Frances (1994) studied that moving toward self-acceptance among Students with Learning Disabilities.

This study describes a course developed at Lesley College (Massachusetts) to help students with learning disabilities accept their disability and develop self-understanding and self-advocacy skills. It describes the course model and major tenets, highlights some course components, and summarizes results of a study of the courses impact.

CHROMIC (1996) Studied the level of acquisition of Self advocacy attribution within a group of High School students with learning disabilities after being exposed to an instructional unit developed to teach Self - advocacy skills.

The subjects were high school students (10th - 12th) with learning disabilities who were receiving services within transition resource classes. The conclusion was that seven week Self advocacy unit was not powerful enough to effect a change in the self advocacy attributes of the students as measured by the CPI qualitative data. Results indicated that most students were able to identify individual strengths and weakness, but were able to describe effectively the nature of their disability.

FREDERICK, VERDINE J (1997) Studied the relationship among acceptance of a learning disability grade level at diagnosis and achievement of students with learning disabilities.

The study sample consists of fifty high schools. Only students whose records indicated that they had been designated as learning disabled by a board of education, special education, team were considered for participation. The tools were given to each of the 50 learning disabled students in their schools. The findings demonstrate that lower the students grade level when a diagnosis of a learning disability is determined, the greater the students Self Acceptance of his or her learning disability.

BRILL (1999) Studied Self Acceptance and a heightened sense of emotional vulnerability.

The transition period from child to adult arrives the adolescents' intense need for emotional security in the form of acceptance by peers. Throughout life emotional needs and fear are interpreted differently. Helpless infants have a moral fear of living abandoned. At childhood, our emotional security requires contribute reassurance of our lovability and acceptability. In adolescence, this core emotional needs become Focused upon Self and social acceptance. The unbearable emotional distress leads the adolescence to a variety of destructive behavior patterns, some may become self-destructive, some may express in anger and violence. Self Acceptance makes a person emotionally balanced. Self accepted person can be well adjusted with the peers and society.

LEVON (2001) Studied Self Acceptance as the ability to see and recognize all aspects of self without judgment, either positive or negative.

Self Acceptance is not about living or approving one's self. It is simply about being aware of all of the parts of the self. It is about being awake and fully conscious. He also says that increase of self acceptance increase the raw material at disposal. It is about adding and expanding. It is the contrasts, conflicts, inconsistencies and polarities in life that make it interesting and awesome.

SIM T.N. (2003) Studied Father and mother linkage in relation to adolescent academic and athletic competence and self worth.

A total of 140 Singapore undergraduates reported on themselves and their parents. Results indicate that some adolescent attributes exist only when mother's characteristics are considered. The link between father's responsiveness and athletic competence existed only when mother's responsiveness was high and that link between father's acceptance of individualization and athletics competence existed only when mother's acceptance of individualization was moderate or high.

STUDIES IN INDIA

ARORA (1981) Studied the problems of students in professional courses of medicine, law, engineering and education in relation to personality factors.

In this study Self Acceptance was taken as one of the variable. A student's problem checklist consisting of 10 areas were administered to a sample of 800 boys & girls preparing for the first professional degree in medicine, law, engineering and education. Result shows that high problem students in general, found to have lower personality adjustment, lawer creative persons, and higher level of aspirations, and high Self Acceptance than low problem students.

WAHEEDA (1989) Studied the behavioral training in improving personality characteristics of juvenile delinquents in relation to Self Acceptance.

The sample was drawn from Government Special Home for boys at Chengelpet and Government special home for girls at Kilpauk, Madras, run by Government of Tamil Nadu. The samples were chosen by administering kakkar's Self Acceptance inventory to a group of 50 male and female delinquents. The samples were given Jerner's personality inventory to assess the personality characteristics of the juvenile delinquents. His major findings were that the high self acceptance experimental low acceptance group, no significant difference was found in both the high Self Acceptance and low self acceptance group among males and females and the high self acceptance group showed improvement in a social index whereas the low self acceptance group had no improvement.

Sunanda. Y. (1991) conducted a study of reaction of frustration as related to life satisfaction and self acceptance among the aged.

The objective is to relate frustration reaction to the acceptance of age-linked changes. The 'Sample comprised under middle age (40-49 years) advanced middle age (50-59 years) young old (60-69 years) and old age (70+ years). The tools used included frustrations reaction of life satisfaction. Scale, Jamuna and Ramamoorthy is Assessment of self acceptance and a bio-data schedule. The collected data was subjected to statistical analysis. Mean, S.D, 't' test, correlation and analysis of variance was calculated. He found that self acceptance among the aged was positively related to life satisfaction.

BHARADWAJ (1998) Studied Parental rejection, acceptance and adolescent value conflict. In a sample of 500 adolescents by employing a two group design. Tools used were parenting scale constructed and standardized by Bharadwaj et al. and value conflicts scale constructed and standardised by Bharadwaj.

STUDIES RELATED TO LOCUS OF CONTROL
STUDIES ABROAD

Guss,-Thomas (1990) Studied Integrating Underemployment and Hardship: Using Locus of Control To Develop a Profile among Married Men. The role of marital issues and individual characteristics in hardship, and the emphasis in the literature of the traditional provider role, there is a need to explore the experience of underemployment among married men. only husbands were selected for this project. A random sample of a non-metropolitan northwest community produced 137 couples with a variety of incomes.. Husbands in hardship were more oriented to chance, while non hardship providers were more internal. Results suggest that locus of control is a distinguishing characteristic among married men.

Thompson,-Josephine-T.(1991) Established the Locus of Control among Ninth Graders: Using Peer Mentors To Reduce Student Disengagement, Absenteeism, and Failures.

An intervention program was implemented to reduce absences, stimulate responsibility for assignments, and increase participation in extracurricular activities among disengaged ninth-grade students (N=18). Mentors felt the greatest benefits were showing disengaged students that someone cares and that if attitudes toward school could be improved needless failures and dropouts could be prevented.

Martin,-Janice-E.; et. al. (1991) Studied the relationship among Internal-External Locus of Control and Rational-Irrational Beliefs.

The study investigated the relationship between Internal-External Locus of Control Scale and Irrational Beliefs Test (IBT) scores. The independent variable was locus of control; the dependent variables were IBT full-scale and subscale scores. Data were collected through administering these instruments to state human service agency employees (N=105). Statistical analyses indicated that there was a significant correlation between internal-external locus of control and IBT full-scale scores and that there were significant correlations between internal-external locus of control and 8 out of 10 IBT subscale scores. Internal locus of control subjects exhibited more rational beliefs. Likewise, external locus of control subjects maintained more irrational beliefs.

Hipps,-Elizabeth-Smith; Halpin,-Glennelle (1991) Studied Job Stress, Stress related to performance-based accreditation, Locus of Control, Age, and Gender As Related to Job Satisfaction and Burnout in Teachers and Principals.

The purpose of the study described here was to: (1) determine the amount of variance in burnout and job satisfaction in public school teachers and principals which could be accounted for by stress related to the state's performance-based accreditation standards; (2) examine the relationship between stress related to state standards and the age and gender of the educators; and (3) develop measures of educator job stress common to both teachers and principals and stress related to the state performance-based accreditation standards. Surveys were sent to teachers (N=445) and principals (N=128). Responses were received from 219 teachers and 58 principals.

Whitney,-Patricia (1991) Studied Children's Locus of Control and Intrinsically Motivated Reading.

Study investigated the relationship between locus of control and intrinsically motivated reading for children. To find the hypothesis that students with an internal locus of control would be more productive readers than those with an external locus of control, a matched sample was drawn. The t-test for matched samples and the Pearson product-moment both indicated non-significant differences between intrinsic motivation of internal and external subjects. The t-test for matched samples and the Pearson product-moment both indicated non-significant differences between intrinsic motivation of internal and external subjects. The most revealing factor was that the students felt they were "too busy" for free-choice reading. To find the hypothesis that students with an internal locus of control would be more productive readers than those with an external locus of control, a matched sample was drawn. The t-test for matched samples and the Pearson product-moment both indicated non-significant differences between intrinsic motivation of internal and external subjects.

Evans,-Jan-Holmgren (1991) Studied the Relationship between Internal Locus of Control and Rehabilitation Prognosis.

Studies involve the subject groups selected and the indexes of outcome, as well as the manipulation of treatment, structures cause limited generalability. Different studies contradict each other probably too frequently for strictly scientific purposes. The importance of internal locus of control on the rehabilitation process of any illness or disability tends to have numerous methodological problems. Questionnaires exist that measure a person's internal locus of control; however, that extra inner essence of a person defies scientific exploration and measurement.

Ayersman,-David-J. (1992) Studied the effect of a Summer Enrichment Program for At-Risk Youths on Locus of Control and the Relation to Motivational Orientation.

Examining locus of control, and showing an effective treatment program for transitioning from externality to internality, it may be possible to predict other behaviors and eliminate negative behaviors (drug use, low self-esteem, poor grades) associated with externality which will assist in keeping children in school. This study examined the relationship between locus of control and motivation. Statistical significance was also found by age and gender with younger females being the most external and older males being the most internal. A moderate negative correlation was found linking one of the five motivation subscales (independent judgment) with locus of control.

Thompson,-Bruce; et.al.(1992) Studied the Nature of Children's Health Locus of Control Beliefs.

The study was to explore the structure of the health locus of control beliefs of children, using the Multidimensional Health Locus of Control Scales. People's beliefs about the origins of their health, sometimes referred to as health locus of control, have been shown to influence a variety of important behaviors. Two samples of 4th- through 6th-grade students were utilized to allow for cross-validation of results. The first group had 780 subjects, the second group had 524 subjects. Confirmatory methods were employed in this study.

Martin,-Janice-E.; et.al (1992) Studied the effects of internal-external Locus of Control and Selected Demographic Variables on Rational-Irrational Beliefs.

This study evaluated whether or not locus of control mediates rational-irrational beliefs. Results support the view that internally oriented individuals maintain more rational beliefs than do externally oriented people. Nine tables present study data. Data were generated investigating the impact of an internal-external orientation and selected demographic variables (age, race, gender, education, and occupation) on rational-irrational beliefs. Independent variables were locus of control and demographic characteristics, and the dependent variable was beliefs. Data were collected by administering the Internal-External Locus of Control Scale and the Irrational Beliefs Test to 105 state human service agency employees (81 internals and 24 externals). A one-way analysis of variance uncovered significant differences in internal and external females. In addition, there were significant differences in beliefs between internal and external subjects at different educational levels.

Sisco,-Sharon-S. (1992) Using Goal Setting To Enhance Self Esteem and Create an Internal Locus of Control in the At Risk Elementary Student.

Study examined the effects of a program designed to enhance the self-esteem of at-risk students by developing an internal locus of control in the students. The Piers-Harris Children's Self-Concept Scale was administered as a pretest and posttest, providing the data from which the discrepancy gap for showing improvement in self-esteem was formulated. The program consisted of six major components: (1) a specified vocabulary and format; (2) goal identification and description by students; (3) student evaluation and selection of alternative actions to accomplish goals; (4) student journal writing showing reflective evaluation and identification of successful and unsuccessful behaviors; (5) a scale to evaluate student goals; and (6) peer encouragement through class meetings. Results indicated that students' self-esteem improved and fewer severe behavior referrals were necessary. However, attendance was not significantly affected. Related materials are appended.

Freedman,-Susan-A. (1992) Studied Sex, Gender and Locus of Control in College Students.

Study was undertaken to examine the relationship between locus of control and gender role. Locus of control has most frequently been measured using Internal versus External measures. A non significant trend for the interaction of sex by locus of control was found. Findings further indicated that Internal locus of control may be over-represented in some college populations.

Enger,-John-M.; et.al (1993) Studied Internal/External Locus of Control and Parental Verbal Interaction of At-Risk Adolescent Black Males.

The academic and discipline problems of young black male students in a small southern town, the Positive Impact Program (PIP) was developed for at-risk black males. Two possible at-risk factors, locus of control and the quality of parental verbal interaction, were studied for participants in the PIP. Locus of control and communications with parents were compared to those of previously nor med groups. The Verbal Interaction Questionnaire (developed by P. C. Blake in 1991) scores were comparable to those for rural predominantly white male and female high school students. In general, students more internally controlled reported having more positive parental verbal communication, while those more externally controlled had more negative parental verbal communication. Eighteen of the 42 boys were in the PIP, but no significant differences were found for these students on either measure, or no locus of control scores were available from the period before PIP participation.

Bernhard,-Judith-K.; Siegel,-Linda-S. (1994) Increasing Internal Locus of Control for a Disadvantaged Group: A Computer Intervention.

Discussion of locus of control (LOC), gender, and mathematics and technical subjects focuses on a study of preschool girls and boys Highlights include treatment of experimental and control groups; gender differences; parent questionnaires; and pretests and posttests.

Reeh,-H.-Elise; Reilly,-Karen-J. (1995) A Quasi Meta Analysis of the Health Locus of Control Construct.

The study about the Internal HEALTH LOCUS OF CONTROL (HLOC) is related to health-promoting behavior, positive health status, health knowledge, information-seeking, and treatment success. The results of this analysis indicate that HLOC research is primarily conducted in the United States by a fairly even distribution of male and female researchers, who are often members of psychology faculties. Studies are mostly published in psychology journals, with some research appearing in medical journals. These studies have included a wide variety of participants, including hospital patients, employees, school children, and university students. HLOC research is generally of an applied nature, and is most often correlational in design.

Fournier,-Genevieve; St-Onge,-Susan (1995) Studied about the Shaping Vocational Locus of Control through Beliefs.

Presents a survey of rudimentary results, and proposes a typology of vocational beliefs. Presents a synthesis of the theoretical foundations implemented in an investigation of the principal vocational beliefs of individuals having difficulty with their career choice. Suggests. Principles of intervention to help young adults facing difficulty in career decisions

Hawkes,-Brent-B (1995) Studied Locus of Control in Early Childhood Education This study discusses research on locus of control, particularly as it relates to early childhood education. Some measures of children's sense of locus of control are discussed, including the Optimism-Pessimism Test Instrument and the Stanford Preschool Internal-External Scale. Factors which inhibit the assessment of children's sense of locus of control are detailed, including: (1) lack of development of children's vocabulary and communication skills; (2) children's tendency to select the last possible answer offered in a structured interview situation; (3) children's tendency to respond "yes" to yes or no questions; and (4) the prevalence of a research bias which assumes that elementary school children do not have well-developed self-awareness. The review concludes by noting that locus of control appears to be an important element of children's experiences and potential success in school.

Tyler,-Doris-Kennedy; Vasu,-Ellen-Storey (1995) Studied Locus of Control, Self-Esteem, Achievement Motivation, and Problem-Solving Ability: LogoWriter and Simulations in the Fifth-Grade Classroom.

The effects of using LOGO, or problem-solving- oriented simulation software on locus of control, self-esteem, and achievement motivation for fifth-grade students. The importance of these variables in predicting LOGO mastery and far-transfer problem-solving ability was also examined.

Santa-Rita,-Emilio (1995) Studied the Effect of Computer-Assisted Student Development Programs on Entering Freshman Locus of Control Orientation.

To determine the effect of SUCCESS programs on students' perceived locus of control and empowerment study was conducted at New York's Bronx Community College of two entering freshmen classes in fall 1995 (n=35). The experimental class received six SUCCESS assignments over 14 weeks related to basic college survival information and calculations of grade point averages and financial aid data. The Nowicki-Strickland Internal-External

Control Scale was administered to both groups at the beginning and again at the end of their first semester to determine differences in student sense of power versus helplessness, persistence with parents in achieving goals, and perception of luck as a determinant in obtaining goals. Comparison of pre- and post-test scores for both groups indicated that students who completed the SUCCESS assignments did not shift significantly with respect to overall perceived control of reinforcement and there were no significant differences between the experimental and control groups' sense of persistence with parents. The SUCCESS students did however perceive luck as having a considerably lesser effect on the attainment of desired outcomes than the control group

Cook,-Ann; Troike,-Roger (1995) Studied Adolescent Parenting: Contrasts in Self-Esteem and Locus of Control.

Of the 17,051 women who become pregnant every day in America, 2,795 or 16% of them are adolescents. The self-esteem and locus of control of 85 pregnant and parenting teens enrolled in the Ohio Graduation, Reality, Dual Role Skills (GRADS) Program were measured and compared to the scores of 85 non-parenting peers. Self-esteem was measured using Rosenburg's Self-Esteem Scale. Locus of control was measured by Rotter's Internal-External Locus of Control

No significant differences in the mean scores were discovered. This supported the assumption that involvement in the GRADS Program allowed pregnant and parenting teens to retain a level of self-esteem and locus of control equivalent to their non-parenting peers. The results of this study substantiate the worth of in-school support groups for high risk adolescents.

STUDIES IN INDIA

PANI, MINA (1991) Studied the effect of culture and locus of control.

The performance among 40 tribal and 40 non-tribal Indian students in grade 3. Both tribal and non-tribal students were divided into internal Vs external locus of control groups. Reading task included both oral comprehension and several metalinguistic tasks. The poorest performance was evidenced by tribal students and students with external locus of control.

SAEEDUZZAFAR AND SHARMA, RAMA (1991) Studied the effect of religion (Hinduism and Islam) on locus of control and dependence proneness among externally oriented and internally oriented individuals.

The results showed that Muslim students were more dependent prone than Hindu Students. Externally oriented students were more depended than internally oriented students. However, the interactional effect of religion and locus of control was insignificant.

CONCLUSION

The survey of the related literature has helped much to have a proper perspective of the problem chosen for the study. The review of related literature has enabled the investigator to formulate relevant literature also resulted in providing insight into the selection and use of effective methods of study, analysis and interpretation.

❐

9

Design of the Study

This chapter describes in detail, the design of the study, nature and selection of sample, a brief description of the tools of investigation and the criteria for their investigation. It also gives a description of the procedure adopted for the collection of data, for its scoring and classification, finally the proposed statistical treatment of the data for testing the hypothesis that were formulated are explained.

HYPOTHESIS

The following hypotheses have been set for the present study:

1. The level of Self Acceptance among High School Student is Average.
2. The internal locus of Locus of Control is predominant among High School Student
3. There is a significant difference between boys and girls of High School students in their self acceptance.
4. There is a significant difference between boys and girls of High School students in their locus of control.
5. There is a significant difference between different ages among High School students in their self acceptance.
6. There is a significant difference between different ages among High School students in their locus of control.

7. There is a significant difference between the high School students studying in different management in their self acceptance.
8. There is a significant difference between the high School students studying in different management in their locus of control.
9. There is a significant difference between joint and nuclear family of High School students in their self Acceptance.
10. There is a significant difference between joint and nuclear family of High School students in their locus of control.
11. There is no significant difference between rural and urban area High School students in their self acceptance.
12. There is no significant difference between rural and urban area High School students in their locus of control.
13. There is a significant difference between English and Tamil Medium of High School students in their self acceptance.
14. There is a significant difference between English and Tamil Medium of High School students in their locus of control.
15. There is a significant relationship of self acceptance and locus of control among High School students.

TOOLS AND MATERIALS USED

To test the hypotheses, two inventories were used for the present investigation viz., Self Acceptance inventory and Locus of control inventory.

THE SELF ACCEPTANCE INVENTORY

The Self Acceptance inventory constructed and standardized by Dr.Kakkar (Patiala, 1984) was used in this study. It consists of 34 statements with positive and negative statements. The nature of items of Self Acceptance Inventory has been presented below.

TABLE. 9.1: Showing the Nature of the Items of Self Acceptance Inventory

S.No.	Nature of Item	Item number
1.	True	3,6,9,11,13,15,16,19,22,23,24,25,28, 30,33,34
2.	False	1,2,4,5,7,8,10,12,14,17,18,20,21,26,27

ADMINISTRATION

The following instructions were given to the students before administrating the inventory. The purpose of this questionnaire is to detect the type of Self Acceptance students have about themselves. There are 34 items in the questionnaire. The subjects were asked to read each statement carefully and respond by putting a tick on "True" column. If it is not applicable, put tick (x) on "False" column.

SCORING

For one correct answer, one score is provided according to key. Scoring through a template is also possible where circles which show through the template are counted and the total entered in the proper cell of the last page is treated as raw score.

LOCUS OF CONTROL INVENTORY

The Locus of Control Inventory constructed and standardized by Stephen Nowicki and Strickland in 1973 was used in this study. It consists of 40 statements. The nature of items of Locus of Control has been presented below.

TABLE. 9.2: Showing the Nature of the Items of Locus of Control Inventory

S. No	Nature of item	Item Number
1.	Yes	1,3,5,7,8,10,11,12,14,16,17,18,19,21,23,24, 27,29,31,33,35,36,37,39
2.	No	2,4,6,9,13,15,20,22,25,26,28,30,32,34,38,40

ADMINISTRATION

The following instructions were given to the students before administrating the inventory. The purpose of this questionnaire is to detect the type of Locus of Control students have about themselves. There are 40 items in the questionnaire. The subjects were asked to read each statement carefully and respond by putting a tick on "Yes" or "No" in all the responses.

SCORING

For one correct answer, one score is provided according to the key. The total umber of agreements between the answers and the ones on the key is a raw score.

PILOT STUDY

A pilot study was conducted to assess the reliability of the tools. Pilot study also helped in understanding the difficulties faced by the subject in answering the questionnaires. The pilot study was conducted on 50 students to assess the reliability and validity

RELIABILITY OF THE TOOLS

The Reliability Coefficient Of The Self Acceptance Inventory Has Been Computed By Using The Odd Even Method. The Reliability Coefficient Was Computed By Spearman Brown Formula. Obtaining A Value Of 0.747 Indicating, That The Tool Was Highly Reliable.

The reliability coefficient of the Locus of Control has been computed by using the odd even method. The reliability coefficient was computed by Spearman Brown formula obtaining a value of 0.866 indicating , that the tool was highly reliable

VALIDITY OF THE TOOLS

The validity of the score was calculated by taking the square root of reliability. In the case of Self Acceptance inventory it is found to be 0.864, also suggesting that tool is valid. In the case of Locus of Control inventory it is found to be 0.93 indicating that the tool is valid.

SAMPLE

A stratified random sampling technique was adopted for the selection of sample. The school selected for this study is divided into different strata, namely Government, Aided and Private schools. 300 students were taken for the study.100 students were drawn from Government schools, 100 from Aided schools and 100 from Private schools.

TABLE. 9.3: Showing The Composition of The Sample Selected For The Study of Gender, Type of School, Medium of Instruction And Locality Of School.

S. No	Name of the School	Gender		Types of School			Medium		Locality of School	
		Boys	Girls	Govt	Aided	Private	English	Tamil	Urban	Rural
1.	Govt. welfare boys Hr.Sec school, Sevvapet.	47		47				47		47
2.	Govt. welfare girls Hr.Sec school , Sevvapet		53	53				53		53
3.	Siddhartha Matriculation school, Sevvapet	34	16			50	50			50
4.	Gnana vidyalaya matric school, Tiruvallur	12	38			50	50		50	
5.	Goudie Hr.Sec school,Tiruvallur	77	23		100		50	50	50	50
Total		**170**	**130**	**100**	**100**	**100**	**150**	**150**	**100**	**200**

MAIN STUDY

Permission was sought from the respective heads of the institution and explanation was given regarding the purpose and nature of the study. After having fixed the day and time for the distribution of questionnaire, the investigator administered the questionnaire to the sample of students selected standard VIII, IX and X.

The students were gathered in a classroom and the purpose of the investigation was explained to them. The nature of the questions and the method of answering was explained. Total confidentiality of views was assured in a bid to stimulate the students to answer freely. They were made to feel one with the purpose of the investigation. More instructions were given on the first page of the questionnaire.

STATISTICAL TECHNIQUES

Suitable descriptive and inferential statistical techniques were used in the interpretation of the data to draw more meaningful pictures of results from the collected data. In the present study the following statistical techniques were used.

1. Mean.
2. Standard Deviation.
3. Critical Ratio.
4. Analysis Of Variance.
5. Correlation Coefficient.
6. Quartile Deviation.

CONCLUSION

This chapter outlines the design of the present study, the procedure followed and the nature of the sample. It describes the hypotheses to be tested, the tools used and method of administration and scoring.

❐

10

Analysis and Interpretation of the Data

Analysis of data means studying the tabulated material in order to determine the facts or meanings. The data, after collection has to be processed and analysed in accordance with the outline laid down for the purpose at the time of developing the research plan. This is essential for a scientific study and for ensuring that we have all relevant data for making contemplated comparisons and analysis. After analyzing the data the researcher has to accomplish the task of drawing inferences followed by report writing.

ANALYSIS AND INTERPRETATION OF THE DATA

The data collected was subjected to statistical calculations and the hypotheses formulated have been verified.

1. Descriptive statistics to understand the nature of Self Acceptance and Locus of control.
2. 't' test to find out the significant difference of Self Acceptance with respect to location, medium of instruction, gender. And same for the other variable Locus of control.
3. ANOVA to find out the significance of difference for self acceptance and Locus of control with respect to age, type of school.

4. Correlation to find out the relationship between Self Acceptance and Locus of control.

Hypothesis – I

The level of Self Acceptance among High School Student is Average.

TABLE. 10.1: Shows the Frequency and Percentage for the Variable Self Acceptance.

Category	Range	Frequency	Percentage
Low self acceptance	Below 14	57	19 %
Moderate self acceptance	From 14- 18	191	63.36%
High self acceptance	Above 18	52	17.3%

From the above table, it is clear that more number of students lie in the category of moderate self acceptance (63.36%). So the level of self acceptance among high school students is moderate in nature. Hence the above hypothesis is accepted.

Hypothesis –II

The internal locus of Locus of Control is predominant among High School Student.

TABLE. 10.2: Showing the Frequency and Percentage for the Variable locus of Control

Category	Range	Frequency	Percentage
Average locus of control	Below 22	27	9%
High locus of control	Above 22	273	91%

From the above table, it is clear that more number of students lie in the category of high locus of control. So the level of locus of control among high school students is external in nature. Hence the above hypothesis is rejected.

Hypothesis –III

There is a significant difference between boys and girls of High School students in their self Acceptance

TABLE. 10.3: Significance of Difference in the Self Acceptance mean Scores of High School Students based on their Gender

Variable	Gender	N	Mean	SD	C.R	L.S
Self Acceptance	Male	170	17.10	2.72	1.221	N.S
	Female	130	16.68	3.12		

From the above table, C.R value (1.22) which is lesser than the table value (1.96). Hence there is no significance difference between the male and female students of high school on their self acceptance. Therefore the above hypothesis is rejected.

Hypothesis–IV

There is a significant difference between boys and girls of High School students in their locus of control

TABLE.10.4: Significance of Difference in the Self Acceptance mean Scores of High School Students based on their Gender

Variable	Gender	N	Mean	SD	C.R	L.S
Locus of control	Male	170	21.30	3.01	3,487	0.01
	Female	130	20.05	3.13		

From the above table, C.R value (3.487) is greater than the table value (2.58). Hence there is a significance difference between the male and female students of high school on their self acceptance. Therefore the above hypothesis is accepted.

Hypothesis–V

There is a significant difference between different ages among High School students in their self acceptance..

TABLE. 10.5: Showing the Significant Difference of Self Acceptance with Respect to their Different ages among high School Students.

Variable		**Sum of Squares**	**DF**	**Mean Squares**	**F value**	**L.S**
Self Acceptance	Between groups	54.845	2	27.423	3.305	0.05
	Within groups	2466.071	297	8.303		
	Total	**2520.917**	**299**			

From the above table it is clear that self acceptance of high school students of different ages has significant difference. So it is consider for further analysis.

TABLE : Showing the Significance Sifference of ages of High School Students for Self Acceptance.

Variable	**Age**	**N**	**Mean**	**SD**	**Sem**	**C.R value**	**L.S**
Self acceptance	14 yrs	115	16.86	2.91	0.37	0.832	N.S
	15 yrs	117	16.54	2.95			
Self acceptance	15 yrs	117	16.54	2.95	0.426	2.629	0.01
	16 yrs	68	17.66	2.71			
Self acceptance	14 yrs	115	16.86	2.91	0.426	1.877	N.S
	16 yrs	68	17.66	2.71			

From the above table, the C.R value is found to be significant difference in the Self Acceptance of high school students with respect to 15 and 16 years of age. So in these group only the hypothesis is accepted. In other groups table value shows no significance. So the hypothesis is partially accepted.

Hypothesis –VI

There is a significant difference between different ages among High School students in their locus of control..

TABLE. 10.6: Showing the Significant Difference of locus of Control with Respect to their Different ages among High School Students.

Variable		Sum of Squares	DF	Mean Squares	F value	L.S
Locus of control	Between groups	5.779	2	2.889	0.295	N.S
	Within groups	2904.941	297	9.781		
	Total	**2910.917**	**299**			

The above table value reveals that the obtained 'f' value is lesser than the table value indicating no significant difference of Locus of control with respect to ages. Hence the hypothesis is rejected.

Hypothesis –VII

There is a significant difference between the high School students studying in different management in their self acceptance.

TABLE. 10.7: Showing the Significant Difference of Self Acceptance with respect to their type of Management among High School students.

Variable		Sum of Squares	DF	Mean Squares	F value	L.S
Self Acceptance	Between groups	30.427	2	15.213	1.814	N.S
	Within groups	2490.490	297	8.385		
	Total	**2520.917**	**299**			

The above table value reveals that the obtained 'f' value is lesser than the table value indicating that the type of schools has no significant difference of self acceptance. Hence the hypothesis is rejected.

Hypothesis –VIII

There is a significant difference between the high School students studying in different management in their locus of control.

TABLE. 10.8: Showing the Significant Difference of Locus of Control with Respect to their type of Management among High School Students.

Variable		Sum of Squares	DF	Mean Squares	F value	L.S
Locus of control	Between groups	66.140	2	33.070	3.453	0.05
	Within groups	2844.580	297	9.578		
	Total	**2910.720**	**299**			

From the above table value it is clear that type of schools has significant difference in Locus of control of high school students. So it is considered for further analysis.

TABLE: Showing the Significance Difference Between Different type of Management with Respect to locus of Control among High School Students.

Variable	Types of School	N	Mean	SD	Sem	C.R value	L.S
Locus of control	Private	100	20.77	3.83	0.478	1.17	N.S
	Aided	100	21.33	2.87			
Locus of control	Aided	100	21.33	2.87	0.374	3.06	0.01
	Govt	100	20.18	2.41			
Locus of control	Private	100	20.77	3.83	0.451	1.30	N.S
	Govt	100	20.18	2.41			

From the above table, the C.R value is found to be significant indicating that there is significant difference in the Locus of control of high school students with respect to their Aided and Government schools. So in these groups only the hypothesis is accepted. In other groups table value shows no significance. So the hypothesis is partially accepted.

Hypothesis –IX

There is a significant difference between joint and nuclear family of High School students in their self Acceptance.

TABLE. 10.9: Significance of Difference Between self Acceptances Means Scores of High School Students based on their type of Family.

Variable	Types of Family	N	Mean	SD	C.R	L.S
Self Acceptance	Joint	139	16.83	2.23	0.47	N.S
	Nuclear	161	16.99	2.97		

From the above table, C.R value (0.47) is lesser than the table value (1.96). Hence there is no significance difference between the type of family of high school on their self acceptance. Therefore the above hypothesis is rejected.

Hypothesis –X

There is a significant difference between joint and nuclear family of High School students in their locus of control.

TABLE. 10.10: Significance of Difference Between locus of Control Mean Scores of High School students based on their type of Family.

Variable	Types of School	N	Mean	SD	C.R	L.S
Locus of control	Joint	139	21.02	3.23	1.35	N.S
	Nuclear	161	20.53	3.02		

From the above table, C.R value (1.35) is lesser than the table value (1.96). Hence there is no significance difference between the type of family of high school on their locus of control. Therefore the above hypothesis is rejected.

Hypothesis –XI

There is no significant difference between rural and urban area high School students in their self acceptance..

TABLE.10.11: Significance of Difference Between self Acceptance mean Scores of High School Students based on their Location.

Variable	Location	N	Mean	SD	C.R	L.S
Self Acceptance	Rural	200	16.68	2.42	1.78	N.S
	Urban	100	17.40	3.66		

From the above table, C.R value (1.78) is lesser than the table value (1.96). Hence there is no significance difference between the self acceptances of high school students on the basis of location. Therefore the above hypothesis is accepted.

Hypothesis –XII

There is no significant difference between rural and urban area High School students in their locus of control.

TABLE. 10.12: Significance of Difference Between Locus of Control mean Scores of High School Students based on their Location.

Variable	Location	N	Mean	SD	C.R	L.S
Locus of control	Rural	200	20.78	2.98	0.15	N.S
	Urban	100	20.72	3.40		

From the above table, C.R value (0.15) is lesser than the table value (1.96). Hence there is no significance difference between the locus of control of high school students on the basis of their location. Therefore the above hypothesis is accepted.

Hypothesis –XIII

There is a significant difference between English and Tamil Medium of High School students in their self acceptance.

TABLE. 10.13: Significance of Difference Between self Acceptance mean Scores of High School Students based on their Medium of Instruction.

Variable	Medium	N	Mean	SD	C.R	L.S
Self Acceptance	Tamil	150	16.48	2.26	2.62	0.01
	English	150	17.35	3.38		

From the above table, C.R value (2.62) is greater than the table value (2.58) at 0.01 level. Hence there is a significance difference between the English and Tamil medium high school students on their Self acceptance mean scores, English medium scores (17.35) being higher than Tamil medium scores (16.48). Therefore the above hypothesis is accepted.

Hypothesis –XIV

There is a significant difference between English and Tamil Medium of High School students in their locus of control.

TABLE. 10.14: Significance of Difference Between Locus of Control mean Scores of High School Students based on their Medium of Instruction.

Variable	Medium	N	Mean	SD	C.R	L.S
Locus of control	Tamil	150	20.40	2.65	2.008	0.05
	English	150	21.12	3.50		

From the above table, C.R value (2.008) is greater than the table value (1.96) at 0.05 level. Hence there is a significance difference between the English and Tamil medium high school students on their Locus of control mean scores. Therefore the above hypothesis is accepted.

Hypothesis -XV

There is a significant relationship of self acceptance and locus of control among High School students

TABLE. 10.15: Shows the Correlation Between Self Acceptance and Locus of Control among High School Students.

Variable	N	Correlation Coefficient	L.S
Self acceptance	300	-0.0241	N.S
Locus of control			

The above table shows that there is no significant relationship between self acceptance and locus of control. Hence the above hypothesis is rejected.

CONCLUSION

The above analysis clearly shows that there is no significant relationship between the self acceptance and locus of control. The analysis and interpretation of data represent the application of deductive and inductive logic to the research process. The data are often classified by division into subgroups and then analyzed and synthesized in such a way that hypotheses may be verified or rejected. The final result may be a new principle of generalization. Like interpretation of results, the formulation of conclusion and generalizations also demands keen observations, wide look and power of logical thinking. A brief report of the present research study together with major findings and conclusions has been presented in the succeeding chapter.

❐

11

Summary, Findings and Conclusion

In this chapter we have tried to assimilate, what we have done so far in the previous chapter by reinstating the statement of the problem, tools used for investigation, about the samples and finally presenting the major findings of the study. In the light of the major findings some useful recommendations for improvements and suggestions for research are proposed.

STATEMENT OF THE PROBLEM

Self acceptance and locus of control among high school students in Tiruvallur district.

OBJECTIVES OF THE STUDY

1. To study the level of self acceptance among High School students.
2. To Study the level locus of control among High School students
3. To find out the significant difference between boys and girls of High School students in their self Acceptance.
4. To find out the significant difference between boys and girls of High School students in their locus of control.
5. To find out the significant difference between different ages among High School students in their self acceptance.

6. To find out the significant difference between different ages among High School students in their locus of control.
7. To find out the Significant difference between the high School students studying in different management in their self acceptance.
8. To find out the Significant difference between the high School students studying in different management in their locus of control.
9. To find out the significant difference between joint and nuclear family of High School students in their self Acceptance.
10. To find out the significant difference between joint and nuclear family of High School students in their locus of control.
11. To find out the significant difference between rural and urban area High School students in their self acceptance.
12. To find out the significant difference between rural and urban area High School students in their locus of control.
13. To find out the significant difference between English and Tamil Medium of High School students in their self acceptance.
14. To find out the significant difference between English and Tamil Medium of High School students in their locus of control.
15. To find out the Significant Relationship of Self Acceptance and Locus of Control among High School students.

HYPOTHESIS OF THE STUDY

1. The level of Self Acceptance among High School Student is Average.
2. The internal locus of Locus of Control is predominant among High School Student
3. There is a significant difference between boys and girls of High School students in their self Acceptance.
4. There is a significant difference between boys and girls of High School students in their locus of control.
5. There is a significant difference between different ages among High School students in their self acceptance.
6. There is a significant difference between different ages among High School students in their locus of control.
7. There is a significant difference between the high School students studying in different management in their self acceptance.
8. There is a significant difference between the high School students studying in different management in their locus of control.
9. There is a significant difference between joint and nuclear family of High School students in their self Acceptance.

10. There is a significant difference between joint and nuclear family of High School students in their locus of control.
11. There is no significant difference between rural and urban area High School students in their self acceptance.
12. There is no significant difference between rural and urban area High School students in their locus of control.
13. There is a significant difference between English and Tamil Medium of High School students in their self acceptance.
14. There is a significant difference between English and Tamil Medium of High School students in their locus of control.
15. There is a significant relationship of self acceptance and locus of control among High School students.

SAMPLE

The present study is concerned with High School Students. Random Sampling technique is used among the Government, Aided and Private Schools in Tiruvallur district. The investigator selected randomly two Government School, Two Private School and one Aided School. The sample composes of 300 High School students.

TOOLS USED

The following tools and techniques were used:

1. Self acceptance inventory. **(Dr.Kakkar ,Patiala, 1984)**
2. Locus of control inventory. **(Dr.Stephen Nowicki, Jr., and Dr.Strickland in 1973)**

MAJOR FINDINGS

1. It is found that the level of self acceptance among High School students is average in nature.
2. It is found that the level of locus of control is high (external) in nature.
3. It is found that boys and girls of High School students have no significant difference in their self acceptance.
4. It is found that boys and girls of High School students have significant difference in their locus of control.
5. It is found that the different ages of High School students has significant difference in their self acceptance.
6. It is found that the different ages of High School students has no significant difference in their Locus of control.
7. It is found that the type of school of High School students has no significant difference in their self acceptance.

8. It is found that type of schools of high school students has significant difference in their locus control.
9. It is found that type of family of High School students has no significant difference in their self acceptance.
10. It is found that type of family of High School students has no significant difference in their local of control.
11. It is found that the locality of High School students has no significant difference in their self acceptance.
12. It is found that locality makes no significant difference in their locus of control
13. It is found that the medium of instruction of High School students has significant difference in their self acceptance.
14. It is found that the medium of instruction of High School students has significant difference in their locus of control.
15. It is found that self acceptance and locus control of High School students correlation is not significant.

EDUCATIONAL IMPLICATIONS

In the educational scenario it is found that the High School part of education in the schools is very significant milestone of a student. This is due to some psychological aspects like emotional, mental, physical changes of High School students. This change gives or paves the way for various problems. During the adolescent stage the students normally find it difficult to adjust with home, school, peer and social setting. They normally possess on unstable self-acceptance. Since the self acceptance is a personality variable the high school students must possess this in their behavior.

This study in self acceptance and locus of control of High School students will throw more light on the impact of self acceptance and locus of control in relation to their education. If the self acceptance is high locus of control also would be better and thus it is found that the students also learn and perform better in their school subjects. Further the students are well adjusted to the school and also develop good habits.

SUGGESTION FOR FURTHER RESEARCH

Some suggestions with regard to possibilities of the record in the field of education are offered with a view to stimulate prospective research works in this area. These are as follows:

1. Self-acceptance in relation to personality and different kinds of adjustment behavior such as personal adjustment, social adjustment etc., can be studied among High School students.

2. A study of self-acceptance and locus of control among the college students.
3. A study of self-acceptance and academic achievement could be conducted among higher secondary students.
4. A study of locus control and personality could be conducted among college students.
5. A study of self-acceptance and leadership behaviour of college students.

CONCLUSION

Self-acceptance plays a vital role in every human being. Self-acceptance requires consistency, stability, and tends to resist change. If self-acceptance changed readily, the individual would lack a consistent and dependable personality. Man is a social being thus self-acceptance helps him to understand the self and what other thinks about himself. When there is an available in self-acceptance it may tend to lead the locus of control. So they help man to live smoothly and at peace with one another. If the locus of control is not good then the person cannot live freely in the society especially in the present fast developing world. So it is extremely necessary to develop high self acceptance, which is turn, would positively complements locus of control.

❐

12

Self-Concept and Emotional Maturity

The best and most perfect creation of the Almighty is man. Shakespeare has described him as an angel, little lower than his creator. The main reason which makes him so, when biologically he does not differ much with monkeys or apes and other similar higher animals, lies in the fact that while the animal can only be trained, man can both be trained and educated. The man who does not have any education is no more different than an animal. It is the education which makes him the noblest and finest creation of the world.

Education is the process of living through a continuous reconstruction of experiences. It is the development of all those capacities in the individual which will enable him to control his environment and fulfil his possibilities.

Education of a human being should begin at birth and continue throughout his life. The main aim of education is to develop harmonious personality of the learner. Education is considered to be the most significant agent of basic change in the status of a human being besides occupation and economic status.

Education is as old as mankind. In every society ancient or modern, simple or complex, primitive or advanced, one finds provision for education. Without education, no society can last more than a generation. The function of education is considered to be the adjustment of man to his environment which means his adaptation and reconstruction of his surroundings for his own benefit and that of society.

So the school, as an agency of education is the training ground for the future citizen in the school. The student learns the process of creating new knowledge as an essential byproduct.

The aim of education is always two fold.

1. There is a collective aspect
2. There is an individual aspect

From the collectively point of view, education is expected to turn the individual into a good citizen, i.e., into a person who has harmonious relations with the other members of the community, who is useful to the society and who fulfils with zeal his obligation as a citizen.

Education will give to the individual a strong and healthy body, helps him in building up his character and attains self mastery and supply him with good opportunities of discovering and developing harmoniously his natural abilities.

Education must promote the well being of those being educated. Education brings out and develops the best in an individual. It leads to self - perfection or fulfillment and improvement of others. It seeks to develop an integrated holistic personality harmonising the head, hands and heart of a person each activated by the educational procedure. Thus the real development is the improvement of the self and the refinement of human perceptions.

Educational research is that activity which is directed towards development of a science of behaviour in educational situations. According to Robert M.W. Travers (1964), the ultimate aim of such a science is to provide knowledge that will permit the educator to achieve his goals by the most effective methods.

SELF-CONCEPT

Self is the conscious reflection of one's own being or identity, as an object separate from other or from the environment. Self-Concept is the cognitive thinking aspect of self and generally refers to "the totality of a complex, organised, and dynamic system of learned beliefs, attitudes and opinions that each person holds to be true about his or her personal existence" (Purkey, 1988).

HISTORY

A milestone in human reflection about the non - physical inner self came in 1644, when Rene Descartes wrote principles of philosophy. Descartes proposed that doubt was a principal tool of disciplined inquiry, yet he could not doubt that he doubted. He reasoned that if he doubted, he was thinking and therefore he must exist. Thus existence depended upon perception.

A second milestone in the development of Self-Concept theory was the writing of Sigmund Freud (1900) who gave us new understanding of internal mental processes. While Freud and many of his followers hesitated to make Self-Concept a primary psychological unit in their theories, Anna (1946) gave central importance to ego development and Self - interpretation.

Self-Concept theory has always had a strong influence on the emerging profession of counselling. Prescott Lecky (1945) contributed the notion that self - consistency is a primary motivating force in human behaviour. Raimy (1948) introduced measures of Self-Concept in counselling interviews and argued that psychotherapy is basically a process of altering the ways that individuals see themselves.

By far the most influential and eloquent voice in Self-Concept theory was that of Carl Rogers (1947) who introduced an entire system of helping built around the importance of the self. In Roger's view, the self is the central ingredient in human personality and personal adjustment. Rogers described the self as a social product, developing out of interpersonal relationships and striving for consistency. He maintained that there is a basic human need for positive regard both from others and from oneself. He also believed that in every person there is a tendency towards self - actualization and development so long as this is permitted and encouraged by an inviting environment (Purkey and Schmidt, 1987).

While most Self-Concept theorists continued to write and conduct research during the 1970s and 1980s, general interest in Self-Concept declined.

Fortunately, there is a new awareness on the part of both the public and professionals that Self-Concept cannot be ignored if we are to successfully address such nagging problems as drug and alcohol abuse, drop-out rates, dysfunctional families and other concerns. In addition to this growing awareness, new ways are being developed to strengthen Self-Concept. For example, research by cognitive theorists McAdam, (1986); Ryan, Short and Weed, (1986) are demonstrating that negative self-talk leads to irrational thinking regarding oneself and the world.

BASIC ASSUMPTIONS

Many of the successes and failures that people experience in many areas of life are closely related to the ways that they have learned to view themselves and their relationship with others. It is also becoming clear that Self-Concept has at least three major qualities of interest : (1) it is learned (2) it is organised and (3) it is dynamic.

Self-Concept is Learned

As far as we know, no one is born with a Self-Concept. It gradually emerges in the early months of life and is shaped and reshaped through repeated perceived experiences, particularly with significant others. The fact that Self-Concept is learned has some important implications:-

1. Because Self-Concept does not appear to be instinctive, but is a social product developed through experience, it possesses relatively boundless potential for development and actualization.
2. Because of previous experiences and present perceptions, individuals may perceive themselves in ways different from the ways others see them.
3. Individuals perceive different aspects of themselves at different times with varying degrees of clarity. Therefore, inner focusing is a valuable tool for counselling.
4. Any experience which is inconsistent with one's Self-Concept may be perceived as a threat, and the more of these experiences, the more rigidly Self-Concept is organised to maintain and protect itself. When a person is unable to get rid of perceived inconsistencies, emotional problems arise.
5. Faculty thinking patterns, such as dichotomous reasoning (dividing everything in terms of opposites or extremes) or over generalising (making sweeping conclusions based on little information) create negative interpretations of oneself.

Self-Concept is Organised

Most researchers agree that Self-Concept has a generally stable quality that is characterised by orderliness and harmony. Each person maintains countless perceptions regarding one's personal existence, and each perception is orchestrated with all the others. It is this generally stable and organised quality of Self-Concept that gives consistency to the personality. This organised quality of Self-Concept has corollaries.

1. Self-Concept requires consistency, stability, and tends to resist change. If Self-Concept changed readily, the individual would lack a consistent and dependable personality.
2. The more central a particular belief is to one's Self-Concept the more resistant one is to changing that belief.
3. At the heart of Self-Concept is the self - as - doer, the "I", which is distinct from the self - as object, the various "me's". This allows the person to reflect on past events, analyse present perceptions, and shape future experiences.

4. Basic perceptions of one are quite stable, so change takes time.
5. Perceived success and failure affect Self-Concept. Failure in a highly regarded area lowers evaluations in all other areas as well. Success in a prized area raises evaluations in other seemingly unrelated areas.

Self-Concept is Dynamic

To understand the active nature of Self-Concept, it helps to imagine it as a gyrocompass: a continuously active system that dependably points to the "true north" of a person's perceived existence. This guidance system not only shapes the ways a person views oneself, others, and the world, but it also serves to direct action and enables each person to take a consistent "stance" in life. Rather than viewing Self-Concept as the cause of behaviour, it is better understood as the gyrocompass of human personality, providing consistency in personality and direction for behaviour.

1. The world and the things in it are not just perceived, they are perceived in relation to one's Self-Concept.
2. Self-Concept development is a continuous process. In the healthy personality there is constant assimilation of new ideas and expulsion of old ideas throughout life.
3. Individuals strive to behave in ways that are in keeping with their Self-Concepts, no matter how helpful or hurtful to oneself or others.
4. Self-Concept usually takes precedence over the physical body. Individuals will often sacrifice physical comfort and safety for emotional satisfaction.
5. Self-Concept continuously guards itself against loss of self esteem, for it is this loss that produces feelings of anxiety.
6. If Self-Concept must constantly defend itself from assault, growth opportunities are limited.

CONCEPTS AND DEFINITIONS

The social psychological conception of the self is based on the idea that people are reflexive, responding to themselves just as they respond to other "objects". Since reflexive thinking requires language, it is assumed that infants and nonhuman animals lack a Self-Concept.

While a number of philosophers and psychologists have addressed the idea that behaviour is influenced by the way people see themselves, investigation into the importance of Self-Concept is most closely associated with the writings and therapeutic practices of Carl Rogers. According to Rogers, one's Self-Concept influences how one regards both oneself and one's environment. The Self-Concept of a mentally healthy person is consistent with his or her thoughts, experiences and behaviour. Social psychologists have pointed out that Self-Concept also plays an important role in social perception - the process by which we form impressions of others.

Self-Concept has been defined by several authors. William James (1890) holds it to be all that a person is tempted to call by the name `me' or `mine'. Murphy (1947) it as the individual as known to the individual. According to Symonds (1951), it is the way or manner in which the individual reacts to himself. He spells out four aspects of self : (1) how a person perceives himself : (2) what he thinks of himself : (3) how he values himself; and (4) how he attempts through various actions to enhance or defend himself.

Sherif and Cantril (1947)

It is the constellation of attitudes of the type "what I think of myself, what I value, what is mine, and what I identify with". According to them, their attitudes when activated, energise, direct and control the person's behaviour.

Franken (1994) states that

"there is a great deal of research which shows that the Self-Concept is, perhaps, the basis for all motivated behaviour. It is the Self-Concept that gives rise to possible selves, and it is the possible selves that create the motivation for behaviour (p.443).

This supports the idea that one's paradigm or world view and one's relationship to that view provide the boundaries and circumstances within which we develop our views about possibilities. This is one of the major issues facing children and youth today.

CONCEPT OF EMOTIONS

A good person, according to Aristotle must have right emotions. Emotion is a complete state of arousal associated with varying degrees of physiological activation, a conscious awareness of feeling with specific cognitive label and tendency to move the organism into action.

The word emotion is derived from a latin term `Emovere' which means to stir up, to agitate or to excite. Emotions influence actions in many ways. The stronger the emotion, the greater the activity to which it will give rise to negative emotion like kicking, biting, scratching, bed wetting, thumb sucking, crying, trembling running away, irritation, resentment, refusal to eat and so on. Emotions like affection, amusement, curiosity happiness and joy are positive emotions which help in carrying out the activities smoothly and earily. Increase in heart rate, rise in blood pressure, changes in blood compensation, increase in respiration, increase in muscle tension, perspiration, dilation of eye pupil are signs of emotions.

Emotions can be considered as a feeling first noticed at the bodily level as arousal; then it is noticed by the mind which interprets and apprehends the world resulting in bodily feelings. Emotions are neither bad nor good as such. But their relation with the situations is that which makes them effective or ineffective.

In India, emotions have always been considered as energies, the vital being which can be constructive or destructive according to the individual's desires and goals.

Definitions of Emotions

David Hume (1711-1776), the emotions are simple un-analysable impression of a non - bodily variety, or in otherwords, a type of psychic feeling - Emotion is a psychic energy that can be put to use in either in a destructive or constructive manner.

According to Jean Paul - Satre, the French philosopher.

Emotion is a manner of apprehending the world. It is not an innocent perception but a conscious strategy of the subject person. It is an intentional social act.

According to Crow and Crow (1973) emotion is an effective experience that accompanies generalised inner adjustment and mental and psychological stirred up status in an individual and that shows itself in his own behaviour.

In Kumball Young's view, emotion is the aroused psychological state of the organism marked by increased bodily activity and strong feelings directed to some subject.

Categories of Emotions

Harold Schools berg speaks of 3 basic dimensions of emotions.

i. Pleasantness - Unpleasantness
ii. Attention - Rejection
iii. Level of activation (sleep - tension)

Others add a fourth dimension to the above three degree of complexity. When these 4 bipolar dimensions are imposed upon the possible emotional states we get several categories of emotions.

(a) Primary goal oriented emotions (anger, joy, fear and grief are also called PRIMARY or basic emotions).
(b) Emotions triggered by sensory stimulation (pain, disgust and delight).
(c) Emotions pertaining to self appraisal and related to one's level of aspiration (pride, shame and guilt).
(d) Emotions related to others.
(e) Appreciative emotions (wonder and awe)

All these increasingly varied and differentiated patterns of emotional expressions are gradually evolved in the course of development and learning from the initial single generalised emotional response of excitement of the new born infant.

EMOTIONAL MATURITY

Psychologists differ considerably in their emphasis on the role of maturation in the development of emotional behaviour. Gessel says that maturation is responsible for the gradual evolution of emotional expression in infants and children. He strongly disagreed with the view that emotional development is largely a phenomenon of social stimulation. According to Gessel, maturation influences the expression of emotion through the development of capacities, rather than through the ripening of a specific innate response pattern. Jones demonstrated that while visceral components of emotional response are not highly correlated with the vigour of vocal and motor components during the neonatal period, this correlation is increased in preschool children, indicating that the integration of various aspects of emotional development are dependent partially upon maturation.

For Gessel, as the individual becomes more adequate physically, intellectually and socially through the development of his capacities there is a concomitant emotional growth. Outside control gradually disappears as the child's emotions mature, and ultimately the emotionally mature individual is able to function on the basis of inner controls.

Emotional Maturity is always relative. A five year old child has Emotional Maturity, if he is capable of the emotional behaviour we judge fit for a five year old.

Emotional Maturity develops throughout life. It is also a form of maturity from which one can regress more quickly. The child becomes more emotionally mature as the parent permits him to accept responsibilities and becomes independent and self sufficient.

Emotional development, like other aspects of development, is gradual and both innate maturational factors as well as learning play a part in the development. Emotional development is linked with other areas of human development like physical, intellectual and social. Any retardation, undue acceleration or abnormal deviation in these areas would inevitably influence normal emotional development resulting in frustration, conflicts and imbalance in behaviour. Frustration is caused by the accumulation of emotional tensions affecting the personality of the individual.

According to Cole, "The most outstanding mark of Emotional Maturity is the ability to bear tension". Besides, an emotionally mature person persists the capacity for fun and recreation. He enjoys both play and responsibility and keeps them in proper balance.

Kaplon and Baron stated that an emotionally mature person has the capacity to withstand delay in the satisfaction of his needs. He has belief in long term planning and is capable of delaying or revising his expectations in terms of demands of situations. An emotionally mature individual has the capacity to make effective adjustment with himself, members of his family, his peers in school, society and culture.

The levels of Emotional Maturity

In the empirically derived hierarchy of emotions, it is observed that there are six fairly distinct behavioural categories which we refer to as `levels of Emotional Maturity'. Each level composed of a number of discrete emotions, represents a different "attitude" or way of perceiving and responding or reacting to all human beings regardless of culture or personality differences. Although the expression of each level always has cultural and personality nuances and variations, the emotions and emotional levels themselves retain both their relationships to each other and their underlying messages.

How individuals deal with change and their effectiveness in making contributions to themselves, their loved ones, an organisation, or to society directly relates to their emotional level. The higher the level at which a person actually functions, the greater their potential for all its positive aspects, increases exponentially as one moves up the levels.

The higher the level, the greater ones ability to easily deal with change both positively and constructively.

Level 6 represents the essence of Emotional Maturity. At this level, an individual communicates and performs with integrity. Levels 5 through 1 reflect varying degrees of emotional immaturity and a corresponding lack of integrity with level 5 being the least immature. As we move down the levels, manifestations of responsible, mature behaviour exponentially decline. As we move higher or lower within a level, we increasingly begin to see more characteristics common to the next higher or lower level.

LEVEL 6 - LEADER / MENTOR

At level 6, individuals are passionate and compassionate, live and demonstrate Emotional Maturity and integrity, and therefore have a positive, expansive effect on their environment. They are responsible leaders and compassionate mentors.

Leaders/Mentors are trustworthy and have forthright, honest communication. They manifest great patience. They have self - respect and respect the dignity of others. They strive for quality and excellence but do not get caught in insatiable demands for perfection. They desire and will honestly listen and be open to many view points, including those that differ from their own. They demonstrate, demand, and reward authenticity and responsibility as well as high performance. They do not tolerate irresponsibility, incompetence injustice, or dishonest behaviour, and they know how to communicate with people exhibiting such behaviour.

Emotionally mature individuals of Level 6 have the entire range of emotions at their disposal. They can and do feel and express the entire range of emotions. They do so without malice, honestly and responsibly.

LEVEL 5 - DOER

Doers have many positive characteristics. They are generally responsible and conscientious. They are open to positive ideas, provided the actions or changes do not upset what has been shown to be workable. Doers are interested enough in positive ideas to check them out thoroughly. Therefore though they are progressive and will move forward, they like things substantiated before doing so. Once enough data and documentation are provided, they will make a decision. If the decision is positive, they will tend to want to "pilot" it rather than commit to fully putting it into effect right away. They tend to be more conservative, and concerned with maintaining the status quo than the expansive, proactive people of Level 6.

Even so, by contemporary standards, the attitudes and behaviours of individuals functioning on Level 5 are above average. Neverthless, these people demonstrate less than they are capable of and therefore show some sighs of Emotional Maturity, rationalized though those signs may be.

LEVEL 4 - COPER

Copers do "just enough". They are not particularly responsible or irresponsible. Theirs attention and interest is mainly on making life easier for themselves. They tend to be observers rather than participants. Although not particularly dependable, they are generally likeable because they try to avoid disagreements and prefer the easier way of "going along". Copers are often described as being "mellow" and "easy going". They tend to be some what non chalant about details and commitments. Not much is a "big deal" at Level 4. However, if life is not made to be "comfortable enough", Level 4 individuals can fairly easily drop into the antagonism of Level 3 and be "testy".

LEVEL 3 ASSERTER

Level 3 is the first level at which an individual's net impact is more destructive than constructive, to both themselves and their environment. The person's certainty and security have gone from positive to negative. Individuals at this level are starting to feel noticeably over whelmed by their environment. Life and the environment are viewed as a threat. Their defense is to lash out, to attack, and oppose “the enemy”. There people range from being “testy” about specific things to being outright bullies about everything.

An asserter’s basic operating mode is to oppose or attack other view points. Asserters will exaggerate some element of truth to divert the attention of others from their goals and strengths onto their “weakness”. Emotionally, asserters will be antagomstic or angry. They are good at pressuring others to the point that others will be concessions just to get the asserters to back off. If others buy into the Asserter’s attempted intimidation, the Asserter has “won”.

LEVEL 2 MANIPULATOR

Manipulators are hostile, insecure and afraid. Consequently, they are too afraid to directly express their fears and hostility. They hide their hostility and destructive intention by artful deceit and covert manipulations. Individuals on the manipulator level are the most dangerous because not only is their underlying hostility vicious, but they are expert at hiding their true intentions and thus different to spot and deal with.

Manipulators have no concept of exchange and little or no real concept of right and wrong. Their attitude is that they are only doing what they need to do to survive in this “obviously hostile world”. They regard others as their enemies, and thus any means to “do others in” are justified in their minds. Manipulators often are able to assume any social level that will meet their destructive, hostile and unscrupulous ends. Manipulators view people who act with comparison, honesty, and integrity as simpletons who deserve to be taken advantage of Manipulators do not take responsibility but instead subtly point fingers. Supervisors may find themselves getting angry with the manipulator but be unable to be precise about why. Everything will always appear to have its reasons, including the Manipulator’s subtlet put - downs.

LEVEL - 1 VICTIM

Victims have an overwhelming sense of power lessness. The Victim - level individual feels he or she is about to - or already has lost. Victims have the view point that the environment has done them in. They have little, if any, sense of responsibility for anything, and truth has little meaning for them. Victims have a very narrow, self centered, and selfish viewpoint. They cry, whine or attempt to appears. Victims often try to feebly gain some sembalance of control by getting others to feel sympathetic toward them. Victims do not see solutions, only problems. If offered a solution, victims will have myriad excuses for how the solutions cannot or will not work. People chronically at the victim level always will have one or more “unsolvable” problems.

SUMMARY OF LEVEL BEHAVIOUR

Individuals or organizations operating chronically at levels 1, 2 and 3 are emotionally challenged and will manifest correspondingly limited viewpoints, attitudes, abilities and behaviours at level 4 this also will be true but less so. Levels 4 and above demonstrate increasing responsibility, integrity, trust worthiness and a win - win viewpoint. It is only sustained Levels 5 and 6 that we find individuals who and organisations that are capable of capitalizing on their true potential.

Level 6 offers the broadest perspective and most consistently responsible mature behaviours. It manifest rational certainly, positiveness and creativity. It represents the ideal of a win - win attitude.

Level 5 is mostly positive and action and results - oriented but with a provision that willingness to move, expand and try new things occurs after thoroughly testing examination and validation.

Level 4 is barely more positive than negative, it is characterised by doing enough things right to get by.

Levels 3 and below are indicative of a lose - lose situation in which individuals are perceiving themselves as being overwhelmed by their environment and are fighting back in the only ways they know how. At level 3 and below, honesty, responsibility and contribution become inverted, and their opposites become the dominant manifestation.

At level 3, individuals are still "strong" enough to overtly lash out at their environment in the form of opposition attack and intimidation, which are emotionally characterized by antagonism and anger. At this level, people are not only obviously hostile but also frightened, despite their bluster.

When individuals become too frightened even to outwardly express their hostility, they go covert. This is level 2, which is the most dangenous level. The underlying hostility is covered up with social necessities, subtle deceits, and invalidation's of others that are always destructive but difficult to spot.

At level 1, individuals feel as though they have already "lost". Their behaviour takes on pathetic forms of helplessness to gain sympathy or gross attempts at appeasement.

Knowing the levels of maturity and their manifestations allows us to more elegantly facilitate the most positive forms of change, helping to create personal satisfaction and organisational success.

STAGES OF DEVELOPMENT OF EMOTIONAL MATURITY

Jersild presents one of the most comprehensive lists of the stages involved in the child's moving toward maturity in the emotional area.

1. A change from being a creature who at first receives much gives little, to one who is capable of giving as well as of receiving and capable of learning to get enjoyment from giving.
2. Development of capacity, to identify with a larger social group, and the ability, to participate emotionally in the fortunes of the larger group.
3. Development from the status of being the child of family to the status ultimately, of being able to have children of one's own and along with this development a capacity to exercise the feeling and attitudes involved in being a parent psychologically, whether or not one is a parent biologically.
4. Progressive sexual development and the capacity after puberty to enjoying mature sex experiences.
5. An increased capacity for bearing the inevitable sufferings and pains connected with life and growth without feeling abused.
6. An increased capacity for sympathy and compassion as one assimulates the meaning for self and others of the joys and vicissitudes of life.

Some of the characteristics of the person, who has achieved maturity, emotionally are suggested here.

1. He accepts criticism gracefully, being honestly glad for an opportunity to improve.
2. He does not indulge in self pity. He has begun to feel the laws of compensation operating in all life.
3. He does not expect special consideration from anyone.
4. He controls his temper.
5. He meets emergencies with poise.
6. His feelings are not easily hurt.
7. He accepts the responsibility of his own actions without trying to `alibi'.
8. He has outgrown the "all or nothing" stages. He recognises that no person or situation is wholly good or wholly bad, and he begins to appreciate the Golden Mean.
9. He is not impatient at reasonable delays. He has learned that he is not the arbiter of the universe and that he must often adjust himself to other people and their convenience.
10. He is a good loser. He can endure defeat and disappointment without whining or complaining.
11. He does not worry about things he cannot help.
12. He is not given to boasting or "showing off" in socially unacceptable ways.

13. He is honestly glad when others enjoy success or good fortune. He has outgrown envy and jealousy.
14. He is open - minded enough to listen thoughtfully to the opinions of others.
15. He is not a chronic "fault - finder".
16. He plans things in advance rather than trusting to the inspiration of the moment.

Last of all, in terms of spiritual maturity :

1. He has faith in a power greater than himself.
2. He feels himself as an organised part of mankind as a whole, contributing his part to each group of which he is a member.

STATEMENT OF THE PROBLEM

"A study of Self-Concept and Emotional Maturity among high school students.

OPERATIONAL DEFINITIONS

Self-Concept

Self-Concepts is the individual's way of looking at himself. It also signifies his way of thinking, feeling and behaving.

Self-Concept is the dominant element in the personality pattern, it governs the individual's characteristics reaction to people and situations and determines the quality of his behaviour.

Emotional Maturity

Emotional Maturity is a process in which the personality is continuously striving for greater sense of emotional health, both intra - physically and intra personally.

OBJECTIVES OF THE STUDY

1. To find out the level of Self-Concept among High School students.
2. To find out the level of Emotional Maturity among High School students.
3. To find out whether there is significant difference in the Total Self-Concept and its dimensions of High School students with respect to their.
   a. Gender
   b. Medium of instructions
   c. Type of Management
   d. Locality

   e. Type of family
   f. Birth Order

4. To find out whether there is significant difference in the Total Emotional Maturity and its dimensions of High School students with respect to their.
   a. Gender
   b. Medium of instructions
   c. Type of Management
   d. Locality
   e. Type of family
   f. Birth Order

5. To find out whether there is any significant association between Self-Concept of High School students and the following variables.
   a. Gender
   b. Medium of instructions
   c. Type of Management
   d. Locality
   e. Type of family
   f. Birth Order

6. To find out whether there is any significant association between Emotional Maturity of High School students and the following variables
   a. Gender
   b. Medium of instructions
   c. Type of Management
   d. Locality
   e. Type of family
   f. Birth Order

7. To find out the relationship between Self-Concept of High School students and their Emotional Maturity.

SIGNIFICANCE OF THE STUDY

In the present day circumstances, youth and children face difficulties in life. These difficulties may lead to many psychosomatic problems such as anxiety, tensions, frustrations and emotional disturbances in the day to day life. Hence the study of emotional life is now emerging as a descriptive science.

As Self-Concept seems to play a significant role in the growth and development of a person, a detailed knowledge about its nature and its relation to other factors of personality provides an objective and encouraging basis for the educators to work on. An emotionally matured person will have a healthy Self-Concept not thinking too highly or too lowly of oneself. Since Self-Concept has acceptably a significant influence of behaviour, it was felt that a knowledge of the relationship between Self-Concept and Emotional Maturity would be very enriching and useful.

DELIMITATIONS OF THE STUDY

The investigator is conscious of the circumstances given below that might to some extent exert influence on the findings of the research.

1. The study was limited to the schools located in Kerala.
2. The study was limited to high school students only.
3. The sample is restricted to 300 students.

CONCLUSION

The first chapter highlights the introduction to the problem and its statement, operational definitions of the terms, objectives and limitations of the study.

A review of related literature, design of the study, analysis and interpretation of the data and summary of the results are dealt with the chapters that follow.

❐

13

Rview of Related Literature

"The review of literature promotes a greater understanding of the problem and its crucial aspects" **Mouly,1964).**

A review of empirical studies in any area indicates not only the relevance and significance of the problem of study but also the appropriateness of the planned methodology and of the techniques of analysis of the research data. Review of the related literature gives a right perspective to understand as well as appreciate every aspect of the work and the procedure followed studying in the problem.

According to Good (1959) In order to be truly creative and original, one must read intensively and critically as a stimulus of thinking.

Therefore careful study is carried out and is presented in this chapter under the following headings.

1. Studies related to Self-Concept
2. Studied related to Emotional Maturity

STUDIES RELATED TO SELF-CONCEPT

Indian Studies on Self-Concept

Paul Bruece (1958) studied the relationship of self acceptance to other variables with sixth grade children oriented in self understanding has pointed out that the child who indicates a marked discrepancy between his Self-Concept and ideal self, feeling his need satisfaction blocked would show evidences of insecurity in his behavior and would yield responses indicating manifest anxiety.

Deo P. and Sharma Sagar (1971) studied the relationship of Self -Concept and Anxiety. Under this study, 700 adolescents from 13 urban higher secondary schools in North India were selected. From the calculated data, Self -Concept and Anxiety was found to be negatively correlated and increase in Self-Concept is accompanied by decrease in anxiety. It was also found that Self-ideal discrepancy increases, Anxiety also increases.

Walia D (1973) made an attempt to study the gifted adolescents and their Self-Concept was affected by intelligence and sex. The gifted have higher idea of self and better insight than the average. The gifted have higher perceived ideal discrepancies as compared to the average adolescence.

Lalithamma and Passi (1973) analysed the relationship of creativity and Self-Concept in terms of low, average and high achievement. No significant difference were found among the groups in Self-Concept but over achievers were more creative.

Mohan (1975) Traced the growth of Self-Concept over years of adolescence and its relationship with intelligence and achievement. The results showed that longitudinal and cross sectional analysis revealed increased trend of female perceived self. Females showed more stability of self than males during adolescence.

Jogawar (1976) conducted a study to find out how the Self-Concept of the adolescence change as a function of age, the relationship of these changes with some family factors and the relationship of sex with these changes. For studying, the significant difference between group analysis for variance was used. The findings showed that the developmental course of Self-Concept and social self stood at higher level at the beginning and at the end stage of adolescence were found to be considerably lower level at the middle of the adolescent period.

Narayanan and Ganesan (1978) developed a Self-Concept check list to measure Self-Concept of Palamalai in Tamil Nadu who are scheduled tribes of that area. The scale consisted of both open ended and closed ended questionnaire and had 44 items. This community people seem to be unaware of expression of self but considered themselves strong and healthy.

Prasad S. (1982) studied certain important factors of stability of the Self-Concept. The samples included 132 college and university tutors, the inventory used was Sharan's ideal Self-Concept, self-satisfaction and role performance. The major findings were social change had been identified as an independent factor of self-consistency and older and younger generation differed significantly on anxiety, insecurity self-role in congruence and self-satisfaction.

Dastoor, H.F. (1982) studied the different types of Self-Concept prevalent among the nurses, to assess the relationship between the types of Self-Concept and job performance and to compare the Self-Concept of the most efficient and the least efficient nurses. Under incidental sampling method 700 samples were collected. About 71% of nurses had high to very high Self -Concept and had little or no doubt about the profession. The nurses with low proficiency and low Self-Concept had definite doubts about their profession.

Pandit I. (1985) studied the psychological needs and Self-Concept of adolescents and their bearing on adjustment. The sample consisted of 640 adults and the tools employed in this study were socio-economic status inventory by Deo, Jogawar and Shekar and Bhagia's school adjustment inventory. The calculated data results that the difference between perceived self and social self was not significant and the results for Self-Concept of adolescent boys and girls showed that boys had a higher Self-Concept than girls.

Ghose P. and Khurana (1986) made a study which aims at assessing socio-economic status and sex on anxiety, adjustments and Self-Concept. The sample consisted of 100 students belonging to different colleges in Delhi. Significant differences were found between the high socio-economic status group and low socio- economic status group as well as males and females with respect to Self-Concept, the high Self-Concept and low Self-Concept groups on anxiety, between high Self-Concept and low Self-Concept groups on adjustment.

Karan, Patricia (1989) studied the relationship of peer group and the Self-Concept of adolescence. This analysis showed that there is a positive relationship existing between the peer group and Self-Concept.

Chanda, Sunanda (1990) conducted a study on Self-Concept, parental influence socio-economic status and sex in education to career choice attitude among high school students. Attitude scale of career maturity inventory and the Self-Concept inventory were used to collect the data from 60 girls and 60 boys of class X. The results showed that parental influence interacted with Self-Concept in the prediction of career choice attitude scores

Ramiah L. (1990) made a relational study involvement and Self -Concept of standard IX students in Devakottai educational district. The objectives of the study were

To assess the level of parental involvement and Self-Concept of standard IX students.

To determine if there is any significant relationship between parental involvement and Self-Concept of standard IX students.

The sample comprised of 303 students from higher secondary schools and 97 students from matriculation schools. Saraswat's tool on Self -Concept and the investigator's questionnaire on parental involvement were used to collect the data.

The major findings showed that there was significant relationship between parental involvement and Self-Concept of the students and the more parental involvement the better the Self-Concept.

Joseph Alexandar E and Rajendran K (1992) analysed the influence of Self-Concept, Sex, Area and Parents education on adjustment problems. Check list were used to collect the data from 671 students of 5 universities of Tamil Nadu. The results showed that students with high Self-Concept are better adjusted than students with low Self-Concept.

Chauhan, Sarita (1992) made a study on values, Self-Concept, creativity and anxiety among professional college students Self-Concept scale of Mukta Rastogi was used to find out the Self-Concept of the students of the colleges of engineering, medicine and teaching. The data was collected from the sample of 405 students. The findings revealed that there was no difference in Self-Concept between students of engineering colleges and medical colleges. There was a little difference in the value of engineering students and teachers – training students.

Barooah, S and Phukan.M. (1999) designed a comparative study of Self-Concept of orphan children and the children with natural parents. The sample comprised 45 children with natural parents from 3 schools in Guwahati of age group 10 to 15 years and 45 orphan children from SOS children's village Azara. A Self-Concept questionnaire was prepared to collect the data. The results revealed that there is no significant difference in the physical, educational and moral Self-Concept of children from the two groups. Intellectual Self-Concept of children with natural parents was found to be higher than Orphan children and the social Self-Concept and the social Self-Concept of orphan children was found to be lower than that of children with natural parents.

Foreign studies Self-Concept

Cross (1991) made a study to investigate the Self-Concept of middle school students and to examine the extend to which selected variables predict the Self-Concept of 293 students in Dade country, Florida. Phase one examined the difference in Self-Concept between music participants and non-participants in music. The Self-Concept scores of these two groups were compared. Phase two involved only the 140 music participants. The data for the choral students responses on the six independent variables were analysed using a step-wise multiple regression design.

Kloomok – Shauna; Cosden – Merith (1992) made a study of 72 elementary children with learning disabilities explored how children maintain a positive Self-Concept despite academic difficulties. Children with high global Self-Concept, compared to low global Self-Concept, perceived themselves as more intelligent, more competent in nonacademic domains, and receiving more special support. Subjects did not discount the importance of academics. (Author / JDD)

Buege – Carol (1993) studied that reverse mainstreaming, creative drama and social skills training used during an academic year with a class of fourth-grade students and emotionally disturbed (ED) students improved the fourth grades attitudes towards emotionally disturbed children and improved the Self-Concept of the ED students.

Sax – Linda (1994) investigated factors associated with development of mathematical Self-Concept in college students. Results showed that some students' background characteristic, college characteristic and student experiences contribute to an overall decline in Mathematics.

Rothman (1995) et al., studied the relationship between self perception of learning disability (L.D.) and Self-Concept and social support among 56 elementary students with L.D. Children with less negative perceptions of their L.D. showed higher Math's achievement scores and perceived more positive Self-Concept, intellectual and behavioral competence and support from classmates and parents.

Kaisa Aunola, Esko Leshnein and Tina Onatsu (2002) studied on 3 methods for developmental changes in the case of reading skills and Self-Concept in the University of Finland on 105 samples 61 boys and 44 girls, 6-7 years from 4 first grade class, pre school shows a uniconstruct Mathew effect for the development of their Self-Concept, but not for the reading skills. However the results showed there was a multi constructed cumulative cycle between children reading skills and their Self-Concept.

Gordon et al., (1995) studied the Self-Concept and motivational patterns of Resilient African American High School students and determined the role of Self-Concept and motivation in aiding resilient African American high school sophomores to obtain academic competence. Results from 138 students suggest resilient African American high school students different from their monresilient peers in the cognitive domain; cognitive ability, cognitive environmental support, cognitive control and cognitive importance.

Jackson et al., (1994) studied about the stereotypic differences and the role of gender attitudes. The gender differences in overall self - evaluation and in specific dimensions of Self-Concept were examined in 470 primarily white college. 501 high school students were examined and it was found that there are gender differences in overall self - evaluation that favour males and that there are differences in specific Self-Concept areas that are consistent with gender sterectypes.

Connolly et al., (1994) examined peer Self-Concept and its association with structural and qualitative features of peer experiences in high school students. Factor analysis supported a three - factor model that differentiated the peer - Self-Concept in terms of the peer group, close friendship, and romantic relationships and found that both peer network structure and friendship quality were significant predictors of Self-Concept.

Pyryt et al., (1994) conducted a comparitive study of gifted and average - ability adolescents. The four dimensions of Self-Concept (academic, social atbletic and evaluative) were evaluated with 97 junior high school students and the results indicated that the gifted students differed in Self-Concept from average ability students, particularly in the area of academic Self-Concept.

STUDIES RELATED TO EMOTIONAL MATURITY

Indian studies on Emotional Maturity

Siddiqui, M.M. (1976) conducted a study on social psychological study of students behaviour" with special reference to indiscipline. The objectives of the investigation was to study the psychological (Emotional Maturity, social maturity, ascendance – submission, security and aggression) and social factors (educational attainment, socio-economic status and rural or urban inhabitation) which affected student behaviour in general; discipline in particular. The measures of Emotional Maturity, social maturity, ascendance submission and social factors showed that disciplined students were emotionally and socially more mature than the indisciplined ones.

Sinha, A.K. and Bhan, R.W. (1978) of Kurukshetra University studied mental health of university students. The sample consisted of 259 male students and 118 female students of Kurukshetra University and 293 male engineering students. The major findings were that the boys and girls of the university did not differ on emotional insecurity. The engineering boys were signficantly superior in mental health to the university boys. Emotional insecurity was more prominent among children from the agricultural community. Emotional insecurity was evenly spread among children from business community and service community.

Arya A (1984) conducted a study on "Emotional Maturity and the value of superior children in the family", A printed scale was administered to 300 superior children (150 males and 150 females) at random. The major findings were (a) superior intelligence showed high relationship with emotional maturiry (v) Agewise there was no significant difference on Emotional Maturity(c) Boys to be more mature (d) Residence did not link with Emotional Maturity.

A study was conducted by Manral, Bheema (1988) of Kaumann University on "The impact of Emotional Maturity and prolonged deprivation on indisciplined behaviour among university students in relation to their academic achievement". The descriptive survey method was used in this study. Stratified random sampling was used to select 472 students. The major findigns were (a) Emotional Maturity was related to disciplined behaviour (b) There was no significant difference between male and female students on Emotional Maturity (c) High deprived students differed from lower deprived students in Emotional Maturity.

Kapil Renu, (1992) investigated on nature and sources of emotional tensions of educated girls of Hindu Society in Agra region. He found that (a) significant difference was found in the level of emotional tensions of highly educated and lower educated girls (b) Higher age group and lower age group educated girls also differed in the levels of emotional tension. (c) parental levels of education had a significant relationship with different kinds of emotional tensions in educated girls of Hindu socieity.

Arora, R.K. (1992) studied international effect of creativity and intelligence on emotional stability, personality adjustment and academic achievement. The major findings were high creative/high intelligence group was significantly higher in emotional stability, than the remaining three creative/ high intelligence group. Those possessing both high convergent and divergent abilities were by far the most accommodative persons among different creative intelligence groups.

Sandhu, Daya Singh (1992) studied "A child's mind in the adult's body". An investigation of perceptual difference between males and females towards Emotional Maturity. The major findings suggested that females seem to consider Emotional Maturity special problem for males, whereas males see it as a problem for both sexes.

Foreign Studies on Emotional Maturity

Allen Jaffe (1981) examined how Illinois state legislators' scores on Emotional Maturity – immaturity measure compared with a similar non political group. The study indicated a higher mean level of Emotional Maturity for the political group.

Bush, Kethryn. J. (1989) conducted research on level of Emotional Maturity in first, second, third grade teachers, investigation of group differences, teachers anxiety, achievement and classroom attitudes. The main purpose of this study and trait emotions before and after administration of standardized tests and to examine the relationship between teacher test Emotional Maturity and teachers anxiety, intelligence, classroom, attitudes and sex differences. The sample consisted of 240, first, second, and third grade teachers and their schools. It was found that the Third grade teachers emotions appeared more positively related to teachers achievement than the second and third grades. Although a casual influence between these occurrences and the administration of GRT cannot be assumed, results provide an impetus for further investigations. Teacher's Emotional Maturity, students Emotional Maturity and environmental variables appear associated with statement achievement.

A study was undertaken by Creamer – Don G (1992) on how to use a developmental model of maturity to enhance student centered teaching. The findings indicated that student – centered teaching must foster the whole student. It presented a developed model involving setting goals in courses and interactive teaching / learning strategies to create student centered classroom. It describe sample course goals for developing and evaluating students maturity, and argues for a model addressing self, values and attitudes.

Heyer, et al., (1993) conducted an investigation on the relationship between parental marital status and the development of identify and emotional autonomy in college students revealed that development approach was used to examine relationship between parental marital status and identity and emotional autonomy to examine relationship between parental marital status and emotional autonomy in 388 college students. Confidence and sexual identity scores revealed that students whose parents were divorced had higher scores than students from intact families. There were no difference in the autonomy scores.

Lawrence P. Michael D. (1993) conducted the study of enablement, alienation, and emotions in middle school classrooms. This study was designed to pursue the question of the relationship between alienation, and emotions in the seventh and eight grade, subjects and 2,159 students taught by 19 teachers in 14 middle schools. There are strong relationship between the student perceptions of classroom structure and their emotions. If they see themselves as having a great deal of control of over events in the classroom, and are less alienated, they have a much better emotions. Boys feel empowered than girls and classes taught by male teachers report themselves to be less in control than those taught by females. Emotions of students with female teachers are more positive than those taught by males.

Gerdes and Hillary et al., (1994) conducted longitudinal study titled emotional, social and academic adjustment of college students. The major findings were new school children completed surveys on expectations about college adjustments; later completed survey of actual adjustments. Six years later, results indicated that two different sets of items best discriminated among good standing persisters and leavers. Emotional and social adjustment items predicted attrition as well as better academic adjustment items.

Allan, Bradford Drake (1997) studied emotions and its influences on mathematical problem solved among 209 under graduates. The major finding stated that the emotions may be more differentiated because psychological responses are stronger for better problem solvers.

Kellner et al., (1995) studied a school based Anger Management program for developmentally and emotionally disabled high school students and described a group program designed for high school students with cognitive, emotional and behavioural disturbances using Novaco's cognitive conceptualization of anger. Multiple techniques allowed multiply handicapped students to learn the physiology, triggers, and consequences of anger as well as to develop coping strategies for managing their anger and to reduce acting out.

Benge et al., (1996) studied the emotional development of twice exceptional rural students and case studies were developed over a 3 years period. The data were interpreted using Kazimierz Dabrowski's Theory of positive Disintegration, in which progressive conflicts and contradictions arise from life experience and become a fundamental and positive factor of development. The study revealed four general categories of behavioural and motivational themes. The students provided evidence of Level - 1 egocentrism, over excitabilities, and asynchronous development, three areas informed by Dabrowski's theory. In addition a fourth theme emerged called acute awareness of manipulation.

CONCLUSION

The survey of related literature has helped the investigator to have a clear perspective of the problem chosen for the present investigation. The review of the related literature has enabled the investigator to formulate the relevant hypotheses for the present study. Based on this review, a suitable methodology and well planned procedure for present investigation is adopted and it is explained in the next chapter.

❒

14

Research Design and Methods

The main aim of research is to provide knowledge that will allow the educator to achieve his goal by the most effective methods. The selection of the method depends upon the nature of the problem, the objectives of study and the population to be studied.

In any research endeavour, methodology occupies a crucial position. Methodology is the art of applying the most suitable procedure to a particular activity. By methodology, we mean the philosophy of research process. This includes the assumption and values that serve as a rational for research and the standard criteria the researcher uses for interpretation, data and conclusion. Research design is a logical and systematic plan prepared for directing a research study. It specifies the objectives of the study, the methodology, and techniques to be allotted.

This chapter gives an overall picture of the design of the study, hypotheses, the psychological tools used for study, nature and selection of the sample, a brief description of the procedure adopted for the collection of data, its scoring and classification.

A research design **(Bryman, 2001)** provides a framework for the collection and analysis of data. A choice of research design reflects decisions about the priority being given to a range of dimensions of the research process. This include the importance attached to

a. Expressing casual connections between variables
b. Generalizing to larger groups of individuals than those actually forming part of the investigation.
c. Understanding behaviour and the meaning of the behaviour in its specific social context.
d. Having a temporal (i.e. overtime) appreciation of social phenomena and their interconnections.

HYPOTHESES

1. The level of Self-Concept among high school students is moderate in nature.
2. The level of Emotional Maturity among high school students is low in nature.
3. There is no significant difference in the total Self-Concept and its dimensions of high school students with respect to their
   a. Gender
   b. Medium of instructions
   c. Type of management
   d. Locality
   e. Type of family
   f. Birth order
4. There is no significant difference in the Total Emotional Maturity and its dimensions of High School students with respect to their.
   a. Gender
   b. Medium of instructions
   c. Type of management
   d. Locality
   e. Type of family
   f. Birth order
5. There is significant association between Self-Concept of High School students and the following variables.
   a. Gender
   b. Medium of instructions
   c. Type of management
   d. Locality
   e. Type of family
   f. Birth order
6. There is significant association between Emotional Maturity of high school students and the following variables.

   a. Gender
   b. Medium of instructions
   c. Type of management
   d. Locality
   e. Type of family
   f. Birth order

7. There is no significant relationship between Self-Concept of high school students and their Emotional Maturity.

DESCRIPTION OF THE TOOLS USED

To verify the framed hypotheses the following tools and techniques were used in the present investigation.

1. Self-Concept Questionnaire
2. Emotional Maturity Scale

SELF-CONCEPT QUESTIONNAIRE

Description

The Self-Concept inventory provides six separate dimensions of Self-Concept viz. Physical, Social, Intellectual, Moral, Educational and Temperamental.

1. Physical Self-Concept measures individuals view of their body, health, physical appearance and strength.,
2. Social Self-Concept measures individual's sense of worth in social interactions.
3. Temperamental Self-Concept measures individual's view of their prevailing emotional state or predominance of a particular kind of emotional reaction
4. Educational Self-Concept measures individuals view of themselves in relation to school, teachers and extracurricular activities.
5. Moral Self-Concept measures individual's estimation of their moral worth; right and wrong activities.
6. Intellectual Self-Concept measures individual's awareness of their intelligence and capacity of problem solving and judgments.

The following table indicates item numbers included in different Self-Concept dimensions.

TABLE. 14.1: Self-Concept Dimensions along with their Item Numbers

Self-Concept Dimensions	Code Number	Item Numbers
Physical	A	2,3,9,20,22,27,29,31
Social	B	1,8,21,37,40,43,46,48
Temperamental	C	4,10,14,16,19,23,24,28
Educational	D	5,13,15,17,25,26,30,32
Moral	E	6,34,35,41,42,44,45,47
Intellectual	F	7,11,12,18,33,36,38,39

Administration of the Test

The following instructions were given to students before administering the inventory. The purpose of the inventory is to detect the Self-Concept of the students. The inventory contains 48 items Each dimension contains eight items. Each is provided with five alternatives. Responses are obtained on the test booklet itself. The students have to read each item carefully and respond to it by marking a tick (√) on any one of the five responses given against that item. There is no time limit but generally 20 minutes have been found sufficient for answering all the items. In the event of the subjects raising any doubts, it must be made clear by the administrator. However the respondent is expected to independently decide and complete the test.

Scoring Method

The sample is provided with five alternatives to give his/her responses ranging from most acceptable to least acceptable description of his/her Self-Concept. The alternatives or responses are arranged in such a way that the scoring system for all the items will remain the same i.e 5,4,3,2,1 whether the items are positive or negative. If the subject put (√) mark for first alternative the score is one. The summated score of all the forty-eight items provide the total Self-Concept score of an individual. A high score on this inventory indicates a higher Self-Concept, while a low score shows low Self-Concept. The score of each item on the front page is transferred against that item. All the scores of eight items given in that column is added. The score obtained is taken as the score for that particular dimension.

EMOTIONAL MATURITY SCALE

Description

Emotional Maturity Scale (Appendix -1) Standardised by Dr.Yashvir Singh and Dr.Mahesh Bhargava (Head, Department of Psychology, St.John's College, AGRA and Dr.Mahesh Bhargava, Director N.P.C. AGRA).

Emotional Maturity is assessed by evaluating the following five aspects of an individual namely.

(a) Emotional unstability
(b) Emotional regression
(c) Social Maladjustment
(d) Personality disintegration
(e) Lack of independence.

(a) Emotional Unstability: This is a broad factor representing syndrome of lack of capacity to dispose off problems, irritability needs, constant help for one's day to day work, vulnerability, stubbornness and temper tantrums.

(b) Emotional Regression: Emotional regression is also a broad group of factors representing such syndromes as feeling of inferiority, restlessness, hostility, agressiveness and self-centredness.

(c) Social Maladjustment: Such a person shows lack of social adaptability and possess hatred, seclusiveness boasting and will be a lier and shirker.

(d) Personality Disintegration: It includes all those symptoms, which represent disintegration of personality, life reaction, phobia formation, rationalization, pessimism, immorality etc. Such a person suffers from inferiorities and hence reacts to environment through aggressiveness, destruction and has distorted sense of reality.

(e) Lack of Independence: Such a person shows parasitic dependence on others is egotic and lack `Objective Interests'. People think of him an unreliable person.

There are 48 positive statements in the Emotional Maturity Scale. Of these, statements 1-10 measure emotional unstability, statements 11-20 evaluate emotional regression, statements 21-30 assess social maladjustment statement 31-40 indicate personality disintegration while statements 41-48 determines the level of independence. The total score of items 1-48 attribute to the total Emotional Maturity of an individual.

The higher the score on the Emotional Maturity scale, lower is the Emotional Maturity and vice versa.

Administration of the test

The scale for psychological investigation consists of statements about what the students feel about emotional unstability, emotional regression, social maladjustment, personal disintegration and lack of independence in various situations. The students were required to select any one of the given five responses to indicate the extent to which they agree or disagree with each statement to describe their own feelings about Emotional Maturity. The students are requested to give their responses frankly and they were told that it would be kept confidential.

Scoring Method

The weightage of 5,4,3,2 and 1 are given for the categories `Very much', `Undecided', `Probably' and `Never respectively. The net score of an individual with respect to Emotional Maturity is the sum of all scores in each of the 48 items.

Sample for the Study

The sample of the study is mainly concerned with high school students studying in Thiruvananthapuram district in Kerala. A sample of 300 were chosen at random from Government, Aided and Private schools.

PILOT STUDY

Before finalizing the final structure of the questionnaires and collection of data for the main study a pilot study was attempted. It was conducted in the month of September 2006 on high school students drawn from each school selected randomly from the whole sample to establish reliability and validity of various tools used in the study.

ESTABLISHING RELIABILITY AND VALIDITY OF TOOLS USED

Self-Concept

Reliability

In order to establish the reliability of Self-Concept inventory, odd-even method of correlation was used. The correlation between the two parts of odd-even question score was calculated by using karl Pearson's Product moment formula and the co-efficient of reliability so obtained is 0.8241 showing that the tool is reliable.

Validity

In the case of Self-Concept inventory, it is found to be 0.9077 suggesting that the tool is valid.

Emotional Maturity

Reliability

This Emotional Maturity scale is a standardized tool. The reliability of the tool in the present study has been found by test-retest method. The obtained reliability coefficient is 0.8647 revealing that the tool is reliable.

Validity

In the present study the validity coefficient is computed as the square root of the reliability coefficient which is 0.9298 revealing that the tool is highly valid.

MAIN STUDY

The tools described below

1. Self-Concept inventory
2. Emotional Maturity Scale are used to collect the information from the samples for the main study following the procedures mentioned for the administration of the tests. The tests were administrated on the samples of High School students in November 2006.

TABLE. 14.2: Showing the time Schedule of Administered

Sl. No	Name of the Tool	Time Taken
1.	Self-Concept	45 minutes
2.	Emotional Maturity Scale	60 minutes

CONCLUSION

This chapter outlines the design of the present study, the procedure followed and the nature of the sample. It also describes the hypotheses to be tested, the tools used and methods of administration and scoring. The collected data were analysed using appropriate statistical techniques described above to study the Self-Concept and Emotional Maturity among the High School students.

❐

15

Analysis and Interpretation of the Data

The collected data have to be processed so that intelligible conclusions may be drawn. Statistical analysis is of great use in this regard. *"Analysis of the data is as important as any other component of the research process"* **Gay** (1976). According to **Mouly** *"Research data becomes meaningful in the process of being analysed and interpreted"*. The purpose of analysis is to summarise the completed observations in such a manner that they yield answers to the research questions. Regardless of how well the study is conducted, an inappropriate analysis can lead to in appropriate conclusions.

In this chapter, an attempt is made to analyse and interpret the collected data. It deals with the statistical analysis of the data with reference to the hypotheses that were formulated. Interpretations are also made to account for the results obtained. The choice of statistical techniques for data analysis was largely determined by the research hypotheses.

Descriptive Analysis

The following table shows the sample under the following variables.

TABLE. 15.1: Showing the Categories and Percentage of the Sample.

Variables	Categories	N	Percentage
Gender	Boys	150	50
	Girls	150	50
Medium of instruction	Malayalam	150	50
	English	150	50
Type of management	Private	100	33.33
	Aided	100	33.33
	Government	100	33.33
Locale	Rural	150	50
	Urban	150	50
Type of family	Nuclear	279	93
	Joint	21	7
Birth order	First	149	49.66
	Second	132	44
	Third and Above	19	633

INFERENTIAL ANALYSIS

Descriptive Analysis

The following table explains the different dimensions of Self-Concept of High School students.

Self-Concept and its dimensions of High School students.

TABLE. 15.2: Mean and Standard Deviation of High School Students for Self-Concept and its Dimensions -Total sample

Self-Concept and its dimensions	Mean Score	Standard deviation	Percentage
Physical	28.12	3.60	70.3
Social	28.44	4.23	71.1
Temperamental	28.22	3.99	70.55
Educational	28.81	4.44	72.02
Moral	29.30	4.48	73.25
Intellectual	25.84	3.86	64.6
Total Self-Concept	**168.73**	**17.30**	**70.30**

From table 15.02 it is observed that the total Self-Concept of high school students was 168.73 (70.30%). The Moral Self-Concept had the highest percentage of mean score (73.25%) and the Intellectual Self-Concept had the lowest percentage of mean score (64.4).

TABLE. 15.3: Emotional Maturity and its Dimensions of High School Students-Total Sample

Emotional Maturity and its dimensions	Mean	Standard deviation	Percentage
Emotional unstability	25.81	6.90	51.62
Emotional regression	22.59	6.50	45.18
Social maladjustment	22.36	5.85	44.72
Personality disintegration	20.25	5.77	40.5
Lack of independence	18.93	4.76	47.32
Total Emotional Maturity	**109.94**	**23.05**	**45.80**

It is observed from table 15.03 that the total Emotional Maturity mean score is 109.94. The dimension emotional unstability had a mean score of 25.81 which was found to be highest and the dimension lack of independence was found to have the least score (18.93).

(i) Self-Concept of High School Students

The variable Self-Concept has been classified into three groups based on quartiles and the frequency and percentage of students in each category is given in table 15.04.

TABLE. 15.4: Showing the Criteria for Classifying the Sample into three Groups Based on Self-Concept

Self-Concept		
Level	**Frequency**	**Percentage**
Low	101	33.67
Moderate	97	32.33
High	102	34.00

It is observed from the above table that (102) students of high school show a high level of Self-Concept indicating that the Self-Concept of high school students is high in nature.

(ii) Emotional Maturity of High School Students

The variable Emotional Maturity has been classified into three groups based on quartiles and the frequency and percentage of students in each category is given in table 15.05.

TABLE. 15.5: Showing the Criteria for Classifying the Sample into three Groups Based on Emotional Maturity

Emotional Maturity		
Level	**Frequency**	**Percentage**
Low	103	34.33
Moderate	97	32.33
High	100	33.33

It is observed from the above table that (103) students of high school show a low level of Emotional Maturity indicating that the Emotional Maturity of high school students is low in nature.

Differential Analysis

(i) Self-Concept with Respect to Gender

The mean, standard deviation and t value have been calculated for Self-Concept and its dimensions with respect to gender and the results are given in table 15.06.

TABLE. 15.6: Mean, Standard Deviation and t value for the Scores of Self-Concept and its Dimensions with Respect to Gender

Self-Concept and its dimensions	Boys		Girls		t-value	Level of significance
	Mean	SD	Mean	SD		
Physical	28.80	3.81	27.45	3.24	3.312	P<0.05
Social	28.97	4.24	27.90	4.17	2.209	P<0.05
Temperamental	29.18	3.68	27.25	4.07	4.302	P<0.05
Educational	29.37	4.36	28.25	4.46	2.185	P<0.05
Moral	29.15	4.19	29.45	4.76	-0.580	P>0.05
Intellectual	26.34	4.20	25.35	3.41	2.247	P<0.05
Total Self-Concept	**171.81**	**17.86**	**165.65**	**16.21**	**3.128**	**P<0.05**

From table 4:06, it is found that the total Self-Concept score was higher for boys (171.81) than for girls (165.65).

The `t' value calculated for the Self-Concept and its 6 dimensions with respect to gender revealed that boys and girls differed significantly in the Total Self-Concept and its dimensions namely Physical Self-Concept, Social Self-Concept, Temperamental Self-Concept, Educational Self-Concept and intellectual Self-Concept at 0.05 level except Moral Self-Concept.

(ii) Self-Concept with Respect to Medium of Instruction

The mean standard deviation and t value were calculated for Self-Concept and its dimensions with respect to their Medium of Instruction and the same are given in the table 15.07.

TABLE. 15.7: Mean, Standard Deviation and 't' value for the Scores on Students Self-Concept with Respect to Medium of Instruction

Self-Concept and its dimensions	Malayalam		English		t-value	Level of significance
	Mean	SD	Mean	SD		
Physical	27.43	3.33	28.81	3.73	3.380	P<0.05
Social	27.24	4.48	29.63	3.61	5.095	P<0.05
Temperamental	27.59	4.36	28.84	3.49	2.735	P<0.05
Educational	28.41	4.37	29.21	4.49	1.551	P>0.05
Moral	27.38	4.47	31.21	3.58	8.195	P<0.05
Intellectual	25.44	4.30	26.25	3.32	1.819	P>0.05
Total Self-Concept	**163.50**	**19.42**	**173.95**	**12.99**	**5.479**	**P<0.05**

From the above table, it is observed that the total Self-Concept is more (173.95) for the students who are studying in English medium schools than the students studying in Malayalam Medium Schools (163.50).

The 't' value calculated for the total Self-Concept and its 6 dimensions with respect to the Medium of Instruction revealed that the students from English medium and Malayalam Medium Schools differed significantly in the total Self-Concept and its dimensions such as Physical Self-Concept, Social Self-Concept, Temperamental Self-Concept and Moral Self-Concept at 0.05 level. The dimensions of Self-Concept such as Educational Self-Concept and Intellectual Self-Concept did not differ significantly even at 0.05 level with respect to Medium of Instruction.

(iii) Self-Concept with Respect to Type of Management

The mean standard deviation and F-ratio were calculated for student's Self-Concept and its dimensions with respect to the Type of Management of the schools where they are studying and the results are tabulated in the table 15.08.

TABLE.15.8: Mean, Standard Deviation and 't' value for the Scores on Self-Concept with rRespect to the Type of Management of School

Self-Concept and its dimensions	Private (1)		Aided (2)		Govt (3)		F ratio	L.S	Groups differed signific antly
	Mean	SD	Mean	SD	Mean	SD			
Physical	28.80	3.85	27.33	3.35	28.24	3.46	4.350	P<0.05	(1,2)
Social	29.53	3.28	26.99	4.65	28.79	4.28	10.095	P<0.05	(1,2) (2,3)

Temperamental	28.88	3.28	26.99	4.05	28.78	4.32	7.408	P<0.05	(1,2) (2,3)
Educational	29.07	4.45	27.73	4.12	29.63	4.57	4.960	P<0.05	(2,3)
Moral	31.30	3.75	27.83	4.55	28.76	4.39	17.919	P<0.05	(1,2) (1,3)
Intellectual	26.75	3.10	24.02	3.85	26.76	3.92	18.772	P<0.05	(1,2) (2,3)
Total Self-Concept	**174.33**	**12.95**	**160.89**	**16.83**	**170.96**	**18.83**	**18.209**	**P<0.05**	**(1,2) (2,3)**

From table 4,08, it is found that the Total Self-Concept was high for the students studying in Private schools (174.33) and the same was low (160.89) for those who are studying in Aided schools.

The F-ratio calculated for the Total Self-Concept and its dimensions with respect to the type of management revealed that students studying in Private, Aided and Government Schools differed significantly in their total Self-Concept and all its dimensions namely Physical, Self-Concept, Social Self-Concept, Temperamental Self-Concept, Educational Self-Concept, Moral Self-Concept and intellectual Self-Concept at 0.05 level.

Further analysis of differences between the age groups through Turkey HSD revealed that in the total Self-Concept, the pupils who are studying in the Aided schools differed significantly from those who are studying in the Private Schools and Government Schools. The same is found to be true for the Social, Temperamental and Intellectual Self-Concept.

With regard to the Physical dimension of Self-Concept, students from Private Schools show significant difference from that of the students of Aided Schools. The pupils from Private Schools showed more Physical Self-Concept (28.80) when compared to those from Aided and Government Schools.

In the case of Educational dimension of Self-Concept, students from Aided Schools showed significant difference from the students of Government School.

It is observed from the table that in Moral dimension of Self-Concept, students from Aided Schools showed significant difference to both the Government School students and the private school students. Here the Private School students scored, more (31.30) than that of Government and Aided School students.

(iv) Self-Concept with Respect to Locality

Mean, Standard Deviation and 't' value for Self-Concept and its dimensions were calculated with respect to locality and the results are given in table 15.09.

TABLE.15.9: Mean, Standard Deviation and 't' value for the Scores of Self-Concept and its Dimensions with Respect to Locality

Self-Concept and its dimensions	Rural		Urban		t-value	Level of significance
	Mean	SD	Mean	SD		
Physical	27.43	3.33	28.81	3.73	3.380	P<0.05
Social	27.24	4.48	29.63	3.61	5.095	P<0.05
Temperamental	27.59	4.36	28.84	3.49	2.735	P<0.05
Educational	28.41	4.37	29.21	4.49	1.551	P<0.05
Moral	27.38	4.47	31.21	3.58	8.195	P<0.05
Intellectual	25.44	4.30	26.25	3.32	1.819	P>0.05
Total Self-Concept	**163.50**	**19.42**	**173.95**	**12.99**	**5.479**	**P<0.05**

From the above table it is found that the Total Self-Concept is more for students from urban area (173.95) than those from the rural area (163.50).

The t value calculated for the Self-Concept and its 6 dimensions with respect to locality revealed that students from rural and urban area differed significantly in the Total Self-Concept and its dimensions such as Physical Self-Concept, Social Self-Concept, Temperamental Self-Concept, Educational Self-Concept and Moral Self-Concept at 0.05 level except intellectual Self-Concept where it did not show any significant difference even at 0.05 level.

(v) Self-Concept with Respect to Type of Family.

The Mean, Standard Deviation and t value have been calculated for Self-Concept and its dimensions with respect to the Type of Family and the results are given in table 15.10.

TABLE. 15.10: Mean, Standard Deviation and 't' value for the Scores of Self-Concept and its Dimensions with Respect to Type of Family

Self-Concept and its dimensions	Nuclear		Joint		t-value	Level of significance
	Mean	SD	Mean	SD		
Physical	28.13	3.55	28.00	4.28	0.139	P>0.05
Social	28.47	4.25	28.05	4.09	0.451	P>0.05
Temperamental	28.20	3.98	28.38	4.20	-0.186	P>0.05
Educational	28.86	4.46	28.19	4.20	0.697	P>0.05
Moral	29.28	4.49	29.52	4.38	-0.246	P>0.05
Intellectual	25.88	3.86	25.33	3.84	0.631	P>0.05
Total Self-Concept	168.82	17.54	167.48	0.414	0.414	P>0.05

From the above table, it is observed that the Total Self-Concept is more for students who come from Nuclear family (168.82) than that of those from Joint family (167.48).

The 't' value calculated for Self-Concept and its dimensions with respect to type of family revealed that the students coming from Nuclear and Joint family did not differ significantly in any of the dimensions of Self-Concept and in the total Self-Concept even at 0.05 level.

(vi) Self-Concept with Respect to Birth Order

The Mean, Standard Deviation and t value have been calculated for the total Self-Concept and its dimensions with respect to birth order and the results are given in table 15.11.

TABLE. 15.11: Mean, Standard Deviation and 'F' ratio for the Scores on Self-Concept with Respect to Birth Order

Self-Concept and its dimensions	First (1)		Second (2)		Third (3)		F value	L.S	Groups differed signifi cantly
	Mean	SD	Mean	SD	Mean	SD			
Physical	27.66	3.60	28.42	3.53	29.63	3.61	3.399	P<0.05	(1,3)
Social	28.19	3.92	28.58	4.39	29.37	5.43	0.773	P>0.05	N.S
Temperamental	27.93	3.97	28.39	3.84	29.26	5.05	1.151	P>0.05	N.S
Educational	28.69	4.55	28.76	4.37	30.11	4.15	0.870	P>0.05	N.S
Moral	29.56	4.23	29.03	4.67	29.11	5.07	0.501	P>0.05	N.S
Intellectual	25.46	3.66	26.15	3.98	26.74	4.32	1.691	P>0.05	N.S
Total Self-Concept	**167.50**	**16.72**	**169.33**	**17.39**	**174.21**	**20.64**	**1.413**	**P>0.05**	**N.S**

From table 15.11, it is observed that the total Self-Concept was highest (174.21) for the students whose Birth Order is third and above when compared to those whose birth order is first or second.

The F ratio calculated for the total Self-Concept and its dimensions with respect to the Birth Order, revealed that there is no significant difference between the groups based on their Birth Orders except physical dimension Self-Concept where the pupils whose birth order is `one' differed significantly from those whose Birth Order is `third' and above.

(vii) Emotional Maturity with Respect to Gender.

The Mean, Standard Deviation and t-value have been calculated for the total Emotional Maturity and its dimensions with respect to Gender and the results are given in table 15.12.

TABLE. 15.12: Mean, Standard Deviation and 'F' ratio for the Scores on Emotional Maturity with Respect to Gender

Emotional Maturity and its dimensions	Boys		Girls		t-value	Level of significance
	Mean	SD	Mean	SD		
Emotional Unstability	25.16	6.88	26.47	6.87	1.645	P>0.05
Emotional regression	22.16	6.54	23.01	6.45	1.138	P>0.05
Social malajustment	22.57	5.98	22.16	5.73	0.601	P>0.05
Personality disintegration	20.77	5.80	19.73	5.71	1.575	P>0.05
Lack of independence	19.11	5.17	18.75	4.32	0.667	P>0.05
Total Emotional Maturity	**109.77**	**23.94**	**110.11**	**22.20**	**-0.128**	**P>0.05**

From the t values shown in table 15.12 it is revealed that boys and girls did not differ significantly in their total Emotional Maturity and in any of its dimensions.

(viii) Emotional Maturity with Respect to Medium of Instruction

The Mean, Standard Deviation and t value have been calculated for the total Emotional Maturity and its dimensions with respect to medium of instruction and the results are given in table 15:13.

TABLE. 15:13: Mean, Standard Deviation and 'F' ratio for the Scores on Emotional Maturity with Respect to the Medium of Instruction

Emotional Maturity and its dimensions	Malayalam		English		t-value	Level of significance
	Mean	SD	Mean	SD		
Emotional Unstability	26.60	7.47	25.03	6.20	1.985	P<0.05
Emotional Regression	22.34	6.90	22.83	6.08	-0.657	P>0.05
Social Malajustment	23.14	6.31	21.59	5.26	2.315	P<0.05
Personality Disintegration	21.64	5.38	18.86	5.37	4.293	P<0.05
Lack of Independence	19.06	4.74	18.80	4.79	0.472	P>0.05
Total Emotional Maturity	**112.78**	**24.52**	**107.11**	**21.18**	**2.145**	**P<0.05**

From table 15:13, it is found that the total Emotional Maturity score is high (112.78) for malayalam medium students indicating that they have less Emotional Maturity than the English medium students.

The 't' value calculated for the total Emotional Maturity and its dimensions with respect to medium of instruction revealed that the students from Malayalam and English medium differ significantly in the scores of their Total Emotional Maturity and its dimensions such as emotional unstability, social maladjustment and personality disintegration. In dimensions such as emotional regression and lack of independence, students from both the medium did not show any significant differences.

(ix) Emotional Maturity with Respect to Type of Management

The Mean, Standard Deviation and F ratio were calculated for the total Emotional Maturity and its dimensions of high school students with respect to the Type of Management and the results are given in table 15.14

TABLE. 15.14: Mean, Standard Deviation and 'F' ratio for the Scores on Emotional Maturity with Respect to the Type of Management of School

Emotional Maturity and its dimensions	Private (1)		Aided (2)		Govt (3)		F ratio	L.S	Groups differed significantly
	Mean	SD	Mean	SD	Mean	SD			
Emotional Unstability	26.57	5.79	22.41	6.24	28.46	7.20	23.118	P<0.05	(1,2) (2,3)
Emotional Regression	23.95	5.76	20.97	6.35	22.84	7.02	5.537	P<0.05	(1,2)
Social Maladjustment	20.77	5.16	21.64	5.39	24.68	6.27	13.315	P<0.05	(1,3) (2,3)
Personality Disintegration	18.08	5.31	20.08	5.44	22.59	5.69	16.982	P<0.05	(1,2) (1,3) (2,3)
Lack of Independence	19.03	4.07	18.05	5.20	19.71	4.84	3.118	P<0.05	(2,3)
Total Emotional Maturity	**108.40**	**20.37**	**103.15**	**21.69**	**118.28**	**24.48**	**11.923**	**P<0.05**	**(1,3) (2,3)**

From table 15.14, it is observed that the Total Emotional Maturity was less for the students coming from Government school (118.28) than those who come from Private and Aided school.

The F ratio calculated for the total Emotional Maturity and its dimensions with respect to the type of management revealed that the students studying in Government Schools differed significantly in the total Emotional Maturity and all its dimensions namely Emotional unstability, Emotional Regression, Social Maladjustment, personality disintegration and lack of independence.

Further analysis of differences between the different school Types revealed that in the total Emotional Maturity, the pupils from Government Schools differed significantly from those of Private and Aided schools.

The same was found to be true for Social Maladjustment.

With regard to emotional unstability, aided school students differed significantly from those who studied in private and government schools. Pupils from Government schools are found to possess more Emotional unstability.

In the case of Emotional regression the Private School students and aided school students differed significantly and the Private School students were found to have more Emotional regression than the other two groups.

With regard to personality disintegration, the pupils belong to all the Private, Aided and Government Schools differed significantly with each other and the Government School students possess more Personality Disintegration (22.59) when compared to the other two groups.

Regarding lack of independence, it is found that the students studying in Aided and Government Schools showed significant difference and the students studying in Government Schools are found to have more lack of independence.

(x) Emotional Maturity with Respect to Locality

The Mean Standard deviation and 't' value were calculated for the total Emotional Maturity and its dimensions of high school students with respect to the locality and the results are given in table 15.15.

TABLE. 15.15: Mean, standard deviation and 't' value for the Scores on Emotional Maturity with Respect to Locality of School

Emotional Maturity and its dimensions	Rural		Urban		t-value	Level of significance
	Mean	SD	Mean	SD		
Emotional Unstability	26.60	7.47	25.03	6.20	1.985	P<0.05
Emotional Regression	22.34	6.90	22.83	6.08	0.657	P>0.05
Social Maladjustment	23.14	6.31	21.59	5.26	2.315	P<0.05
Personality Disintegration	21.64	5.83	18.86	5.37	4.293	P<0.05
Lack of Independence	19.06	4.74	18.80	4.79	0.472	P>0.05
Total Emotional Maturity	**112.78**	**24.52**	**21.18**	**21.18**	**2.145**	**P<0.05**

From the table 15.15, it is observed that the Emotional Maturity scores is more for the pupils coming from rural area, indicating that they are having less Emotional Maturity than the pupils from Urban Area.

The 't' value calculated for the Total Emotional Maturity and its dimensions with respect to Locality revealed that students coming from rural and Urban Areas, differed significantly in their total Emotional Maturity and its dimensions such as Emotional Unstability, Social Maladjustment and personality disintegration. In emotional regression and lack of Independence the students from Rural and Urban area did not differ significantly.

(xi) Emotional Maturity with Respect to Type of Family.

The mean, Standard Deviation and t value were calculated for the total Emotional Maturity and its dimensions of high school students with respect to type of family and the results are given in table 15:16.

TABLE. 15.16: Mean, Standard Deviation and 't' value for the Scores on Emotional Maturity with Respect to Type of Family

Emotional Maturity and its dimensions	Nuclear		Joint		t-value	Level of significance
	Mean	SD	Mean	SD		
Emotional Unstability	26.07	6.86	22.43	6.65	2.412	P>0.05
Emotional Regression	22.78	6.45	20.05	6.71	1.802	P>0.05
Social Maladjustment	22.44	5.97	21.29	3.90	1.255	P>0.05
Personality Disintegration	20.35	5.86	18.90	4.32	1.437	P>0.05
Lack of Independence	19.07	4.82	17.05	3.38	2.553	P>0.05
Total Emotional Maturity	**110.71**	**23.16**	**99.71**	**19.11**	**2.503**	**P>0.05**

From the table 15:16, it is observed that the mean score of Emotional Maturity is more (110:71) for students coming from nuclear family which shows that they are having less Emotional Maturity than those who are coming from Joint Family.

The 't' value calculated for the total Emotional Maturity and its dimensions with respect to Type of Family, revealed that the students coming from nuclear and Joint Families did not differ significantly in their total Emotional Maturity and any of their dimensions such as Emotional Unstability, Emotional Regression, Social Maladjustment, Personality disintegration and lack of Independence.

(xii) Emotional Maturity with Respect to Birth Order

The Mean, Standard Deviation and 'F' ratio were calculated for the total Emotional Maturity and its dimensions of High School students with respect to the Birth Order and the Results are given in table 15:17.

TABLE. 15.17: Mean, Standard Deviation and 'F' Ratio for the Score on Emotional Maturity with Respect to the Birth Order of the Students

Emotional Maturity and its dimensions	First (1)		Second (2)		Third and Above (3)		F value	L.S	Groups differed significantly
	Mean	SD	Mean	SD	Mean	SD			
Emotional Unstability	24.93	6.58	26.56	7.11	27.58	7.24	2.659	P>0.05	N.S
Emotional Regression	22.11	6.25	22.98	6.69	23.63	7.10	0.889	P>0.05	N.S
Social Maladjustment	21.56	5.62	22.84	5.93	25.37	6.07	4.456	P<0.05	(1,3)
Personality Disintegration	19.91	5.63	20.41	6.02	21.84	5.01	1.039	P>0.05	N.S
Lack of Independence	18.67	4.63	19.08	4.81	19.95	5.45		P>0.05	N.S
Total Emotional Maturity	**107.17**	**21.45**	**111.86**	**24.00**	**118.37**	**26.08**	**2.843**	**P>0.05**	**N.S**

From the table 15.17, it is found that the total Emotional Maturity score was high for the pupils whose birth order is `third and above' which indicates that they have a less Emotional Maturity than the other two groups.

The F ratio calculated for the total Emotional Maturity and its dimensions with respect to the birth order revealed that the students belonging to different birth orders did not differ significantly in the total Emotional Maturity and its Dimensions such as Emotional Unstability, Emotional Regression, Personality Disintegration and Lack of Independence. The total Emotional Maturity score was high for the students whose Birth Order is third and above which shows that they show less Emotional Maturity.

With regard to Social Maladjustment, students whose Birth Order is first and `third and above' differed significantly. The Children whose Birth Order is first was found to have less Social Maladjustment and Emotional Maturity.

ASSOCIATION ANALYSIS

(i) Association between Self-Concept and the background variables

The significant association between the variable Self-Concept and the background variables have been assessed through chi-square test, the details of which are represented in the following table.

TABLE. 15.18: Showing the Chi-Square Distribution to find out the Association between Self-Concept and Background Variables

Self-Concept & Variables	X^2	df	L.S.	Contingency Coefficient
Gender	5.497	2	P>0.05	0.134
Medium of Instruction	32.972	2	P<0.01	0.315
Type of Management	38.511	4	P<0.01	0.337
Locale	32.972	2	P<0.01	0.315
Type of Family	1.464	2	P>0.05	0.070
Birth Order	3.003	4	P>0.05	0.100

From the above table it is observed that there is a Significant Association between Self-Concept and medium of instruction; Self-Concept and Type of Management; and Self-Concept and locality as seen from the X^2 value.

(ii) Association between Emotional Maturity and the back ground variables

The significant association between the Emotional Maturity and the back ground variables have been studied through Chi-Square test, the details of which are represented in the following table15.19.

TABLE. 15.19: Showing the Chi-Square Distribution to find out the Association Between Self-Concept and Background Variables

Emotional Maturity Vs variables	X^2	df	L.S.	Contingency Coefficient
Gender	0.385	2	P>0.05	0.036
Medium of Instruction	2.173	2	P>0.01	0.085
Type of Management	21.785	4	P<0.01	0.260
Locale	2.173	2	P>0.01	0.085
Type of Family	7.615	2	P<0.05	0.157
Birth Order	4.574	4	P>0.05	0.123

From the above table, it is observed that there is a significant association between Emotional Maturity and type of management; and Emotional Maturity and type of family as seen from the X^2.

Correlation Analysis

Relationship between Self-Concept and Emotional Maturity

The correlation between Self-Concept and Emotional Maturity has been calculated and results are presented in table 15.20.

TABLE. 15.20: Table Showing `r'-Value and Level of Significance for the Variables, Self-Concept and Emotional Maturity

Variables compared	r - value	Level of significance
Self-Concept and Emotional Maturity	0.051	NS

From the above table, we can conclude that there is no significant correlation between Self-Concept and Emotional Maturity.

CONCLUSION

A brief report of the research study together with major findings and conclusions arrived at along with their educational implications have been presented in the succeeding chapter.

❐

16

Summary, Findings & Conclusions

The present chapter gives a brief summary of the various findings of the entire study and it also gives the statistical analysis of data presented in the previous chapter. The implications along with suggestions for replicating the study or for investigating of other closely related problems in other settings with different samples and tools are also presented.

STATEMENT OF THE PROBLEMS

The present study has been specifically inducted to study the relation between Self-Concept and Emotional Maturity of High School students. The relative contribution of personal variables (Gender, Locale, Type of family and Birth Order) school related variables (medium of instructions and type of management) and research variables (Self-Concept and Emotional Maturity) among high school students are investigated in this study.

The problem is stated as "A study of Self-Concept and Emotional Maturity among high school students".

KEYWORDS IN THE STATEMENT

Self-Concept

Self-Concept is the individual's way of looking at himself. It also signifies his way of thinking, feeling and behaving.

Self - Concept is the dominant element is the personality pattern, it governs the individual's characteristic reaction to people and situations and determines the quality of his behaviour.

Emotional Maturity

Emotional Maturity is a process in which the personality is continuously striving for greater sense of emotional health, both intra physically and intra personally.

If the emotional development of the individual is relatively complete his adaptability is high, his regressive tendencies are low, and his vulnerability is minimal.

OBJECTIVES OF THE STUDY

1. To find out the level of Self-Concept among high school students.
2. To find out the level of Emotional Maturity among high school students.
3. To find out whether there is significant difference in the total Self-Concept and its dimensions of high school students with respect to their.
    a. Gender
    b. Medium of instructions
    c. Type of Management
    d. Locality
    e. Type of family
    f. Birth Order
4. To find out whether there is significant difference in the total Emotional Maturity and its dimensions of high school students with respect to their.
    a. Gender
    b. Medium of instructions
    c. Type of Management
    d. Locality
    e. Type of family
    f. Birth Order
5. To find out whether there is any significant association between Self-Concept of high school students and the following variables.

   a. Gender
   b. Medium of instructions
   c. Type of Management
   d. Locality
   e. Type of family
   f. Birth Order

6. To find out whether there is any significant association between Emotional Maturity of high school students and the following variables.
   a. Gender
   b. Medium of instructions
   c. Type of Management
   d. Locality
   e. Type of family
   f. Birth Order

7. To find out the relationship between Self-Concept of high school students and their Emotional Maturity.

HYPOTHESES

1. The level of Self-Concept among high school students is moderate in nature.
2. The level of Emotional Maturity among high school students is low in nature.
3. There is no significant difference in the total Self-Concept and its dimensions of high school students with respect to their
   a. Gender
   b. Medium of instructions
   c. Type of management
   d. Locality
   e. Type of family
   f. Birth order

4. There is no significant difference in the Total Emotional Maturity and its dimensions of high school students with respect to their.
   a. Gender
   b. Medium of instructions
   c. Type of management
   d. Locality
   e. Type of family
   f. Birth order

5. There is significant association in Self-Concept between high school students and the following variables.
    a. Gender
    b. Medium of instructions
    c. Type of management
    d. Locality
    e. Type of family
    f. Birth order
6. There is significant association in Emotional Maturity between high school students and the following variables
    a. Gender
    b. Medium of instructions
    c. Type of management
    d. Locality
    e. Type of family
    f. Birth order
7. There is no significant relationship between Self-Concept of high school students and their Emotional Maturity.

TOOLS AND TECHNIQUES

The following tools have been used to verify the hypotheses.

i. Self-Concept questionnaire prepared by Dr.Rajkumar Saraswat.
ii. Emotional Maturity scale prepared by Dr.Yashvir Singh and Dr.Mahesh Bhargava.

SAMPLE

Stratified random sampling technique has been adopted to choose the sample. A representative sample of 300 students were drawn from different high schools in Thiruvananthapuram District of Kerala.

MAJOR FINDINGS OF THE STUDY

1. The level of Self-Concept among high school students is high in nature.
2. The level of Emotional Maturity among high school students is low in nature.
3. There is significant difference in the Self-Concept of high school students with respect to their
    a. Gender
    b. Medium of instruction
    c. Type of management

   d. Locality

4. There is significant difference in the Emotional Maturity of high school students with respect to thus
   a. Medium of instruction
   b. Type of management
   c. Locality
5. There is significant association between Self-Concept of high school students and the following variables.
   a. Medium of instruction
   b. Type of management
   c. Locality
6. There is significant association between Emotional Maturity of high school students and the following variables.
   a. Type of management
   b. Type of family
7. There is no significant relationship between Self-Concept of high school students and their Emotional Maturity.

EDUCATIONAL IMPLICATIONS

A person's concept of his self is one of the best predictions of his successful achievement. The relationship of Self-Concept to school achievement is very specific. The level of school success predicts the level of regard of self and one's own ability. Hence the teachers need to concentrate on the academic successes and failures of the students. It is the student's history of success and failures that gives them the information with which to assess themselves. Developing proper emotions and controlling them is another important objective of education during adolescence. Emotional Maturity is reflected in an individual's ability to be responsive to the entire hierarehy of emotions - as they are the communciations that provides the basis for differentiation and discernment of just what our impact is. Emotional Maturity is a result of conscious choice, our conscious choice to be responsible for our impact. As Self-Concept and Emotional Maturity are both constructed by one's conscious reflections, the educators and parents should provide experiences that students can master rather than attempting to boost self esteem directly through other means. It is the responsibility of the teachers and school to facilitate adjustment and learning. In this research the findings of the study will be helpful for the teachers as well as curriculum planners to work out innovative strategies in improving the Self-Concept and Emotional Maturity of the students.

DELIMITATIONS OF THE STUDY

1. The study was limited to the schools located in Kerala.
2. The study was limited to high school students only.
3. The sample is restricted to 300 students.

SUGGESTIONS FOR FURTHER RESEARCH

Following are some of the suggestions put forward by the investigator for further research.

1. This study was confined only with the students of high school. To make the findings of this study more universal, a comprehensive study of this type involving different standards of students could be undertaken.
2. This study was conducted only in a few selected schools. It can be extended to many districts.
3. A comparative study can be undertaken among primary, secondary and higher secondary school students.
4. Investigation may be made on identifying various ways to improve the Self-Concept and Emotional Maturity of the students.

❒

17

Problem and its Perspectives

Emergence of the Problem

Every difference of environment means a difference in one's habit and one's way of living in so far as these differences create a different environment, a dynamic equilibrium of life is maintained through a processing of constant selections and constant adaptations. The society is not the world but is directly related to every one's life and maturity. The more complex the adaptation with society becomes, the more complex the social maturity of intelligence, maturity according to the need.

Society is significant medium where certain quality of life and certain types of activity and occupation are provided with the aim of securing child's development based on the social needs. Since is a stem of growth characteristics of teacher trainees should adapt to the society which we live and to which he is expected to adjust and contribute, the social maturity receives importance at the present context. The conduct of many individual in the society tells about the trainees social maturity through which he can respond right according to the teaching situation.

At the present age of competitive world, every human being meets a lot of problems in his daily activities. The root of most of human psychological problems is more socially based that psychologically based. It is in social situation a lack of competence as well as social maturity. So, every human needed knowledge about teaching competence and social maturity for leading a very healthy life in this world.

The present study takes a position the teaching competency and social maturities are very important to the students who live and grow in the complex social environment. Hence there is a need to find out if there is any correlation between teaching competency and social maturity. Hence the problem emerged to study the two variables teaching competency and social maturity.

STATEMENT OF THE PROBLEM

The title of the problem is a follows: Social Maturity and Teaching Competency of Students Social Maturity Teachers in TTI and DIET in Chennai

OPERATIONAL DEFINITION

Maturity assumes accountability, constantly assesses, judges and takes appropriate decisions. Maturity develops a balanced emotional outlook, helping the individual to accept himself, his talents and limitation and to accept others as they are. It analysis values and internalizes them consistently. It helps towards progressive advancement in spiritual growth, impelling the individual to adapt himself to change and to life without emotional crisis.

Abraham Sperling (1967) defined social maturity in the following words, "An adolescent should get along with others. He ought to develop self-reliance in matter of taste and ought to develop tolerance of human differences".

Nazarath Maria E. Waples (1978) defines as, "Maturity is the belossoming of man's character into a unified totality. It discerns the process that contributes to the psychological and physical growth and well being of man".

Henry E. Garrett (1969) states "Social maturity is the degree of social participation as measured by child's activities, attitudes and play interests. It is related to physical growth and maturity and to mental ability. Every individual develops his own unique way of adjustment in the society. An individual, since his birth attempts to adjust to his environment".

EDUCATION AND THE SOCIETY

Education is the fulcrum upon which hangs the peaceful evolutionary transition of society. It plays a vital role in building a society. A modern society cannot achieve its aim of economic growth, technical development and cultural advancement without fully harnessing the talents of its citizens. For the advancement in education proper social maturity, values and adjustment pattern should be there. Social maturity is related to value that are found in the society. Teacher educators are very well associated with the cultivation of social maturity among the student teachers. Then only they will develop an integrated personality, proper cultivation of values of cope with the environment amicably.

Society does not come out of an oak or a rock; it is the product of human mind reflecting the multi-dimensional hues of human personalities. The society throbs, grows and progresses in tune with the development of the human potentialities. So the "man" and the "society" do not confront each others as antagonistic concepts. The human mind and its potentialities are extending through its cognitive, emotive and affective capacities. But all these capacities flower into realties in the context of the society and social interaction. So the human mind finds its ideal foil in the society, which is instrumental in the actualization of the immeasurable human potentialities.

Man doesn't stand – alone; he is only and essentially a social animal. Otherwise he may be described as a "beast" or a "god" but not as a "man". Similarly society is just an abstraction unless it mirrors the human values, norms, ambitions and goal society is never an aggregate of individuals. Its, in the sense, no predictable string of unity. Tandra Patanic (1986) states, 'The society is rather a peculiar amalgamation of unity in diversity, which characterizes the society that again reflects the nature of human mind" (p.04). Mind can be judged from various dimensions. It is considered powerful as a cognitive tool reflecting sensitivity and emotionality. Separately none of these qualities of the mind can be called to constitute the proper essence of the mind. So man and the society and their relation have been viewed here as a prism throwing multi-colored spectrum of light. Yet the arrangement of colour may change in the direction of the light. Society is a prism; it is multiple facets along with its unique ability of adapting to the change of circumstances.

EDUCATION AS AN AGENCY OF SOCIETY

The process of education is deep significance to the growth and welfare of society. If the people are to keep pace with the fast changing social order, with scientific discoveries and with the explosion of knowledge in all parts of the world, the hidden talents of youth must be brought to the surface and be exploited for the good of the society. There is a great demand for creative ideas and creative talents, and education is the best means for the development of such talents. The events of out time are moving continually, accelerating the rate and if the people are to keep pace with them, the people must make sure that the talents of the youth are thoroughly developed.

Alexander. A. Scheidrs (1965) defines "Education is the total experiences that can transform the life of the individual person". Education can contribute much and in many different ways to the social, moral and religious growth of the adolescent to healthy social perspectives to adequate vocational attitudes and goals, and to the future roles that the adolescent will expect to play. By means of active participation on the playing field and through extracurricular activities such as oratory, debating, newspaper reporting or yearbook editing the adolescent can pick up many ideas, skills and general know-how that may be of great help to him later in his social relations and vocational aspirations.

MATURITY AS A DETERMINANT OF PERSONALITY

Henery. E. Garrett (1968) says, "Social maturity is the degree of social participation as measured by child's activities, attitudes and play interests. It is related to physical growth and maturity and to mental ability".

One of the components of social maturity is adjustment. Maturity is the determinant of personality. A man's personality is the total picture of his organized behavior, especially as it can be characterized by his fellow men in a consistent way.

An individual, since his birth attempts to interact with his environment. Behaviour of an individual can be defined as an adjustment to his environment. Every individual develops his own unique way of adjustment in the society. Socially matured individuals are better able to adjust to the various changes in the environment and react appropriately thus making the right type of adjustment.

STAGES OF SOCIAL MATURITY

An individual takes times in his social development. So, we may think of some stages of social maturity according to the physical, mental, emotional and language development of the individual. They are,

1. Awareness of the presence of another person.
2. Mixing with others
3. Understanding of social relationships.

Understanding of all the above three things refers to human stages of social maturity.

SOCIAL MATURITY AND ITS CHARACTERISTICS

Social maturity is the final expected outcome of social development and socialization, certain characteristics of social maturity are,

1. A social matured person has a sense of his proper place and roles as a member of the social group. He is willing and able to orient himself in the various activities and customs to the group.
2. He is able to assume a reasonable amount of responsibility, to adjust him to the inevitable limitations and restrictions of the community life.
3. He can be original and yet conform to the board pattern of his social environment.

4. He evaluates social problems not form a purely selfish point of view but has regard to the right opinion of others.
5. He accepts responsibility for his actions, does not indulge in self-pitying.
6. He has a realistic self- concept being conscious of his assets and limitations.
7. He is relatively secure and so open to new experiences, which contribute, to his continuous development.

In short, co-operations, pleasing manner, consideration for others, positive and optimistic outlook on life and teaching competence are signs of socially matured individual.

CHARACTERISTICS OF SOCIALLY MATURED INDIVIDUAL

Social maturity is evidenced in the capacity of the individual to maintain friendships that meet the needs of others as well as his own. Vatssyan (1990) states "A matures individual form the social stand point is one who co-operates with all those with whom he comes into contact and contradicts them only when such a course of action becomes inevitable. He is never ill-mannered choosing instead to appear very well mannered, considerate and friendly to all and sundry" (p.119), consequently has a large circle of friends. An adult who has attended that stage as required by the standpoint, evinces great interest in art, study, games etc.

He studies the works of greatest authors and takes interest in games and forms of recreation suitable to his station in life. His activities and conduct are scrupulously in conformity with his age and sex. He has the power of independent decision and judgement. He gives every evidence of being well balanced and adjusted with himself and his behavior towards other individuals.

Elizabeth B. Hurlock (1959) says, "The socially mature individual has sense of his proper place and role as a member of a group. He is willing and able to orient himself in the various activities with others and customs of the group, to make the proportionate contribution to the work to be done, to take a suitable part in the social exchange to assume a reasonable amount of responsibility and to adjust himself to the inevitable limitations and restrictions of community life without waste of energy or loss or satisfaction". He can be original and yet conform to the broad pattern of the cultural environment.

Taneja R.P. (1989) says, "Social maturity refers to degree of growth in social and vocational abilities". The socially mature individual treats the members of his family as friends. In this role he shows the affection, loyalty, consideration and respect for all family members. As a citizen the socially mature person accepts his obligations and performs them faithfully". He makes good adjustments to all types of people without prejudice based on their religion, race or skin colour.

The matured accepts his friends as they are and does not criticize or try to change them as a socially immature person does. He is loyal to them and feels a sense of responsibility towards them when they need his help. Although social may add greatly to his happiness, the mature persons is self-sufficient enough that he can be happy when circumstances make it possible for him to be with his family, friends or acquaintances.

The mature individual can be found to posses the trait of good humour and pleasantness. The important point is that he keeps himself alive, with vigorous interests that make him interesting to be with. The mature individual posses a feeling of social concern and gets very involved in situations that call for obedience to social norms too. The person equipped with the human sensitivities that make for maturity will usually have powerful concern with social problems and ways of alleviating them. For all his social-mindedness, for all his scoring of human relationships, the maturing individuals is not dependent on always having company.

The mature person knows that he has to go on choosing alternatives, that each alternative costs him something, and there are things he will never be able to do and experience. He also knows that there are things he will never be able to do again, that he can never recapture his youth or relive his first encounters with certain experience. He knows that his integrated is continually threatened by practical demands, by seductive temptations, by concessions and compromises, by conflicting values, and can only be preserved at the cost of some psychic stream. He knows that the only real reward in life come with continued growth, and that there is no room in the material life he has for major regrets. This individual who has approached maturity can know that he has loved, had done his work, has made his mark on people.

IMPORTANCE OF SOCIAL MATURITY

Social maturity has been defined as an indication of willingness and ability to orient. Oneself in the various activities and customs of the group to make a proportionate contribution to the work to be done, to take a suitable part in the social exchange, to assume a reasonable amount of responsibility and to adjust oneself to the inevitable limitations and restrictions of community life without waste of energy or loss of satisfaction.

Nazarath Maria. E. Waples (1978) defines, "Maturity is the blossoming of man's character into a unified totality. It discerns the process that contribute to the psychological and physical growth and well being of man".

Maturity assumes accountability, constantly assesses, judges and takes appropriate decisions. Maturity develops a balanced emotional outlook, helping the individual to accept himself, his talents and limitations and to accept others as they are. It analyses values and internalizes them consistently. It helps towards progressive advancement in spiritual growth, impelling the individual to adapt himself to change and to life without emotional crises. Abraham Sperling (1967) states social maturity in the following words "An adolescent should get along with and well with others. He ought to develop self-reliance in matters of taste and ought to develop tolerance of human differences". Maturity is a gradual process that comes with self-knowledge and with self-realization shaping man into a responsible adult.

CHALLENGES AND PROBLEM OF TEACHER EDUCATION

Teacher education has to support the efforts for the solution of problem of education of the country. These problems may be divided into two categories. First one is problems of education as a whole with special reference to school education and the second is problems of teacher education itself. The latter includes general problems as well those caused by school education curricula and teacher effectiveness which put the responsibility of its implementation on teachers.

The education system now faces challenges from neo-colonialism which is not the same as its traditional counterpart. It is economic, ideological and cultural. If not checked, it will lead to further 'educational divide'. Teacher education has to understand its many dimensional consequences and take appropriate safeguards against it.

The country has to fulfill its constitutional commitment of article 45 providing universal elementary education to all and a achieve the goal. To meet this obligation many programmes have been initiated. For achieving the target, the country needs well qualified and properly trained teachers. The system, has to prepare them and also train under qualified teachers professionally.

Population explosion of school going children, rising aspirations of the people and their greater desire for more useful knowledge, complete with explosion of knowledge and techniques for imparting knowledge have emerged as new challenges to teacher education. The possibility of acquiring knowledge from sources other than the teacher, books and from outside educational institutions has increased tremendously. Then educational system has to respond in full measure to this development. Technological development impact knowledge within a short span of time and use of new transactional strategies including all the resources. Students should be encouraged to pursue independent learning and make us of the skills of 'learning to learn'.

In the emerging context the possibility of teachers and educators becoming outdated and professionally less effective has increased. Constant re-education and in-service programmes for teachers and their educators have become the need for this present century.

Teacher education institutions need to forge stronger links with the system of education and also with the community they serve. Community linked teacher education, research and extension programmes need to be undertaken. The exports from community, if available, may be invited by teacher education institutions and teachers and educators may be encouraged to participate in the activities of the community and vice-versa.

Education requires interdisciplinary approach. For its enrichment it needs cross fertilization and active support from allied subjects, and teacher education is no exception to this. Sociology and social and cultural anthropology can help in developing need based pedagogies. Economics and management science can add value and meaning to the courses of educational finance, economics of education, educational planning, management, administration and supervision. There is a need to harness inputs from these areas to courses of education for teachers. By doing so, the theoretical and practical component of teacher education will certainly become more meaningful and contemporary. Alternative programmes with increased duration may be tried out for qualitative improvement of teacher education.

Children process information acquire knowledge and learn in a cultural context and their personalities and mental make-up are influenced by cultural factors. There are difference in the levels of aspiration and perception of children coming from a metropolis and of those from a tribal background. They may interpret the some event or concept differently according to their socio-cultural backgrounds. Cultural specificity therefore, needs to be utilized to improve children's learning. Since there is no uniform process of learning and forming concepts, acquisitions of values, morality and character and personality development, there is a need for teachers and educators to understand how cultural traditions and factors outside the school affect pedagogical practices. To ignore these factors can adversely affect educational and learning out comes. To evolve culture-specific pedagogy and empower the teacher to do so in their specific context becomes an important function of teacher education.

Culture-specific pedagogy is influenced by many tangible and intangible factors operating in society. Chief among these are the practices of child rearing in the family and the community, well-established methods of teaching and learning, indigenous educational practices and the ideas of thinkers and educationists of the society. India provides valuable opportunity for blinding all these together for evolving culture-specific pedagogy not only because it has preserved a rich cultural heritage, a large variety of educational practices outside the school in different regions but also because it has its own thinking on matters pertaining to education. The thought and practices of Indian educationists can be useful for reconstructing a need-based indigenous national and culture specific pedagogies considerable research has been carried out in teacher education, and some of its findings relevant to Indian context can help in the development of quality teacher education programmes. Mass copying and leakage of question papers and unruly behaviour of students during after examinations demand that teachers should evolve a more reliable and continuous evaluation system. Misconceptions about decentralization of education with special reference to Panchayati Raj need to be removed from the minds of the teachers. Mismatch in the supply and demand of teachers in certain sectors and states demand need-based manpower planning. Teacher education has to convince the state about it. Special attention needs to be paid to inculcating professionalism, its values and skills and to improve teachers work culture.

TEACHING COMPETENCY

The teacher has a major role in the educational development Gandhiji remarked that "no country can make any progress without good teachers". The quality and standard of education depends on the quality and standard of teachers. Teacher is the torch bearer of the race and guardian of the feature of the mankind.

According to Humagun Kabir: "Teachers are literally the architects of a nations destiny" Mrs.Indira Gandhi stated, "The nations well being depends upon the teachers well being our teachers are the 'custodians' of future. No society can afford to neglect them".

"Competency" ordinarily is defined as "Adequate for the purpose; suitable, sufficient, or as capable". In a sense it refers to adequate preparation to begin a professional career, and has a direct linkage to verification requirements.

Cooker (1976) defined "competence is seen as the ability to cope with a certain class of problems encountered on the job. A teacher who can deal with problems in certain area is said to be competent in that area a fully competent teacher is one who can cope successfully with any "propositional problem". Competency in teaching stems forms the capacity to reach out differing children and to create a rich and multidimensional environment for them (Joyce and Well 1985).

To study the effectiveness "competency based teacher training (CBTT) strategy" for developing following basic teaching competencies among pre service teacher,

1. Cognitive - based teaching competency
2. Performance - based teaching competency
3. Affective - based teaching competency
4. Consequence - based teaching competency
5. Managerial - based teaching competency

CONCEPTS OF TEACHING COMPETENCY

A competent teacher has good command of subject matter and solid core of teaching skills. They have excellent instructional strategies supported by methods of goal setting, instructional planning and classroom management. They know how to motivate, communicate and work effectively with students. The teachers play an important role in molding and shaping the attitudes, habits, and manners and above all, the character and personality of the students. The teacher with competency does the planning, organization, reading and controlling of teaching. He is free to perform various activities to provide a learning experience to the learners.

We expect scholars and leaders to be able to effectively communicate with others, and to be able to teach. Students can take coursework related to teaching and engage in a teaching mentorship with a faculty mentor. During the mentorship, students practice didactic, interactive and experimental teaching strategies in classroom setting. They also learn approaches to other forms of knowledge dissemination such as teaching and presentation. Teaching involves a conceptual understanding of how people learn and the ability to translate this understanding into constructing and delivering learning opportunities to diverse audiences.

According to Joki (1982), school boards can help improve the quality of teaching by writing strong, clear policies on administrative accountability (including provisions for instructional leadership); on teacher recruitment, supervision, and evaluation, on an instructional model keyed to specific objectives; and on in service training for administrators and teachers. Superintendents also might provide principals with clerical assistance to free more time for classroom observation, clinical supervision, demonstration teaching, and staff development (Joki 1982).

Teacher evaluation, in addition to its customary function of establishing basis for promotion, retention, inservice training of teachers can also be a valuable tool for improving instructional effectiveness. A good evaluation program should emerge from the cooperative efforts of teachers and their evaluators in identifying broad areas of responsibility and specific objectives (Joki 1982). Thus teachers will "own" an evaluation program, rather than have one arbitrarily imposed.

Besides monitoring teacher's performance, a specific objective of teacher evaluation should be to set measurable job improvement targets (Sweeney and Manatt 1982). Once targets are set, the principal and teacher work out a specific plan of action within a given time frame, and then review the teacher's progress in conference. Such clinical supervision promotes a school climate in which continuous improvement becomes an essential part of every teacher's job.

In addition to setting and clarifying expectations, administrators can also employ incentives to induce teachers to excel in their profession. These include merit pay plans, career options (including career ladders), enhanced professional responsibilities (for example, master teacher plans), non monetary recognition such as annual awards, and improved working conditions.

The University of Waterloo's Competency portfolio Project emphasizes the need for student "to learn in ways that help deal with a range of contexts, many, if not all, unique" (Bowden and Marton, 1988) and be able to demonstrate that knowledge in a variety of learning contexts. This means that faculty members need to model desired competencies for students in their teaching. For history, it is important that students learn, not just about the "facts" but also about how historians really "do" history. In other words, we need to teach them about what it means to be a historian.

In my own practice, this has translated into a much more skilled-based approach to my teaching. This should not be taken to mean, however, that I see history courses as being just about "skill-building" I believe that by helping students to "see" their own competence in history they will be able to transfer their knowledge to other learning contexts. In order to foster this change in students 'behaviour I go beyond simply articulating my learning goals for the them in terms of the competencies that they will develop in my courses to encouraging (and, in fact, requiring) them to reflect on how they can use their knowledge (both content and skills) in other learning contexts (in the work place in their community and in other academic courses). You can find examples of student reflections in the "methods that prompt thoughtful and responsible learning" link below.

The approach to teaching history, we believe, translates into a more powerful learning experience because it encourages students to view learning as a life-long experience, rather than just a course – based experience. Below we will see the professional and discipline-specific competencies that are part of teaching excellence in higher education. Links to example of how the model these competencies for our students are provided.

The University of Wateloo's Competency Portfolio Prject emphasizes the need for students "to learn in ways that help them deal with a range of contexts, many if not all, unique" (Bowden and Marton, 1998) and be able to demonstrate that knowledge in a variety of learning contexts. This means that faculty members need to model desired competencies for students in their teaching. For history, it is important that students learn, not just about the "facts" but also about how historians really "do" history. In other words, we need to teach them about what is means to be a historian.

DEFINITIONS

In the words of Murthy and Lulla, "Competence based teacher education is that type of professional education of class room teachers that takes the pre-determined competence of teaching behaviours as the base of teacher education programs".

The Education Commission (1964-66) observed, "Of all the different factors, which influence its quality of education and its contribute to national development, the quality, competence and characters are undoubtedly the most significant".

COMPETENCIES TO BE DEVELOPED

Competence in the use of any methodology involves being able to choose intelligently with the knowledge, experience and skill to make chosen methods work effectively. This can only be acquired by experience, which requires confidence, risk taking and reflection on what happens, so the competencies that are to be developed among the teacher trainees are as follows.

1. Competence to understand the sight process of learning, including learning, learning by doing, learning to be, learning to do and learning to become.
2. Competence to devise dynamic methods in the day-to-day situations based on the needs and interests of children.
3. Competence to organize the class room in such a manner that different kinds of activities may be organized in it so that children may receive required guidance from teacher.
4. Competence to become an example of qualities that he/she wants to develop among his/her students, realizing that example is superior to mere instruction and preaching.
5. Competence in regard to language, delivery of speech and other method of communication.
6. Competence in regard to the contents of the subject that he / she is supposed to teach. The teacher should be able to answer questions that belong to the immediate reason or even to some remotely related subject matter, which may occur in subsequent reason.

7. Competence to engage children in a meaningful manner so that children my develop capacity to ask question and may be inspired to find out the answers by themselves.
8. Competence to innovate so as to create proper environment in the classroom to enable children to develop wider horizons of perceptions.
9. Competence to develop among students a scientific temper, which is often confined to cultivation of various attitudes, includes objective observation, experimentation and consideration of every point of view relevant to the enquiry in a logical manner.

The competencies mentioned above suggest that the school teacher in the developing countries may inspire a change in the impulses of the pupils growing personality so as to have a balanced blending of knowledge, power, love and skills that are required for his / her development as a good individual and useful member of the society. The teacher has to develop competence to innovative methods oriented and learner's need based. The teachers may be apprised what they are supposed to teach.

COMPETENCY AREAS

National Council for Teacher Education (NCTE) has identified ten competency areas in teacher preparation:

1. Contextual competencies including development of education in society and teacher's role in it.
2. Conceptual competencies comprising various concepts of education and learning and psychological, sociological and physiological aspects of education.
3. Curricula and content competencies relating different stages of education like primary, upper-primary and secondary.
4. Transitional competencies as regards general subject-wise and stage-wise dimensions.
5. Competencies in other educational activities such as planning and organizing morning assembly, etc.
6. Competencies relating to teaching-learning materials.
7. Evaluation competencies including preparation, selection, use of tools, justice etc.
8. Management competencies including organization of classroom, school and community activities.
9. Competencies related to working with parents understand the role; discuss the problems; active co-operation; organize parent teacher meetings; explore and utilize educational resources etc.

10. Competencies related to working with the community and other agencies through understand the importance; contribute for improvement; realize the objectives; develop wholesome relationship; explore and exploit community educational resources activities etc.

A TO Z OF TEACHING COMPETENCIES

Teaching is an interactive process involving many aspects of teacher, student, learning process and learning situations. So in order to be a competent teacher one must have competent in the following dispositions.

'A' is for alertness.
'B' is for business like attitude to keep busy in worthwhile tasks.
'C' is for clarity and co-operative teaching learning.
'D' is for devotion and discovery.
'E' is for enthusiasm, expecting children to learn and evaluation.
'F' is for feedback for the guidance of the learner and evaluation.
'G' is for goal setting and achieving.
'H' is for hard work, honest work, humility and humor.
'I' is for involvement of children.
'J' is for judicious attitude and just action.
'K' is for knowledge of the students, subject-mater of oneself.
'L' is for linking learning with daily experiences and life.
'M' is for motivation.
'N' is for need-based learning.
'O' is for objectivity and providing out of classroom learning experiences.
'P' is for practice and praising children when needed.
'Q' is for quiz organizing for monitoring learning progress.
'R' is for relationships and review.
'S' is for stimulation.
'T' is for tolerance and the technology of teaching learning.
'U' is for unbiased attitude and unexpected encounters and situations.
'V' is for a variety of learning experience.
'W' is for warmth and wisdom.
'X' is for x-ray of the learning process.
'Y' is for yearning and eagerness.
'Z' is for zeal.

ESSENTIAL QUALITIES OF A COMPETENT TEACHER

In order to be a competent teacher, he must possess certain special qualities such as

1. Qualities relating to professional requirements.
2. Qualities relating to character and personality.
3. Qualities relating to human relationship.
4. Qualifications relation to professional educational / training.

JOB FUNCTIONS AND COMPETENCY

Competence refers to a state of being well qualified to perform an activity, task or job function. When a person is competent to do something, her or she has achieved a state of competence that is recognizable and verifiable to a particular community of practitioners. A competency, then, refers to the way that a state of competence can be demonstrated to the relevant community. According to the International Board of Standards for Training Performance and Instruction (IBSTPI), a competency involves a related set of knowledge, skills and attitudes that enable a person to effectively perform the activities of a given occupation or function in such a way that meets or exceeds the standards expected in a particular profession of work setting (Richey et al., 2001).

The structure and assessment of competencies may differ form one community of practice to another and even within a community. To facilitate a common understanding of competencies in the / context / if mobile and distributed learning some specifications have been elaborated (IMS, 2001). Typically, as competency is divided into specific indicators describing the requisite knowledge, skills, attitudes and context of performance.

There are different ways to validate that a person has demonstrated the relevant competencies (Le Boterf, 1998, 2000, 2001). One of them is through a certification process (Levy-Leboyer, 1999). Teacher certification is a common practice, and the notion of teacher competencies is fairly well established. However, competencies are generally associated with highly formalized professional activities and not applied to ill-defined tasks (those involving variable and uncertain circumstances, procedures and outcomes). III-defined tasks certainly include many forms of teaching.

This narrow view of competence runs counter to common sense and professional practice, but brings into attention the mainstream approach to elaboration of teacher competencies where it is essential to clearly identify the conditions of teaching (Paquay et al., 1998). The delivery environment (classroom-based, internet-based, laboratory-based, hybrid environments and so on) is a particularly relevant condition to identify competencies for online teaching.

COMPETENCY AND CLASS ROOM TEACHING

Information technology can be integrated into both online and classroom setting, but the interaction between these technologies and new approaches to learning and instruction may very (Spector and Anderson, 2000). The range of activities available in online settings and the multiple conditions of time in which they take place are evidence that the technology demands placed on online teachers are some what more significant than those associated with classroom teachers.

Much of what has already been published with regard to online teaching has focused on technical skills and requirements of successfully moderating and facilitating online discussion and chat sessions (e.g. Collision et al., 2000; Kersley, 2000; Rosenburg 2001). This body of literature suggests that becoming an effective online moderate requires training and that there are competencies unique to online environments.

In online discussions, the moderator's competencies involve (1) allowing learners time for reflection, (2) keeping discussion alive and on a productive path, and (3) archiving and organizing discussion to be used in subsequent lesions.

In online synchronous discussion (e.g., chat), the moderator must (1) establish ground rules for discussion, (2) animate interactions with minimal instructor intervention, (3) sense how online text message may appear to distant learners, and (4) be aware of cultural differences.

At the school level animating discussions, displaying cultural sensitivity and so on, apply to all teachers. At the environment level, however, the ways in which a teacher demonstrates such competence is quite different, which suggests that there are competence is quite different, which suggests that there are competencies unique to online settings. According to Belisle and Linard (1996) the use of technology in teaching calls for additional competencies adapted to new roles and circumstances. Teaching competencies and online teaching competencies have generally been considered separately. Problems and challenges in teacher education.

SIGNIFICANCE OF THE STUDY

A new concept social maturity with its significance is more important for one's daily life. It may be defined as one's unitary ability to know, feel, judge, behave and cooperate with a person's thinking process for behaving in a proper way with the ultimate realization of happiness in him and in others. In view of its wide significance from the individual as well as social angles, it becomes quite imperative that serious efforts should be made for its proper development right from early childhood among human beings.

A person's social maturity helps him much in all spheres of life. social maturity also helps a person to understand and give direction to live a very healthy life. Social maturity is related to teaching competency. A competent teacher can execute their work very effectively. So teachers should have good teaching aptitude and teaching competency. The primary level of education is a significant stage to import various skills like listening, speaking and writing. Unless the teachers are very competent they may not perform their work properly. So it is significant to know the teaching competency of the teacher trainees at this level.

Teaching is an interactive process, involving four aspects teacher, students, learning process and learning situation. A competent teacher possesses all the necessary qualities to interact with the school and community. Teacher with social maturity will be able to teach students with all capabilities. So the present study has been conducted to verify how social maturity is correlated with the teaching competency of the B.Ed. teacher trainees. It is expected that every teacher trainee should have social maturity and it will influence their teaching competency. Hence this study has been conducted to verify these interesting aspects.

OBJECTIVES OF THE STUDY

The following objectives are set for the present study.

1. To find out the significant difference between male and female teacher trainees on their social maturity.
2. To find out the significant difference between male and female teacher trainees on their components of teaching competency.
3. To find out the significant difference between TTI and DIET teacher trainees on their social maturity.
4. To find out the significant difference between TTI and DIET teacher trainees on their components of teaching competency.
5. To find out the significant difference between teacher trainees belonging to nuclear and joint families on their social maturity.
6. To find out the significant difference between teacher trainees belonging to nuclear and joint families on their components of teaching competency.
7. To find out the significant difference between teacher trainees from rural and urban area on their social maturity.
8. To find out the significant difference between teacher trainees from rural and urban area on their components of teaching competency.
9. To find out the significant difference of teacher trainees on their social maturity based on their parental income.

10. To find out the significant difference of teacher trainees on their components of teaching competency based on their parental income.
11. To find out the significant difference on social maturity of teacher trainees based on their communities.
12. To find out the significant difference on components of teaching competency of teacher trainees based on their communities.
13. To find out the significant difference on social maturity of teacher trainees based on their fathers qualification.
14. To find out the significant difference on components of teaching competency of teacher trainees based on their fathers qualification.
15. To find out the significant difference on social maturity of teacher trainees based on their mothers qualification.
16. To find out the significant difference on components of teaching competency of teacher trainees based on their mothers qualification.
17. To find out the significant difference on social maturity of teacher trainees based on their age.
18. To find out the significant difference on components of teaching competency of teacher trainees based on their age.
19. To find out the significant relationship between social maturity and components of teaching competency.

❒

18

Review of Related Literature

The research takes the advantage to the knowledge, which has accumulated in the past as a result of constant human endeavour. Research can never be undertaken in isolation of the work that has already been done on the problem, which is directly or indirectly related to study proposed by a researcher. One of the important steps in the planning of any research study is careful review of the research journals, books, dissertations, and other series of information on the problem to the investigated. A review of the related literature must precede any well-planned research study.

Review of the related literature allows the researcher to acquaint him with current knowledge in the field or area in which he is going to conduct his research. The important specific reason for reviewing the related literature is to know about the recommendation of previous researchers for further research, which they have listed in their studies. The present summary of research studies are related to problem "Social Maturity and Teaching Competency among TTI and DIET students".

IMPORTANCE OF REVIEW OF RELATED LITERATURE

Review of literature related to the problem is essential in order to determine three things.

1. Whether studies already exists similar to what the purpose to undertake.

2. Whether existing research provides guidance or sheds further light on the problem.
3. Whether existing research provides a point of departure or a platform upon which the new research can build.

The investigations have added much to our knowledge. Thus the knowledge of related literature also enables investigator to define the frontiers of their field.

STUDIES RELATED TO SOCIAL MATURITY

Indian Studies

Ghosh. S (1975) has investigated social maturity of pre school Bengali children of Calcutta city belonging to different social-economic groups. Thirty five, nursery and kinder garden schools were randomly selected from the different regions of Calcutta and 40 pre-school children were selected from each school at random equally distributed in each are group. Data were also collected by using a standardized interview schedule on the mothers of these selected children. The final sample included 1410 cases. The study revealed that sex had very insignificant role in imbibing social maturation. Economic status was insignificant as testimony of ability to enrich the social maturity level.

Rao. N. (1978) conducted a research work on social maturity of high school children in Bangalore city. A sample of 1020 students was chosen from 50 secondary schools in Bangalore. The self-constructed questionnaire was used in this study. The major findings were as follows; (I) Positive correlation between social maturity and intelligence (II) Positive relationship between social maturities and self-esteem (III) Girls generally scored higher than boys on social maturity (IV) There are class differences in social maturity among the children of lower grades (V) Private school children scored more on social maturity than Government Schools.

Puranik, S.D. (1985) has studied the relationship of social maturity of pupils with organizational climate and teachers' morale in the primary schools in Bangalore city. The sample consists of 70 schools 2634 students and 712 teachers. The study indicated the development of social maturity; autonomous climate, private management and unaided students and urban location of schools were most conductive factors. No effect of moral of teachers of both senses was noticed on the development of social maturity of male (or) female students (or) on the students of both sexes even under the influence of organizational climate, school organization and localities.

Asthana, Anju (1989) conducted a study of social maturity among school going children in city of Lucknow. The objectives were (I) To study whether social maturity increases with grade level (II) To study association of intelligence, socio-economic status academic achievement, adult dependence and sex of the child with social maturity. It was found that the social maturity increased with inverse in grade level, the growth rate being highest in the first school years. Intelligence, academic achievement and adult dependence were significantly associated with the social maturity of children although adult dependence and a negative association and SES was not found to contribute to social maturity at any of the five grade levels.

Sarojamma, Y.H. (1990) has conducted a comparative study of reaching ability and social maturity of over normal and underachievers of standard VIII, the final sample comprised of 476 boys and 524 girls. The social maturity scale by Sathyanarayana and Swadha was used. It was found that, there was significant difference in the reading ability of,

1. Normal and under achievers,
2. Over and normal achievers,
3. Girls and boys,
4. Students having high and low social maturity
5. Students in private and government schools.

The interaction effect of the variables on reading ability, hypothesized was not significant.

Malin, A.J. (1990) conducted a study on the relationship of social maturity with classroom climate and academic achievement. The sample consisted of 1200 students of classes VIII and IX. The tools used were Edward's social maturity state and achievements tests. The research points out students studying in classes IX had high maturity as compared to students of class VIII. The mean maturity scores of students having low achievement for both classes. Classroom climate and achievement has a significant effort on maturity scores of students of both the class.

Agnihotri, C.S. (1991) has conducted a cross cultural comparative study between tribal and non tribal first generation and traditional learners in relation to their social maturity and educational adjustment. The sample consisted of 113 first generation tribal learners and 108 traditional tribal learners. Social maturity was independent of traditions of learning. The tribal and non-tribal differed in terms of their placements on attribute of social maturity. The traditions of learning were found to be contributing to social maturity. It was found that, the social maturity and educational adjustment were only social ingredients. Psychological characteristics also influenced the social maturity and educational adjustment of children and social maturity was independent of traditions of learning.

Bhusham, A. (1994) conducted a study on social maturity across sex and family vocations. The sample comprised of 200 student teachers from two colleges, equally divided between two sexes. Major variable used were sex values, and family vocations. The tools used for data collections were the form D of value survey. The study highlights, male and female uniformly assigned highest importance to social maturity. Both male and female from service and non-service class had politeness as a subdivision on their maturity.

Foreign Studies

Vora, J.I. (1980) in his research work on social maturity of B.Ed., students in Gujarant. The sample size was 855 student teachers from Gujarat University, South Gujarat University and M.S. University. Some of the major findings were (I) The male students were superior to the female students in their social maturity (II) Age had no relation with social maturity (III) The arts students were more socially mature than science students (IV) The higher socio-economic status had better social maturity.

Savoluk Thongngamkhom (1983) has investigated the social maturity as a function of some psycho socio – adjustment factors of B.Ed., college students of north central region of Thailand. The scale was standardized on a sample of 922 students – including boys and girls. The study states that boys and girls having dominant personality traits were more socially matured than those having submissive personality traits. The two groups of B.Ed., students having high suggestibility and low suggestibility trait did not differ on social maturity. The study revealed that the college students with high SES background were found more socially matured than those of coming from low SES strata. The students having dominant personality trait were more socially matured than those of having submissive personality trait. The students having high leadership personality trait were more socially matured than those of having low leadership personality trait.

Pattramon JumpamGern (1986) investigated the social maturity of teachers, college students of western region of Thailand and found that the teachers – college student coming from urban areas were found to be more matured than those coming from rural areas. Students having good family adjustment were more socially matured than those having poor family adjustment. It was found that the higher secondary students coming from urban areas were found to be more matured than those coming from rural areas. The male higher secondary students were found superior to the female students. The higher secondary students with high SES were more socially matured than those with low SES.

Bances Ann Leslie (1995) conducted a study on measuring the effect of participation in a peer facilitation project on sixth graders self esteem, social maturity and patterns of social choice. The population chosen for the study was rural mainstream sixth grade students. The sample was tested by sociometric pattern of choice. It was found that some significant difference in social maturity for gender and there was significant relationship between self-esteem and social maturity.

Mulia, R.D. (1991) A comparative study of the social maturity of higher secondary students in the contest of their streams, sex and IQs. The objectives were (I) To study the stream effect on social maturity. (II) To study the sex effect on social maturity. (III) To study the effect of levels of IQs on social maturity. (IV) To study the interaction effect among independent variables on social maturity. It was found that there was no significant relationship in social maturity among students of three streams and between the two sexes, while IQ had main significant effect on social maturity streams and sex and no interaction effect of streams and sex as well as sex and IQs was found significant on social maturity.

Flymin Xavier, J., (2003) attempted a study on social maturity and academic achievement among higher secondary school students. The sample of 300 were taken from government, government aided and private higher secondary schools in Trivandrum. The sample were tested by Rao's social maturity scale. Some of the major findings were ((I) Gender has no influence on social maturity (II) Type of schools had no influence on social maturity (III) Social maturity and academic achievement are positively correlated.

Mani, M., (2004) did has study on social maturity and adherence to school regulation of higher secondary students. Taken the sample of 300 higher secondary school students studying in 5 different schools in Chennai. Rao's social maturity scale was used for administration. Some of the major findings were (I) Gender has significant bearing on social maturity (II) There is significant relationship between social maturity and adherence to school regulations (III) There is significant relationship between social maturity and academic achievement.

Saravanan, K., (2005) attempted a research on social maturity on self-concept among higher secondary school students. The sample of 249 boys and girls who studied XI standard in various schools in Chennai was taken. Rao's social maturity scale was used for administration. Some of the major findings were (I) Social maturity is found to be moderate (II) Gender has no influence on social maturity (III) Type of school had no significant difference on social maturity.

STUDIES RELATED TO TEACHING COMPETENCY

Indian Studies on Teaching Competency

Chatter Jee, B.B. et al. (1965) studied about the predication of teaching competency as a function of sharing a common frame of reference. The major findings were: The range of the scaled teaching competency scores given by the staff judges increased in the post-presentation assessments as compared to the pre-presentation predication, while the post-presentation scaled scores of teaching competency given by the instructors themselves were found to have low range compared two scores distributions obtained from the staff judges.

Saraswathi, L.S. (1973) conducted a study about the jobs held by home scientists and the competencies needed on the jobs held as perceived by the employed home scientists and their employees in the District. The major findings were: The high competency perception proportion indicated that majority of the items included in the competency tests were perceived by the two sets of respondents (Teachers and research workers and those on miscellaneous job) as required as the job with an exception of those of the jobs of the assistant lecturers in colleges and teachers in secondary schools.

Nair, S.R. (1974) reported about and impact of certain sociological factors on teaching ability in the classroom of government training college in Tiruchur. The major finding of this work was that private school teachers in general were found to have better teaching ability than the government school teachers. Sex was not found to be affecting teaching ability. A positive relationship existed between age and teaching ability. Caste and religion were not found to be affecting teaching ability.

Sharma, S.K. (1981) analyzed the various relationship of teaching effectiveness in terms of competency. The study was carried out at three different stages. In the final study 220 classrooms teaching learning situations were observed. The major findings were: There were no significant relationship between the ages of Hindi teachers, their attitude, interest and intelligence and their teaching competency. Male and female Hindi teachers did not differ significantly in their teaching competency. There was significant negative correlation the self-perception of Hindi teachers teaching at higher secondary level and their teaching competency. There was a significant positive correlation between the teaching competency of teachers at higher secondary level and academic achievement of their pupil of grade XI in Hindi. The teaching competencies identified were: giving assignments, loud reading, asking questions, introducing lessons, pacing, managing the classroom, presenting verbal mode, clarification, using the black board, using appropriate reinforcement, achieving closure, probing question, creation interest and improving pupils reading behaviour.

Rajan, S. Sathyagiri (1985) conducted a study about the competency, personality, motivation, perception and profession of college teachers. The major findings were: Teacher competency was related to intelligence, emotional stability, conscientcasness, tender mindedness, trusted nature, and placed nature, self-sufficiency, and placed nature, self-sufficiency and relaxedness factors of Cattell's 16PF questionnaires. It was significantly related to creativity, dynamism, organized demeanors and warmth and acceptance, self-actualization and professional perception of teachers. The more competent teachers significantly differed from the less competent teachers in all the above variables. Those variables that correlated significantly with teacher competence inter correlated with one another significantly.

Das, B.C. (1993) conducted a study about the effectiveness of concept attainment model in terms of teaching competency of pre-service student teachers. It was found that concept attainment model effectively developed the teaching competency of pre-service students teachers.

Naseema, C. (1994) reported about a teaching competence of secondary schools physical science teachers in relation to satisfaction of teaching physical science. The major findings were: It was found that 30.92 percent of physical science teachers differed in perceived teaching competence which can be attributed to work (0.01) rewards (1.73), context of work (0.87), self (0.61), others (0.56), 26.89 percent of physical science teachers different in observed teaching competence which can be attributed to work (0.86), reward (0.002) context of work (1.5), self (2.32), others (1.91).

Kukreti, B.R. (1994) reported about a correlation study between job motivation and teaching competency. The major findings were: the competent teachers had joined the teaching profession because they regarded teaching as a prestigious job. They believed that the teaching profession provided them reasonable salary, security, opportunity of social service, to establish human relation and enhance their knowledge. Incompetent teachers entered the teaching profession because they thought that their profession would get fame, personal freedom, influencing opportunity and enough leisure with little burden of work.

Thigarajan, A. et al. (1995) conducted a study about the teaching competency and achievement. The major findings were: The teaching competency and achievement of boys had significant relationships. The relationship between teaching competency and achievement of boys and girls differed significantly.

Panda, S.C., (1996) conducted a study about the effect of competency-based instruction in achieving MLL competencies in grade IV Oriya medium schools. The major findings were: There was remarkable difference in the achievement of both the groups. The competency-based instruction yielded significantly better results than the traditional method of teaching.

Shamala, S.K. (1997) reported about enhancing teaching competency through integration of art education for effective language teaching at the primary stage. The major findings were: Prior the implementation of MLL based curriculum, it was highly essential to orient the primary school teachers to know how to develop local specific competencies based different activities. There was a positive impact of module to empower primary school teachers in developing competency based local specific curriculum. The main objective are: To determine the value of high school teachers place on these elements; classroom climate, questioning, set induction, stimulus variation, reinforcement and closure. In this study classroom climate, questioning, set induction, stimulus variation, reinforcement and closure are sported as a set of selected elements for improving instruction.

Thamilmani, P. (2000) conducted a study on teacher competency, teacher personality and teacher attitude on student achievement in science in high schools. The study included a sample of 100 teachers (58 male, 42 female teaching science and 300 students X studying under those teachers). The tools used were: Teacher Competency – Student Rating Scale, Teacher personality and teacher attitude of science teachers are related to the academic achievement of X standard students in science. They revealed male and female teachers differed significantly in their personality traits and attitude towards teaching.

Palaniyandi, R. (2001) investigated the competency needs of pre-serve teacher trainees. The teacher educators and student teachers from six DIETs constituting 273 pre-service teacher trainees 106 teacher educators and 462 practicing teachers working in these districts were the samples for the study. To identify the competency needs of pre-service teacher trainees as perceived by the pre-service trainees. They revealed learning process related competencies emerged as a group having the highest number of competencies.

Manjula P. Rao (2002) studied Teacher Competencies and learners' achievement in Tribal areas of Karnataka. Twenty schools belonging to 3 taluks, 261 students of third standard and 31 teachers teaching the same students constituted the sample of this study. The researcher tool used in this study are: The achievement test developed based on the competencies specified for class III in Languae, Mathematics, EVS-I and EVS-II to assess teachers' competence in subject areas. To study the relationship between teachers' competency and students achievement: in language, Mathematics, EVS-I and II. They found that majority of the teachers do not have to knowledge competencies in EVS-I (66.5%) and EVS-II (89.9%).

Amaladoss Xavirer, S. and Amlraj, A. (2002), conducted a correlative study on teaching competency and its dimensions in post-graduate chemistry teachers. The study included data from 89 post-graduate chemistry teachers of higher secondary schools in Kanyakumari District in Tamil Nadu. A Teaching Competency Rating Scale was used to assess the teaching competency of chemistry teachers. They revealed that there exists significant relationship between the low-level of post-graduate chemistry teachers with regard to the teaching competency dimensions: content, organization, knowledge, clarity, communication, rapport, audio-visual aids and personality.

Jayakanthan, S. (2003) conducted a study of general teaching competency of secondary school teachers in relation to their attitude in teaching. The study included samples of 3000 teacher from 14 schools. The General Teaching Competency Scale of Passi et al, and Teacher Attitude Scale of Ahulwalia were used to carry out the study found that Government and aided school teachers differed significantly in general teaching competency. Male and female teaches different significantly in teaching competency.

Krishna Prasad, B. and Mthiah, P.N. (2003) carried out a study on teacher effectiveness and temperament variables of secondary school teacher. The study was carried out to a sample of 300 teachers of various secondary schools in Thirunelveli District in Tamil Nadu. MTA-test of personality for measuring the variables of Temperament, Checklist on Teacher Effectiveness developed and validated by the investigators, and a Personal Information Schedule were used. They found that there exist significant differences among high, average and low effective teachers in five variables (inferiority, self sufficiency, sociability, stability, objectivity) of temperament.

Laxmidhar Bhara (2004) made an attempt to find out the performance of B.Ed trainees of IASEs and CTEs. Six fifty student-teachers (259 male and 391 female) drew purposively from tow CTEs and one IASE of Orissa in two consecutive sessions 1995-96 and 1996-97. The major findings were: that women student teachers excel their male counter parts in their aggregate (theory and practical performance.

Jeba, A., (2005) studied that the teaching competency and mental health of student teachers in DIETs. The size of the sample was 300 student-teachers in a DIET undergoing D.Ed. Elementary Teachers Training course. Tools used in this study are: Mental Health status scale constructed by M.Abraham and K.C.B. Praszanna. Teaching Competency Scale the study was conducted to find out gender and group (Arts, Science) difference in teaching competency and mental health status, the relationship between teaching competency and mental health status of student teachers in DIET. Major findings was that there is no significant difference between man and women student teacher.

Foreign Studies on Teaching Competency

Gregrersen and Traves (1968) used the projective technique for making a study of the child concept of the teachers. They made use of drawing of children, environment, which have special significance for them. Choeng and Devault at University of Wisconsin also made similar study in 1966.

Richard M. Galger and Tom. D. Freyo (1974) investigated to two research questions (a) would rewarding items on a questionnaire for evaluating faculty teaching effectiveness substantially affect students ratings (b) would students ratings of professors teaching quality be totally consistent with their ratings of benefits derived from courses? Results shows that students' ratings were affected very little by a major rewarding of items and that a substantial degree of linear independence existed between students perception of the quality benefited from the instructional process.

Garrett and George, W. (1978) studied the teachers perception of selected factors affecting the success of teaching process. A study sought to determine how various groups of teachers rated selected factors in teaching success. A review of literature of the topic indicated that both teachers and non-teacher was conducted to collect data from teachers of 64 elementary and secondary schools that were part of the test.

Lawrenz, Frances (1987) studied the gender effects for students' perception of the classroom psycho-social environment. This study compared to classroom environments as perceived by fourth grade, seventh grade and high school boys and girls in classes taught by males and females to determine if any perceptual differences existed. The analyses showed no difference for fourth grade students, one for seventh grade students, and three for high school students.

Brosious Janice A. and Smith R. Lyle (1990) studied the impact of Teachers Attractiveness and Gender on Students Perception of the Teacher's Ability. A group of seventh grade maths students (N=28) was chosen for the experiment, the students rated photograph of teachers in the area of organization, classroom management, motivation, communication, sensitivity, imagination and competence. The results of this analysis revealed a significant main effect of student perceptions due to the attractiveness of the teacher in the area of organization, classroom significant main effect on student's perceptions due to the gender of the teacher. The students rated the female photographs higher than male photographs in the area of organization. Finally, there was a significant interaction between the attractiveness of the teacher and gender of teacher in the areas of organization, sensitivity and imagination. Overall, females rated higher than males and teachers considered attractive were given higher ratings than teachers considered average and unattracrtive.

Ocepek, Linda Jeanne (1993) tested some "selected elements of effective teaching: A study of perception of high school teachers in Illinois, Indian and Ohio". This study utilized an export co-relational design. A 42 item Value

Rating Scale (VRS) was mailed to a stratified random sample of 384 public high school teachers in Illinois, Indian and Ohio. The teachers rated 42 indicator behaviours subsumed under the six elements of effective teaching.

Kim Keyng Suk (1999) studied "Teacher's perceptions of competencies needed for working inclusive early childhood education programs". A survey using five-point Likert scales included 7 teacher competency domains, each with a set of competency statements, and 12 teachers roles needed for working in inclusive pre-school program. 23 ECE teachers and 52 ECSE teachers in non-inclusive programs and 39 ECE teacher and 25 ECSE teachers inclusive program participated in this study. To determine the early childhood education (ECE) and Early Childhood. Special Education (ECSE) teacher's perceptions of importance teacher competencies, current levels of these competencies and appropriate teacher roles for working in inclusive early childhood programme. They found the ECSE teacher had significantly higher perceptions than the ECE teachers of their self-proficiency of competencies related to child development, curriculum and instruction, assessment procedures, working with other adults, and professionalism.

Kastair, Jamal (1999) carried out a study on "An evaluation of professional teaching competency of the instructors of the institute of Agriculture Sabah, Malaysia". A survey was carried out at the institute involving the instructors, the principal and the first and second year students as respondents. Each instructor and the principal completed a questionnaire containing 40 competency items of 7 categories, while each of the first and the second year students completed a questionnaire containing 33 competency items on 5 categories. The respondents were asked to assess the competence level of the instructors based on a five point Likert type scales. Evaluation by the professional teaching competency of the instructors of the Institute of Agriculture Sabah, Malaysia. They found that instructors' competence level was relatively high was respect to personal characteristics / attribute category, and lower with respect to planning and application of the principles of teaching-learning process.

CONCLUSION

The survey of related literature has helped the investigator to have clear perspective of the problem chosen for the above review of related literature that very few studies had been carried out using both variables "Social Maturity and Teaching Competency". Hence the investigator has chosen to study these two variables on TTI and DIET students. The reviews based on Indian and Foreign studies, had helped the researcher to frame appropriate hypotheses.

In the light of the literature studied, the third chapter has been designed.
❐

19

Research Design and Methods of Investigation

This chapter gives an overall picture of the design of the study, research tools used for the study, nature and selection of the sample and a brief description of the procedure adopted for the collection of data, in the light of the other research studies.

Thyer (1993) defined research design as "a blue print for how research study is to be completed operationalising variables so they can be measured, selecting a sample of interest to study collecting data to be used as a basis for testing hypothesis and analyzing the results".

Research is always directed towards solution to a problem. It is a producer from known to unknown. The ultimate goad of any research work is to find out the cause and effect relationship between the variables.

HYPOTHESES OF THE STUDY

The following hypotheses are set for the present study.

1. There is a significant difference between male and female teacher trainees on their social maturity.
2. There is a significant difference between male and female trainees on their components of teaching competency.

3. There is a significant difference between TTI and DIET teacher trainees on their social maturity.
4. There is a significant difference between TTI and DIET teacher trainees on their components of teaching competency.
5. There is a significant difference between teacher trainees belonging to nuclear and joint families on their social maturity.
6. There is a significant difference between teacher trainees belonging to nuclear and joint families on their components of teaching competency.
7. There is a significant difference between teacher trainees from rural and urban area on their social maturity.
8. There is a significant difference between teacher trainees from rural and urban area on their components of teaching competency.
9. There is a significant difference of teacher trainees on their social maturity based on their parental income.
10. There is a significant difference of teacher trainees on their components of teaching competency based on their parental income.
11. There is a significant difference on social maturity of teacher trainees based on their communities.
12. There is a significant difference on components of teaching competency of teacher trainees based on their communities.
13. There is a significant difference on social maturity of teacher trainees based on their fathers qualification.
14. There is a significant difference on components of teaching competency of teacher trainees based on their fathers qualification.
15. There is a significant difference on social maturity of teacher trainees based on their mothers qualification.
16. There is a significant difference on components of teaching competency of teacher trainees based on their mothers qualification.
17. There is a significant difference on social maturity of teacher trainees based on their age.
18. There is a significant difference on components of teaching competency of teacher trainees based on their age.
19. There is a significant relationship between social maturity and components of teaching competency.

DESCRIPTION OF THE TOOLS USED

To verify the framed hypotheses the following tools and techniques were used in the present investigation.

1. Social Maturity Scale
2. Teaching Competency Scale

DESCRIPTION OF THE TOOL

The maturity outcomes of school going population can best be estimated in the light of paucity of such essential increasing instruments. The social maturity scale was developed by "Dr.Nalini Rao", Department of Education, Bangalore University. The frame work for the integrated conceptual virtues of social maturity was adapted from the psychological structure.

It was formulated by Green Berger et al. The final form of the questionnaire consists of 90 items known as "Rao's SOCIAL MATURITY SCALE" RSMS).

ADMINISTRATION

The social maturity scales were administered to the respondents in groups in the regular classroom situation. The instruction provided on the first page of the scale booklet is self-explanatory. Reading of the instructions by the examiner to the group however ensures better conditions for responding to the items of the scale. The answers were recorded by the respondent on the scale protocol.

The item required to complete the scale items are between 45 minutes and one hour classification sought by the student regarding any item is to be handled by the examiner through encouraging the respondents. In this way the administration procedure is carried out.

SCORING PROCEDURE

The final form of the questionnaire consists of 90 items. Each item was accorded a four point response speed, the intervals of which are labeled.

1. Strongly agree
2. Agree
3. Disagree
4. Strongly disagree

The successive response intervals were subsequently scored as 4, 3, 2 and 1 with the high score represents mature response. There were no right or wrong answers. The answer were checked against the key and point is given for each item ticked as per the key. The total point obtained gives a measure of social maturity. By this way the scoring is carried out for social maturity.

TABLE. 19.1: Scoring Key of the Questionnaire According to the Nature of Items

Nature of Item	Strongly Agree	Agree	Strongly Disagree	Disagree
Positive 17, 21, 24, 26, 36, 39, 41, 42, 50, 51, 52, 54, 56, 57, 59, 63, 74, 77, 89, 90	4	3	2	1
Negative 1, 2, 3, 4, 5, 6, 7, 8, 9, 10, 11, 12, 13, 14, 15, 16, 18, 19, 20, 22, 23, 25, 27, 28, 29, 30, 31, 32, 33, 34, 35, 37, 38, 40, 43, 44, 45, 46, 47, 48, 49, 53, 55, 58, 61, 62, 63, 64, 65, 66, 67, 68, 69, 70, 71, 72, 73, 75, 76, 78, 79, 80, 81, 82, 83, 84, 85, 86, 87, 88	1	2	3	4

PILOT STUDY

A pilot study was conducted on 50 students to establish the reliability and validity of the different tools used in the present study.

ESTABLISHING RELIABILITY AND VALIDITY

The reliability of a test may be defined as the degree of consistency with which the test measures what it does measure. A test score is called reliable to be stable and trustworthy.

The reliability of the tool was calculated using Spearman Brown's formula for split half method.

$$r_{11} = \frac{2r_{hh}}{1 + r_{hh}}$$

r_{11} = Reliability coefficient of the whole test.

r_{hh} = Reliability coefficient of the half-test, found experimentally.

SOCIAL MATURITY SCALE

Reliability

In order to establish the reliability of the social maturity scale, the split half method was used. The reliability of social maturity scale was found to be 0.76. Hence social maturity is considered as a reliable tool.

Validity

The index of validity, which is the square root of reliability, was found to be 0.78. Hence social maturity scale selection for the study was considered to have high valid.

TEACHING COMPETENCY SCALE: B.K.PASSI AND M.S.LALITA

Teaching constitutes one of the major tasks of a teacher. Competency over this task of teaching is the essence of successful educational system. The development of teaching competency among teachers necessitates a clear understanding of the term as well as the method for its assessment. With more than half a century of research in this area, there has been no consensus regarding the meaning of the terms "teaching competency" and hence 'teaching competency' itself. As regards the term teaching although defined in different ways (Bhattacharaya, 1974) there has been a trend in perceiving the process analytically as constituting a host of activities (Brown, 1975; Gage, 1972). This analytical approach to perceive teaching has given a basis for innovations in teacher education, like microteaching (Alien and Ryan, 1969). The term 'competency' has also been a debatable term. It refers to the criteria that determine teacher effectiveness. Although the reviews of research on teacher effectiveness (Ebel, 1969) point out the futility of efforts in identifying teacher effectiveness criteria, the recent upsurge in research provides a cautious optimism (Rosen-shine, 1971). It can now be started with fairly high confidence that pupil outcomes like pupil achievement, student liking may be taken as the criteria of teacher effectiveness (Flanders and Simon, 1969). But the term Teaching Competency's as defined by various authors includes more than mere teacher effects or pupil outcomes. According to some authors it includes knowledge, attitude, skill and other teacher characteristics (Haskew, 1956, Wilson, 1973). Some others perceive teacher competence as teacher behaviours that produce intended effects (Medley and Mitzel, 1973; Biddle, 1964) arriving at a more comprehensive definition, Rama (1979) defines teacher competency as 'the ability of a teacher manifested through act of over teacher classroom behaviours which is a resultant of the interaction between the presage and the product variables of teaching within a social setting. This lack of consensus of the term 'teaching competency' highlights and difficulty of it measurement. The measurement of teaching competency has to be valid; objective and reliable one has to delimit to such variables.

THE GENERAL TEACHING COMPETENCY SCALE

This scale is generally used for measuring teaching competency of a teacher individually by a reliable observer or a group of reliable observes making different observation of his class room behaviour for the entire teaching period.

As the teacher teaches, the observer sits at the back for observations. At the end of the teaching period, he gives his ratings in the GTC scale against all the items. To facilitate this process, he may either mark frequencies or write verbal descriptions against each item which would help him in giving ratings more objectively.

SCORING PROCEDURE

The sum of the ratings against all the items constitutes the score on General Teaching Competency (GTC Score) of the teacher being observed. The maximum possible score is 147 and minimum is 21.

MAIN STUDY

The validated scales were used to collect the necessary data for the main study. The study was carried out on sample of 400 TTI and DIET students.

The sample was stratified on the basis of type of management viz, Government and Private Institutions and type of location viz, rural and urban environment.

It was also stratified on the basis of type of institution viz, boys only, girls only and co-education, type of family community viz, age viz, income viz, qualification viz.

TABLE. 19.2: The Table Shows the Background Variables of the Samples

Institution Name	Type of Institution	Institution Location	Type of Management	No. of Samples
Rajalakshmi Teacher Training Institute	Girls only	Rural	Private	100
Stella Matutina Teacher Training Institute	Girls only	Urban	Private	100
DIET – Chennai	Co-education	Urban	Government	200

STATISTICAL TECHNIQUES USED

Suitable descriptive and inferential statistical techniques were used in the interpretation of data to draw out a meaningful picture of results from the collected data. In the present study the following statistical measures were used.

1. Mean

$$X = A + \frac{\sum fd}{\sum f} x I$$

here,

A = Assumed mean

F = Frequency

D = Deviation from the assumed mean

I = Class interval

2. Standard Deviation

$$SD = \sigma\sqrt{\frac{\sum fd}{N} - \left(\frac{\sum fd}{N}\right)^2}$$

Where,

F = Frequency

D = Deviation from arithmetic mean

I = Class internal

σ = Standard deviation

3. Quartile Deviation

$$Q_1 = L1 + \left(\frac{N/4 - CF1}{F1}\right) x1$$

$$Q_2 = L3 + \left(\frac{3N/4 - CF3}{F3}\right) x1$$

$$Q_3 = \frac{Q_3 - Q_1}{2}$$

QD = Quartile Deviation

Q_1 = First QD

Q_3 = Third QD

L_1, L_3 = Lower limit of medium class

N = Total Frequency

CF1CF2 = Cumulative frequency

F1, F2 = Frequency of the medium class

4. Standard Error Deviation

Standard error of mean deviation.

$$SEMD = \frac{Standard\ error\ of\ mean\ deviation}{\frac{\sigma_1^2}{N_1} + \frac{\sigma_2^2}{N_2}}$$

σ_1 = SD of group I variable

σ_2 = SD of group II variable

N_1, N_2 = Total number of sample for group I, ii

5. Critical Ratio

To compare the significance of difference between mean, critical ratio was used. Critical ratio was calculated from the relation.

$$C.R. = \frac{M_1 - M_2}{\sqrt{\frac{\sigma 1^2}{N_1} + \frac{\sigma 2^2}{N_2}}}$$

Where,

M.M = Mean of group, I, II variable

σ_1, σ_2 = Standard Deviation

N_1, N_2 = Total number of class

6. Analysis of Variance

Correlation coefficient (r)

$$r = \frac{N\sum xy - \sum x \sum y}{\sqrt{\left(N\sum x - (\sum x)^2 - \left(N\sum x - (\sum y)^2\right.\right.}}$$

7. F-Ratio

$$F\text{-ratio} = \frac{Variance\ between\ group}{Variance\ within - group}$$

Correlation

$$term\ C = \frac{\sum x_1 + \sum x_2 + \sum x_3}{N}$$

Tss = X_2-C

Bss =

Wss = Tss - Bss

Where

$\Sigma x_1, \Sigma x_2, \Sigma x_3$ are scores in different groups.

C = Correlation term

Tss = Total sum of squares

Bss = Between sum of squares

Wss = Within sum of squares

CONCLUSION

This chapter indicates the details regarding the design of the study, hypothesis, pilot study and statistical techniques used. A detailed discussion of analysis of study and interpretation of the study follows in the next chapter.

20

Analysis and Interpretation of the Data

Research consists of systematic observation and description of the characteristics of properties for the purpose of discovering relationship starts with the description of the measures of the variables and goes on the higher level of statistics analysis. To develop the research plan, processing and analysis of data is necessary. It covers all the technical matters related to research work. This chapter describes the analysis of data and testing of hypotheses that have been framed on the basis of objectives using appropriate statistical techniques.

The data collected was carefully edited, systematically classified tabulated, analyzed interpreted and rationally concluded.

TESTING OF HYPOTHESES

Hypothesis : 1

There is a significant difference between male and female teacher trainees on their social maturity.

TABLE. 20.1: The table Showing the 't' Value of Male and Female Teacher Trainees on their social Maturity

Variable	Gender	No. of student	Mean	Std. Deviation	Std. Error Mean	't' Value	Level of Sig.
Social Maturity	Male	100	203.46	23.645	2.364	4.617	0.01
	Female	300	214.58	19.859	1.147		

Interpretation

The calculated value of "t" 4.617 is greater than the table value, so there is significant difference occur at 0.01 level. Thus the Hypothesis is accepted.

Hypothesis: 2

There is a significant difference between male and female teacher trainees on their components of teaching competency.

TABLE. 20.2: The Table Showing The 't' Value of Male and Female Teacher Trainees on their Components of Teaching Competency

Variable Teaching Competency	Gender	No. of student	Mean	Std. Deviation	Std. Error Mean	't' Value	Level of Sig.
Planning	Male	100	18.03	5.981	.598	1.737	NS
	Female	300	19.32	6.553	.378		
Presentation	Male	100	46.88	13.409	1.341	2.329	0.05
	Female	300	50.64	14.178	.819		
Closing	Male	100	10.32	4.075	.407	.256	NS
	Female	300	10.50	6.496	.375		
Evaluation	Male	100	9.92	3.784	.378	1.154	NS
	Female	300	9.48	3.160	.182		
Management	Male	100	9.66	3.742	.374	.017	NS
	Female	300	9.65	3.186	.184		

Interpretation

From the table it is observed that there is significant difference occur on the teaching component of presentation. So the empirical hypothesis partially accepted. All other components in teaching competency do not differ each other. As far as presentation is concerned the female teacher trainees perform well than their male counterparts.

Hypothesis: 3

There is a significant difference between TTI and DIET teacher trainees on their social maturity.

TABLE. 20.3: The Table Showing the 't' Value of Ttia and Diet Teacher Trainees on their Social Maturity

Variable	Type of Institute	No. of student	Mean	Std. Deviation	Std. Error Mean	't' Value	Level of Sig.
Social Maturity	DIET	199	217.37	20.251	1.436	5.35	0.01
	Private	201	206.29	21.105	1.489		

Interpretation

The calculated value of "t" 5.35 is greater than the table value, so there is significant difference occur at 0.01 level. Thus the Hypothesis is accepted.

Hypothesis: 4

There is a significant difference between TTI and DIET teacher trainees on their components of teaching competency.

TABLE.20.4: The Table Showing the 't' Value of Tti and Diet Teacher Trainees on their Components of Teaching Competency

Variable Teaching Competency	Type of Institution	No. of student	Mean	Std. Deviation	Std. Error Mean	T Value	Level of Sig.
Planning	DIET	199	20.76	5.268	.373	5.66	0.01
	Private	201	17.25	6.992	.493		
Presentation	DIET	199	55.37	11.812	.837	8.73	0.01
	Private	201	44.09	13.899	.980		
Closing	DIET	199	11.68	7.393	.524	4.18	0.01
	Private	201	9.23	3.770	.266		
Evaluation	DIET	199	10.22	2.985	.212	3.82	0.01
	Private	201	8.97	3.533	.249		
Management	DIET	199	10.42	2.975	.211	4.70	0.01
	Private	201	8.90	3.491	.246		

Interpretation

The calculated value of 't' is greater than the all table value, so there is significant difference occur at 0.01 level. Thus the Hypothesis is accepted.

Hypothesis: 5

There is a significant difference between teacher trainees belonging to nuclear and joint families on their social maturity.

TABLE.20.5: The Table Showing the 't' Value of Teacher Trainees Belonging to Nuclear and Joint Families on their Social Maturity

Variable	Category	No. of Students	Mean	Std. Deviation	Std. Error Mean	't' Value	Level of Sig.
Social Maturity	Nuclear	211	215.53	22.749	1.566	3.74	0.01
	Joint	189	207.64	18.971	1.380		

Interpretation

The calculated value of 't' 3.74 is greater than the table value, so there is significant difference occur at 0.01 level. Thus the Hypothesis is accepted.

Hypothesis: 6

There is a significant difference between teacher trainees belonging to nuclear and joint families on their Components of Teaching Competency.

TABLE.20.6: The Table Showing the 't' Value of Teacher Trainees Belonging to Nuclear and Joint Families on their Components of Teaching Competency

Variable Teaching Competency	Category	No. of Students	Mean	Std. Deviation	Std. Error Mean	't' Value	Level of Sig.
Planning	Nuclear	211	19.21	6.276	.432	.701	NS
	Joint	189	18.76	6.609	.481		
Presentation	Nuclear	211	51.10	13.721	.945	2.115	0.05
	Joint	189	48.14	14.320	1.042		
Closing	Nuclear	211	10.13	4.974	.342	1.131	NS
	Joint	189	10.81	6.927	.504		
Evaluation	Nuclear	211	9.49	3.027	.208	.600	NS
	Joint	189	9.69	3.638	.265		
Management	Nuclear	211	9.67	2.960	.204	.114	NS
	Joint	189	9.63	3.706	.270		

Interpretation

From the table it is observed that there is significant difference occur on the teaching component of presentation. So the empirical hypothesis partially accepted. All other components in teaching competency do not differ each other.

Hypothesis: 7

There is a significant difference between teacher trainees from rural and urban area on their social maturity.

TABLE.20.7: The Table Showing the 't' Value of Teacher Trainees from Ruraland Urban Area on their social Maturity

Variable	Category	No. of Students	Mean	Std. Deviation	Std. Error Mean	't' Value	Level of Sig.
Social Maturity	Rural	214	216.42	20.239	1.383	4.750	0.01
	Urban	186	206.49	21.499	1.576		

Interpretation

The calculated value of 't' 4.75 is greater than the table value, so there is significant difference occur at 0.01 level. Thus the Hypothesis is accepted.

Hypothesis: 8

There is a significant difference between teacher trainees from rural and urban area on their Components of Teaching Competency.

TABLE. 20.8: The Table Showing the 't' Value of Teacher Trainees from rural and Urban Area on their Components of Teaching Competency

Variable Teaching Competency	Category	No. of Students	Mean	Std. Deviation	Std. Error Mean	't' Value	Level of Sig.
Planning	Rural	214	20.36	5.382	.368	4.653	0.01
	Urban	186	17.43	7.160	.525		
Presentation	Rural	214	54.32	12.289	.840	7.519	0.01
	Urban	186	44.39	14.138	1.037		
Closing	Rural	214	11.41	7.221	.494	3.470	0.01
	Urban	186	9.35	3.847	.282		
Evaluation	Rural	214	10.01	3.006	.206	2.773	0.01
	Urban	186	9.10	3.608	.265		
Management	Rural	214	10.21	3.031	.207	3.601	0.01
	Urban	186	9.02	3.546	.260		

Interpretation

The calculated value of 't' is greater than the all table value, so there is significant difference occur at 0.01 level. Thus the Hypothesis is accepted.

Hypothesis: 9

There is a significant difference of teacher trainees on their Social Maturity based on their parental income.

TABLE. 20.9: The Table Showing the 't' Value of Teacher Trainees on their Social Maturity Based on their Parental Income

Variable	Category	No. of Students	Mean	Std. Deviation	Std. Error Mean	't' Value	Level of Sig.
Social Maturity	Low income	330	211.54	21.474	1.182	.534	NS
	High income	70	213.04	21.094	2.521		

Interpretation

The calculated value of 't' (.534) is less than the table value, so there is not significant difference at 0.01 level. Thus the Hypothesis is rejected.

Hypothesis: 10

There is a significant difference of teacher trainees on their Components of Teaching Competency based on their parental income.

TABLE.20.10: The Table Showing the 't' Value of Teacher Trainees on their Components of Teaching Competency Based on their Parental Income

Variable Teaching Competency	Category	No. of Students	Mean	Std. Deviation	Std. Error Mean	't' Value	Level of Sig.
Planning	Low income	330	18.68	6.448	.355	2.165	0.05
	High income	70	20.50	6.176	.738		
Presentation	Low income	330	48.84	13.885	.764	2.675	0.01
	High income	70	53.76	14.318	1.711		
Closing	Low income	330	10.43	6.140	.338	.161	NS
	High income	70	10.56	5.191	.620		
Evaluation	Low income	330	9.51	3.267	.180	1.023	NS
	High income	70	9.98	3.601	.430		
Management	Low income	330	9.58	3.659	.437	1.034	NS
	High income	70	10.03	3.255	.179		

Interpretation

From the table it is observed that there is significant difference occur on the teaching components of planning and presentation. So the empirical hypothesis partially accepted. All other components is teaching competency do not differ each other. As far as presentation is concerned by the parental income.

Hypothesis: 11

There is a significant difference on social maturity of teacher trainees based on their community.

TABLE. 20.11: Anova Showing the Difference in social Maturity of Teacher Trainees to Different Communities

Variable	Source of variation	Sum of Squares	Degree of Freedom	Mean Squares	F	Level of Sig.
Social Maturity	Between Groups	4753.860	2	2376.930	5.308	0.01
	Within Groups	177793.54	397	447.843		
	Total	**182547.40**	**399**	---		

Interpretation

From the above table the calculated value of 'F' (5.308) is greater than the table value is significant difference at 0.01 level. Thus the Hypothesis is accepted.

Hypothesis: 12

There is no significant difference on components of teaching competency of teacher trainees based on their communities.

TABLE. 20.12: Anovashowing the Difference in Teaching Competency of Teacher Trainees toDifferent Communities

Variable Teaching Competency	Source of Variation	Sum of Squares	Degree of Freedom	Mean Squares	F	Level of Sig.
Planning	Between Groups	209.560	2	104.780	2.553	NS
	Within Groups	16294.430	397	41.044		
	Total	16503.990	399	-		
Presentation	Between Groups	97.368	2	48.684	.245	NS
	Within Groups	78870.230	397	198.666		
	Total	78967.598	399	-		
Closing	Between Groups	142.240	2	71.120	1.999	NS
	Within Groups	14120.858	397	35.569		
	Total	14263.098	399	-		
Evaluation	Between Groups	19.731	2	9.865	.891	NS
	Within Groups	4397.207	397	11.076		
	Total	4416.937	399	-		
Management	Between Groups	14.658	2	7.329	.660	NS
	Within Groups	4407.732	397	11.103		
	Total	**4422.390**	**399**	-		

Interpretation

The calculated value of 'F' for all the components of teaching competency is not significant at any level and thereby the hypothesis is rejected.

Hypothesis: 13

There is no significant difference on social maturity of teacher trainees based on their fathers qualification.

TABLE.20.13: Anova Showing the Difference in Social Maturity of Teacher Trainees Based on Fathers Qualification

Variable	Source of variation	Sum of Squares	Degree of Freedom	Mean Squares	F	Level of Sig.
Social Maturity	Between Groups	1865.813	2	932.907	2.050	N.S
	Within Groups	180681.58	397	455.117		
	Total	**182547.40**	**399**	-		

Interpretation

The calculated value of 'F' (2.050) is less than the table value is not significant difference at 0.01 level. Thus the Null Hypothesis is retained.

Hypothesis: 14

There is no significant difference on components of teaching competency of teacher trainees based on their father's qualification.

TABLE.20.14: Anova Showing the Difference on Components of Teaching Competency of Teacher Trainees Based on Fathers Qualification

Variable Teaching Competency	Source of Variation	Sum of Squares	Degree of Freedom	Mean Squares	F	Level of Sig.
Planning	Between Groups	104.960	2	52.480	1.270	NS
	Within Groups	16399.030	397	41.307		
	Total	16503.990	399			
Presentation	Between Groups	1338.179	2	669.089	3.422	NS
	Within Groups	77629.419	397	195.540		
	Total	78967.597	399			
Closing	Between Groups	76.679	2	38.339	1.073	NS
	Within Groups	14186.419	397	35.734		
	Total	14263.098	399			
Evaluation	Between Groups	15.522	2	7.761	.700	NS
	Within Groups	4401.415	397	11.087		
	Total	4416.938	399			
Management	Between Groups	2.229	2	1.115	.100	NS
	Within Groups	4420.161	397	11.134		
	Total	**4422.390**	**399**			

Interpretation

The calculated value of 'F' is less than the table value is not significant difference at 0.01 levels. Thus the null hypothesis is retained.

Hypothesis: 15

There is no significant difference on social maturity of teacher trainees based on their mother qualification.

TABLE.20.15: Anova Showing the Difference in Social Maturity of Teacher Trainees Based on Mother Qualification

Variable	Source of variation	Sum of Squares	Degree of Freedom	Mean Squares	F	Level of Sig.
Social Maturity	Between Groups	3484.033	2	1742.016	3.862	0.05
	Within Groups	179063.36	397	451.041		
	Total	**182547.40**	**399**	-		

Interpretation

The calculated value of 'F' (3.862) is greater than the table value is significant difference at 0.05 level. Thus the null hypothesis is not accepted.

Hypothesis: 16

There is no significant difference on components of teaching competency of teacher trainees based on their mother's qualification.

TABLE. 20.16: Anova Showing the Difference on Components of Teaching Competency of Teacher Trainees Based on Mothers Qualification

Variable Teaching Competency	Source of Variation	Sum of Squares	Degree of Freedom	Mean Squares	F	Level of Sig.
Planning	Between Groups	97.106	2	48.553	1.175	NS
	Within Groups	16406.854	397	41.327		
	Total	16503.990	399			
Presentation	Between Groups	344.359	2	172.179	.869	NS
	Within Groups	78623.239	397	198.043		
	Total	78967.598	399			
Closing	Between Groups	33.438	2	16.719	.466	NS
	Within Groups	14229.659	397	35.843		
	Total	14263.098	399			
Evaluation	Between Groups	.398	2	.199	0.18	NS
	Within Groups	4416.540	397	11.125		
	Total	**4416.938**	**399**			

Management	Between Groups	10.361	2	5.181	.466	NS
	Within Groups	4412.029	397	11.113		
	Total	**4422.390**	**399**			

Interpretation

The calculated value of 'F' for all the components of teaching competency is not significant difference at any level. Thus the null hypothesis is retained.

Hypothesis: 17

There is no significant difference on social maturity of teacher trainees based on their age.

TABLE. 20.17: Anova Showing the Difference in Social Maturity of Teacher Trainees Based on Different Age

Variable	Source of variation	Sum of Squares	Degree of Freedom	Mean Squares	F	Level of Sig.
Social Maturity	Between Groups	1832.424	2	916.212	2.013	NS
	Within Groups	180714.97	397	455.201		
	Total	**182547.40**	**399**	-		

Interpretation

The calculated value of 'F' (2.013) is less than the table value is not significant difference at 0.01 level. Thus the null hypothesis is retained.

Hypothesis: 18

There is no significant difference on components of Teaching competency of teacher trainees based on their age.

TABLE. 20.18: Anova Showing the Difference in Teaching Competency of Teacher Trainees Based on Different Age

Variable Teaching Competency	Source of Variation	Sum of Squares	Degree of Freedom	Mean Squares	F	Level of Sig.
Planning	Between Groups	23.277	2	11.639	.280	NS
	Within Groups	16480.713	397	41.513		
	Total	16503.990	399			
Presentation	Between Groups	575.098	2	287.549	1.456	NS
	Within Groups	78392.500	397	197.462		
	Total	**78967.598**	**399**			

Closing	Between Groups	21.151	2	10.575	.295	NS
	Within Groups	14241.947	397	35.874		
	Total	14263.098	399			
Evaluation	Between Groups	42.534	2	21.267	1.930	NS
	Within Groups	4374.404	397	11.019		
	Total	4416.937	399			
Management	Between Groups	30.707	2	15.353	1.388	NS
	Within Groups	4391.683	397	11.062		
	Total	**4422.390**	**399**			

Interpretation

The calculated value of 'F' is less than the table value is not significant difference at 0.01 level. Thus the null hypothesis is not accepted.

Hypothesis: 19

There is significant relationship between social maturity and components of teaching competency.

TABLE. 20.19: Correlation Matrix Between Social Maturity and Components of Teaching Competency

Variable	Social maturity	Pla	Pre	Clo	Eva	Manage
Social Maturity	*	-	-	-	-	-
Teaching competency Planning	.041	-	-	-	-	-
Presentation	.156	.481	-	-	-	-
Closing	.091	.289	.200	-	-	-
Evaluation	.061	.356	.492	.330	-	-
Management	.041	.353	.447	.332	.717	*

Interpretation

The calculated correlation co-efficient is significant at 0.01 level. So the hypothesis is accepted.

DISCUSSION OF THE RESULTS

The results of statistical analysis of the present investigation interpreted here in terms of the purpose of the study and with respects to other studies, which have been conducted in related areas of research.

It was found that there is no significant difference on social maturity of teacher trainees on their father's qualification and mother's qualification and teacher trainee's age. But significant difference was found based on their gender, type of institution type of family, area, parental income, and community. To find out the relationship between social maturity and teaching competency of TTI and DIET students.

CONCLUSION

This chapter summaries the analysis of data, testing of hypothesis description and discussion of the table. A brief report of the research study together with the major findings and conclusion along with their educational implications has been presented in the succeeding chapter.

❐

21

Summary of Finddings and Conclusion

In this chapter, after presenting briefly the statement of the problem and the description of the procedure used in the investigation, the findings and the conclusions are presented. In the light of the findings of the present study, a few suggestions have been proposed at the end of the chapter for further research in this field.

STATEMENT OF THE PROBLEM

The problem is titled as *"SOCIAL MATURITY AND TEACHING COMPETENCY OF STUDENTS TEACHERS IN TTI AND DIET IN CHENNAI"*.

OBJECTIVES OF THE STUDY

1. To find out the significant difference between male and female teacher trainees on their social maturity.
2. To find out the significant difference between male and female teacher trainees on their components of teaching competency.
3. To find out the significant difference between TTI and DIET teacher trainees on their social maturity.

4. To find out the significant difference between TTI and DIET teacher trainees on their components of teaching competency.
5. To find out the significant difference between teacher trainees belonging to nuclear and joint families on their social maturity.
6. To find out the significant difference between teacher trainees belonging to nuclear and joint families on their components of teaching competency.
7. To find out the significant difference between teacher trainees from rural and urban area on their social maturity.
8. To find out the significant difference between teacher trainees from rural and urban area on their components of teaching competency.
9. To find out the significant difference of teacher trainees on their social maturity based on their parental income.
10. To find out the significant difference of teacher trainees on their components of teaching competency based on their parental income.
11. To find out the significant difference on social maturity of teacher trainees based on their communities.
12. To find out the significant difference on components of teaching competency of teacher trainees based on their communities.
13. To find out the significant difference on social maturity of teacher trainees based on their fathers qualification.
14. To find out the significant difference on components of teaching competency of teacher trainees based on their fathers qualification.
15. To find out the significant difference on social maturity of teacher trainees based on their mothers qualification.
16. To find out the significant difference on components of teaching competency of teacher trainees based on their mothers qualification.
17. To find out the significant difference on social maturity of teacher trainees based on their age.
18. To find out the significant difference on components of teaching competency of teacher trainees based on their age.
19. To find out the significant relationship between social maturity and components of teaching competency.

HYPOTHESES OF THE STUDY

1. There is a significant difference between male and female teacher trainees on their social maturity.
2. There is a significant difference between male and female trainees on their components of teaching competency.

3. There is a significant difference between TTI and DIET teacher trainees on their social maturity.
4. There is a significant difference between TTI and DIET teacher trainees on their components of teaching competency.
5. There is a significant difference between teacher trainees belonging to nuclear and joint families on their social maturity.
6. There is a significant difference between teacher trainees belonging to nuclear and joint families on their components of teaching competency.
7. There is a significant difference between teacher trainees from rural and urban area on their social maturity.
8. There is a significant difference between teacher trainees from rural and urban area on their components of teaching competency.
9. There is a significant difference of teacher trainees on their social maturity based on their parental income.
10. There is a significant difference of teacher trainees on their components of teaching competency based on their parental income.
11. There is a significant difference on social maturity of teacher trainees based on their communities.
12. There is no significant difference on components of teaching competency of teacher trainees based on their communities.
13. There is no significant difference on social maturity of teacher trainees based on their fathers qualification.
14. There is no significant difference on components of teaching competency of teacher trainees based on their fathers qualification.
15. There is no significant difference on social maturity of teacher trainees based on their mothers qualification.
16. There is no significant difference on components of teaching competency of teacher trainees based on their mothers qualification.
17. There is no significant difference on social maturity of teacher trainees based on their age.
18. There is no significant difference on components of teaching competency of teacher trainees based on their age.
19. There is a significant relationship between social maturity and components of teaching competency.

SAMPLE

The population consists of students who are studying in TTI and DIET institutions.

The investigator randomly selected 400 students from 3 TTI and DIET institutions.

TOOLS USED IN THIS STUDY

The following tools were used.

1. Social maturity scale by Dr.Nalini Rao
2. Teaching competency scale by B.K.Passi and M.S.Lalita.

MAJOR FINDINGS OF THE STUDY

The major findings are presented below.

1. It was found that significance difference occurred on the social maturity and teaching competency of male and female teacher trainees.
2. It was found that significant difference occurred on the social maturity and teaching competency of TTI and DIET students.
3. It was found that significant difference occurred on the social maturity and teaching competency of teacher trainees from joint and nuclear family of the teacher trainees.
4. It was found that there is a significant difference between TTI and DIET teacher trainees with respect to their social maturity and teaching competency on the basis of their community.
5. It was found that there is a significant difference between TTI and DIET teacher trainees with respect to their social maturity and teaching competency on the basis of their urban and rural area.
6. It was found that there is no significant difference between TTI and DIET teacher trainees with respect to their social maturity and teaching competency on the basis of parental qualification.
7. It was found that there is no significant difference between TTI and DIET teacher trainees with respect to their social maturity and teaching competency on the basis of parental income.
8. It was found that there is no significant difference between TTI and DIET teacher trainees with respect to their social maturity and teaching competency on the basis of their age.
9. It was found that significant relationship occurred between social maturity and components of teaching competency of TTI and DIET students.

EDUCATIONAL IMPLICATIONS

Social maturity and teaching competency is an aspect that makes an individual adjusted to the society at large. It is related to the development of the personality of a student. Students studying in TTI and DIET are forced to adhere to institution regulations as well as social activities. We find that if the students fall in line with the social relationship system and obeying its regulations they may possess a higher social maturity and teaching competency. Therefore for teacher trainees social maturity and teaching competency is essential for their daily life to adopt the classroom situation.

Hence, the study has a direct impact on the educational practice. The following are some of the major recommendations to be implemented for the social maturity and teaching competency of the students.

1. Educators and Administrators should bring about awareness among students to give more importance to develop social maturity and teaching competency.
2. In order to develop social maturity and teaching competency intensive training should be provided.

SUGGESTIONS FOR FURTHER RESEARCH

1. This study was conducted to 400 TTI and DIET students only. To make the study more comprehensive further studies can be conducted on a larger sample.
2. The present is confined only to the TTI and DIET students. This study may be conducted B.Ed. teacher trainees and nursery school teacher trainees.

CONCLUSION

This study is aimed to know the social maturity and teaching competency of TTI and DIET students. In this chapter the hypotheses and major findings were given also further analysis has been recommended.

❐

Bibliography

1. Alebaikan, R., and S. Troudi (2010). Blended learning in Saudi universities: Challenges and perspectives. ALT-J, Research in Learning Technology Vol.18, p. 49–59
2. Abbott, M. (1997) Effective Teaching and Learning. New Delhi: Prentice Hall.
3. Ajjan, H., & Hartshorne, R. (2014) Investigating faculty decisions to adopt Web 2.0 technologies: Theory and achievement in higher education. Journal of Computer Assisted Learning, Vol.29,p. 220–234.
4. Arun. (2008) ICT skill of the M.Ed., scholars. Journal of Computer Assisted Learning, Vol.20,p.46-54.
5. Anderson Harper, Mason and Poporich (1988) The Trends in Teaching Circle. American Educational Research Journal,Vol.18, p. 13–24
6. Arbaugh, J.B. (2008) Introduction: Blended learning: Research and practice. Academy of Management Learning & Education, Vol .7, p. 13–24.
7. Ausburn, L.J. (2004) 'Course design elements most valued by adult learners in blended online education environments: An American-perspective', Educational Media International, vol. 41, pp. 328-337
8. Berson M.J. (1996) Effectiveness of computer technology in the social studies: a review of the literature, Journal of Research on Computing in Education,Vol. 28,p. 486-500.
9. Bleed, R. (2001)A hybrid campus for a new millennium. Educause Review, Vol.36, p. 16–24
10. Best, J.W. and Khan, J.V. (2004) Research in Education, New Delhi: Prentice Hall of India Pvt. Ltd.

11. Boyle, T. (2003) Developing Models through Blended Learning Strategy. Language Learning and Technology, Vol.7,p.104-110.
12. Chodavarapu jalaja kumari, Digumarti Bhaskara Rao (2004) Methods of Teaching Educational Technology, New Delhi: Discovery Publishing House.
13. Cuban, L., H. Kirkpatrick, and C. Peck. (2001) High access and low use of technologies in high school classrooms: Explaining an apparent paradox. American Educational Research Journal, Vol.38, p. 13–34
14. Chun Meng Tang, Lee Yen Chaw (2014) attitude of students towards different learning aspects could influence their readiness for blended learning, Research in Learning Technology, Vol.20, p.11–22.
15. Dan, C., Sivo, S and Brophy, J.(2003) Pattern of Learning in a Web Based Class Room, Language Learning and Technology, Vol. 7, p.119 – 140.
16. De Freitas, S. & Mayes, T. (2004) Review of E-learning Theories, Frameworks and Models, Unpublished project report, Essex University.
17. Dr inż. Colin F. Hales and Dr Barbara Fura (2014) attitude of students' towards a wider use of ICT in the education process, International Journal, vol. 52, , p. 227-236
18. Driscoll, M. (2002) Blended Learning: Let's Get Beyond The Hype E-Learning Retrieved from, http://www.8.ibm.com/ blended learning. pdf.
19. Elke Mader, Philipp Budka and Elisabeth Anderl (2008) Blended Learning Strategies for Methodology Education. Educause Review Vol.7, p. 86–99.
20. Farouq H. Aziz Al-Rahman (2013) quality of Blended Learning courses. ALT-J, Research in Learning Technology Vol.22, p. 45–52
21. Graham, Allen and Ure. (2003) The Key to Teach Through Blended Learning Strategy in Higher Education. Beston, Harward Business School Press.
22. Graham, C.R. (2006) Blended Learning Systems, Definitions, Current Trends, and Future Directions. In C.J Bonk and C.R Graham (Eds), The Hand Book of Blended Learning, Global Perspectives, Local Designs San Francisco: Pfeiffer.
23. Hannon, J. (2008) Doing staff development: Practices, dilemmas and technologies. Australasian Journal of Educational Technology, Vol. 24, p. 15–29.
24. Heinze, A., & Procter, C. (2006) Online communication and information ,technology education. Journal of Information Technology Education,Vol. 5,p. 235-237

25. Hofmann,J.(2001)BlendedLearningCaseStudy.www.learningcircuits.org/2001/apr2001/hofmann.html.
26. Hong Kian-Sam and Julia Ai Cheng Lee. (2008)Using Blended Learning in Higher Education. Buckingham: Open University Press.
27. Jagannath mohanty (2003) Modern Trends in Educational Technology, New Delhi : Neelkamal Publication Pvt.Ltd.
28. Julie Willems. (2011) Qualitative Research in Education. Sanfrancisco, Jossey Bass Publishers. Kumar.K.L (1997) Educational Technology, New Delhi: New Age International (p) Ltd., Publishers.
29. Kothari C.R (2010) Research Methodology, New age International Publishers, New Delhi.
30. Lidia Bilbatua and Alfredo Herrero de Haro (2014) Teachers' attitudes towards Computer- Assisted Language Learning in Australia. Australasian Journal of Educational Technology Vol.24, p. 20–34.
31. Mohammad A. Alseweed (2014) effects of the traditional learning, blended learning and virtual classes learning on university students, International Journal of e-Learning, Vol.6,p.71–84.
32. Mohammad Ataur Rahman. (2013) teacher educators use of computer technology in Teachers Training Colleges, Journal of Educational Technology Vol.64, p. 10–15.
33. Nallusamy, T. (2014) Attitude towards Blended learning among student-teachers, Indian Journal of Educational Technology, Vol.44, p. 30–44.
34. Nichols, M.(2003) A theory for e-learning, Retrieved from: http://www ifets.inf/ journals/6_2/1.pdf.
35. Ooms, A., L. Burke, T. Linsey, and C. Heaton-Shrestha. (2008) Introducing e-developers to support a university's blended learning developments, ALT-J, Research in Learning Technology Vol.16,p. 111–22.
36. Özgen Korkmaz and Ufuk Karakuş. (2009) impact of blended learning model, Australasian Journal of Educational Technology Vol.4, p. 30–39.
37. Pinelopi Zaka. (2011) blended teaching and learning, Journal of Distance Education Vol.16, pp. 70-84
38. Pandy.V.C(2005) Educational Technology, New Delhi: Isha books.
39. Philip Rotich (2013) Barriers to the uptake of web-based technology by university teachers, Journal of Distance Education Vol.66, p. 61–69.
40. Parthasarathy.M., Ananthasayanam.R and Ravi.R (2013) Usage of Internet Applications among B.Ed Students, Indian Journal of Education, Vol.74, p.56-65.

41. Rama Chandra Dhir (2014) e-learning, attitude of graduating students, International Journal of e-Learning, Vol.12,p.51–64.
42. Raina.M.K (2009) Educational Technology, New Delhi: Ashim Printline.
43. Rovai, A.P., and H.M. Jordan. (2004) Blended learning and sense of community: A comparative analysis with traditional and fully online graduate courses. The International Review of Research in Open and Distance Learning Vol.5, p. 1–13
44. Seema Sharma (2005) Advanced Educational Technology, New Delhi: Anmol Publication Pvt.Ltd.
45. Shih, Ch. and Gamon, J. (2001) Web-Based Learning, Relationships .among Student Motivation, Attitude, Learning Styles and Achievement .Journal of Agricultural Education, Vol 42, p.45-53
46. Sharma, P.,Barrett, B., (2007) Blended Learning: Using Technology in and Beyond the Language Classroom, Oxford: Macmillan.
47. Saminathan, G. (2014) Student attitude towards Audio- Visual Aids used by the teacher, Journal of Distance Education Vol.23, p. 33–41.
48. Thiyagu, K. (2013) B.Ed., Trainees perceptions towards Blended learning in teaching learning of mathematics, Indian Journal of Education, Vol.43, p. 13–21.
49. Vaughan, N. (2010) Perspectives on blended learning in higher education. International Journal of e-Learning, Vol.1, p.81–94.
50. Vilma Bijeikienė, Svetlana Rašinskienė, Lina Zutkienė. (2011) studies about languages. kalbų studijos, Vol. 18, p.78-86
51. Valiathan, P. (2012) Blended Learning Models, Retrained from www. learningcircuits.com.
52. Vanaja.M (2004) Educational Technology, New Delhi: Neelkamal Publication Pvt.Ltd.
53. Venketaraman,S and Nellaiyappan,N.O. (2008) Computer assisted Instruction, The International Review of Research, Vol. 15, p.14-23.
54. Vijay Jaiswal .(2014) Perspectives on blended learning in higher education, International Journal of e-Learning, Vol.1,p. 81–94.
55. Wan, F. ,Shafie, A. and Janier, J. B. (2008) Students' perceptions towards Blended Learning in teaching and learning Mathematics, Application ,of integration, Technologies for E-Learning and Digital Entertainment.Vol 5093,p.162-170.
56. Wing AU, Dr., Greg C. R. Dr and Yates. (2013) A study of student's perceptions in blended learning environment based on different learning styles, Educational Technology & Society, Vol. 11, p. 183-193.

57. Wu, J.H., R.D. Tennyson, and T.L. Hsia. (2010) A study of student satisfaction in a blended- learning system environment, Computers & Education,Vol. 55, p.155-64.
58. Yilmaz, M. B. and Orhan, F. (2010) Pre-service English Teachers in .Blended Learning Environment in Respect to their Learning Approaches The Turkish Online Journal of Educational Technology, vol.9, p. 157-164.
59. Ya-Ting, Bonk and Kyong (2013) The trend of blended learning in Taiwan, perceptions of HRD practitioners and implications for emerging competencies. Human Resource Development International; Vol. 12, p69-84.
60. ZAIDI.S.M (2004) Modern Teaching of Educational Technology, Delhi: Anmol publications Pvt.Ltd.
61. Arora R.K.,(1981), *"An investigation into the problems of study in professional courses of medicine law, engineering and education in relation to personality factors"*, Third survey of Research in Education, National Council of Educational Research and Training, p.105.
62. Ayersman,-David-J. (1992), *" Effect of a Summer Enrichment Program for At-Risk Youths on Locus of Control and the Relation to Motivational Orientation"*.
63. Baker, Eugene .M (1977), *"Psychological Education to enhance Self Understanding and Self Acceptance in college students"*, http://WWW.spd.org/sdp/diss
64. Brill, Ronala .R, *"Dealing with the hazards of adolescence"*, http://www.emotionalhonesty.com/arthazadoles.html
65. Bharadwaj .R (1998), *"Perceived parenting of rejection – Acceptance and adolescents value conflicts"*, Indian psychological review, Vol L1 special issue p.256
66. Bernhard,-Judith-K.; Siegel,-Linda-S. (1995) , *"Increasing Internal Locus of Control for a Disadvantaged Group: A Computer Intervention"*. Journal: Computers-in-the-Schools; v11 n1 p59-77 1994
67. Chromic Daria, Theresa (1996), *"The American Dream and Self advocacy for students with learning disabilities"*, Theory: Curriculum and Learner outcome, Dissertation Abstracts International DAI-A 57/08, p.3455.
68. Chaube S.D, (1981), *"Adolescent Psychology"*, M/S Vikas Publishing house, New Delhi.
69. Furnham, A. and Henry, J. (1980). Cross-cultural locus of control studies: experiment and critique. Psychological Reports, 47, 23-29.

70. Freud, S. (1900). *"The interpretation of dreams. In the complete psychological works of Sigmund Freud."* London: The Hogarth Press, 1962.

71. Fraley,-Stephen-E. (1992) From, *"Self-Blame to Self-Acceptance: Freeing Myself in a Prison Undergraduate Program".* Journal-of-Correctional-Education; v43 n4 p178-81 Dec 1992

72. Frederick, Veedine .j (1997), *" The relationship among acceptance of a learning disability, grade level of diagnosis and achievements of students with learning disabilities",* Dissertation abstract international, DAI –A 58/05, p.3083

73. Garrison, Albert j, and Kingston (1976), Educational psychology, Bombay : Vakils, Feffer and Simons pvt. Ltd.,p.448

74. Hurley, John .R (1990) , *"Constructive thinking and elevated of self in interpersonal groups",* Journal of Psychology Vol. CXXIIV, No.5, pp.563-575.

75. Jersild Arthur, (1963), *"The Psychology of Adolescence",* New York, T.Macmillan company, p.63

76. Kao, G. and Thompson, J. S. (2003). Racial and ethnic stratification in educational achievement and attainment. In K.S. Cook and J. Hagan (Eds.), Annual Review of Sociology (Vol.29,pp.417-442). Palo Alto, CA: Annual Reviews.

77. Krampen, G. and Weiberg, H. (1981). Three aspects of locus of control in German, American, and Japanese university students. Journal of Social Psychology, 113, 133-134.

78. Lynch, Shirley; Hurford, David P.; and Cole, AmyKay. (2002) *Parental Enabling Attitudes and Locus of Control of At-Risk and Honors Students. Adolescence,* 37(147) 527- 549.

79. Levon, Dirk (2001), *"Self Acceptance, Ace up your sleeve",* http://www.masermuse.com/columistsreylogs/archives/00000056

80. Rotter, J.B. (1954). Social learning and clinical psychology. Englewood Cliffs, NJ: Prentice Hall.

81. Rotter, J. B. (1966). Generalized expectancies for internal versus external control of reinforcement. Psychological Monographs: General and Applied, 80 (1, Whole No. 609).

82. Rogers, C. R. (1947). Some observations on the organization of personality. American Psychologist, 2, 358-368

83. Randolph,-Elizabeth (1993), *"Developing Self-Awareness and Self-Acceptance in Emotionally Handicapped Students through the Bibliotherapeutic Process".*

84. Reeh,-H.-Elise; Reilly,-Karen-J. (1995), *"A Quasi Meta Analysis of the Health Locus of Control Construct".*
85. Shelton, T. L., Anastopoulos, A. D., & Linden, J. D. (1985). An attribution training program with learning disabled children. Journal of Learning Disabilities, 18, 261-265
86. Sim T.N (2003), "The father – adolescent relationship in the context of the Mother – adolescent relationship, exploring moderating linkages in the late adolescent sample in Singapore", Journal of Adolescent Research,Vol XVIII, No.4, pp.383-403
87. Sisco,-Sharon-S. (1992), *"Goal Setting To Enhance Self Esteem and Create an Internal Locus of Control in the At Risk Elementary Student".*
88. Sheerer, Elizabeth (1949), *"An analysis of the relationship between acceptance and respect for theself acceptance of and respect for others in ten counseling cases",* Journal of counseling psychology, Volume XIII, pp.169-175.
89. Sisco,-Sharon-S. (1992), *"Using Goal Setting To Enhance Self Esteem and Create an Internal Locus of Control in the At Risk Elementary Student".*
90. Sunanda Y (1991), A study of reactions to frustration as related to life Satisfactions and self acceptance among the aged, Ph.D Sri Venkateswara university IV survey, ii p.977
91. Santa-Rita,-Emilio (1995), *" The Effect of Computer-Assisted Student Development Programs on Entering Freshman Locus of Control Orientation".*CS: Bronx Community Coll., NY. Dept. of Student Development.
92. Starn Richard Lic (1993), *"Californial Psychological inventory profiles of male adolescents with learning disabilities",* A comparison with norm group scores dissertation abstracts international DAI –A 54/04 p.296
93. Statman,-Daniel (1993), *"Self-Assessment, Self-Esteem, and Self-Acceptance".* Journal-of-Moral-Education; v22 n1 p55-62 1993
94. Thompson,-Josephine-T. (1991), *"Establishing Locus of Control among Ninth Graders: Using Peer Mentors To Reduce Student Disengagement, Absenteeism, and Failures"*
95. Thielker, V. et al. *The relationship between positive reinforcement and locus of control.* [Electronic version]. Retrieved December 5, 2004, from
96. Tyler,-Doris-Kennedy; Vasu,-Ellen-Storey (1995), *"Locus of Control, Self-Esteem, Achievement Motivation, and Problem-Solving Ability: LogoWriter and Simulations in the Fifth-Grade Classroom".* Journal-of-Research-on-Computing-in-Education; v28 n1 p98-120

97. Waheeda .M (1998), *"Behavioral Training in improving personality characteristics of Juvenile delinquents in relation to Self Acceptance"*, M.Phil Thesis in Psychology, Madras University p.63.
98. Whitney,-Patricia (1991), *"Children's Locus of Control and Intrinsically Motivated Reading"*.
99. Allan Brad Brake (1997). *Emotion and its influence on problem solving. Dissertation abstract.*
100. Allen Jaffe, (1981). *A study of emotional maturity on the legislators of Illionis state; Dissertation abstract.*
101. Arya - A, (1984). *Emotional maturity and value of superior children in family.* Buch, 1327 IV (2).
102. Barooh .S and Phukan M, (1999). *Self concept of Orphan children and the children with natural parents.*
103. Benge et al., (1996). *Understanding the emotional development of twice exceptional rural student.* Dissertation abstract.
104. Bryman, Alan, (2001), *Social Research Methods, Oxford University* Press, pp.28 - 30.
105. Bush Kethryn, (1989). *Studies of emotional maturity.* Dissertation abstract.
106. Chanda, Sunanda, (1990). *Study on self-concept parental influence of socio economic status and sex in education to carreer choice attitude among high school students.* Dissertation abstract
107. Chauhan, Sarita, (1992). *A study of valves, self - concept, creativity and anxiety among professional college students.* Journal of education and psychology.
108. Connolly et al., (1994). *Peer self - concept of adolescence : Analysis of factor structure and association with peer experiences;* Journal of research on adolescence; V4n3, p.385-403.
109. Creamer, Don .G : *Using a developmental model of emotional maturity.* Dissertation abstract from, New Directions for community colleges; Vol.20, n3/p.73-82.
110. Cross, (1991). *A study of self - concept of middle school students,* Dissertation abstract.
111. Dastoor, H.F. (1982). *A study of different types of self concept prevalent among nurses,* Fifth survey of educational research. Dissertation abstract.
112. Deo P et al., (1971). *A study of relationship of self - concept and anxiety, Fifth survey of educational research.*
113. Dhami, G.S. (1974). *Intelligence, emotional maturity and socio - economic status and factors indicative of success in scholastic Achievement;* Buch, V/II/P-1885.

114 Kaisa Aunola, et al., (2002). *Developmental changes in reading skills and self* - concept; University of Finland.

115. Karan, Patricia, (1989). *Relationship of peer group and the self* - concept of adolescence, Dissertation abstract.

116. Kellner et al., (1995). *A school based Anger Managmeent programme for developmentally and emotionally disabled high school students;* Adolescence; V30n120, p.813-25.

117. Kloomok, et al., (1992). *Positive self - concept on academic difficulties; International;* Dissertation Abstract.

118. Manral Bheema (1988). *The input of emotional maturity and prolonged deprivation on indisciplined behaviour among university students in relation to their academic achievement.* Dissertation abstract.

119. Mohan (1975); *Self concept over years of adolescence :* Dissertation abstract.

120. Narayanan and Ganesan, (1978). *Self concept of scheduled tribes of Palamalai in Tamil Nadu,* Dissertation abstract.

121. Pandit, I (1985). *Self acceptance of sixth grade of adolescence;* Journal of Psychology.

122. Paul Bruece (1958). *Self concept of sixth grade students :* Journal of Psychology.

123. Gerdes et al., (1994). *Emotional social and academic adjustment of college students. A longitudinal study of retention.* Journal of Counselling and Development, v.72n3/ p.281 - 88.

124. Ghose P and Khurana (1986). *A study of socio economic status and Self* - Concept. Journal of education and psychology.

125. Gordon et al., (1995). *Self-Concept and motivational patterns of Resilient African American High School Students. Journal of black psychology*; v21 n3, p.239-55.

126. Heyer and et al., (1993). *The relationship between parental marital status and development of identify and emotional autonomy in college students.* Journal of college student development. v. 34, n6, p.432 - 36.

127. Jogawar, V.V. (1983). *Self-Concept and family relation in India,* Fourth Survey of Research, Vol.27.

128. Joseph Alexander E and Rajendran, K. (1992). *Influence of self - concept, sex, area and parents education on adjustment problems;* Dissertation abstract.

129. Prasad S, (1982). *Important factors of stability of self - concept,* Dissertation abstract.

130. Pyryt et al., (1994). *The multi dimensional Self-Concept :* A comparsion of gifted and average ability adolescents.

131. Ramiah. L (1990). *A relational study of parent involvement and self - concept of standard IX students in Devakottai Educational District* - Alagappa Univ. Fifth Survey of educational Research, Volume II, page 922.
132. Sandhu, Daya Singh, (1992). *A child's mind in the adult body.* Journal of Adult development Spec. Issue, p.23 - 35.
133. Sax Linda, (1994). *Development of Mathematical Self-Concept in college students,* Dissertation abstract international.
134. Siddiqui M.M. (1976). *Social pscyhological study of student behaviours with special reference to indiscipline,* Buch, 1327, iv/2.
135. Walia, D, (1973). *Gifted adolescent and their self concept;* India, Faculty of Education & Psychology.
136. Abraham Sperling (1967). *Definition of Social Maturity,* Vikas Publications, New Delhi.
137. Adams, Linda (1989). Be your best, New York: Putnam.
138. Adhiesehiah, W.T.V. and Pavanasam,R. (1974). Sociology in Theory and Practice, Shanthi Publishers, New Delhi, p.38.
139. Adi Seshiah W.T.A. and Mrs.Sulochana Sekar (1977). *Educational and Social Research,* Nekan Pathipagam, Coimbatore.
140. Agnihotri. L.S. (1991). Conducted a cross-cultural comparative study between tribal and non-tribal first generation and traditional learners in relation to their social maturity and educational adjustment, M.Phil Theses in Psychology.
141. Albert and James Gardon ward. *"Teacher competency and testing: A natural affinity".* Educational Measurement: Issues and Practice I (Summer 1982): 6-9, 26. 1982 ED 223-716.
142. Arthur, L. (1957). *"Educational Goals".* Ed. Res. Bull 36: 29-36.
143. Barr A.S. (1950). *"Teaching Competencies".* Encyc. Ed. Res. New York, Macmillam, p.1446-1454.
144. Bauses Ann Leslie (1995). Measured the effect of participation in a peer facilitation project on sixth grades self esteem, social maturity and patterns of social choice. Ph.D. Kent State University.
145. Bhusan. A. (1994). Conducted a study done on the social maturity across sex and family vocations. Buch, M.B., The Educational Research, Volume II.
146. Bruce (1985). *"Models of Teaching".* New Delhi, Prentice Hall of India.
147. Cron Bach, L.J. and Gleser, G.C. (1954). Review of the study of behaviours, Psychometric 19, 329-333.
148. Cuber, J.F. (1995). Sociology, New York: Appleton Century.

149. Das, R.C. et al. (1976). *A study of effectiveness of micro teaching of teachers dept of teachers education.* NCERT, New Delhi (Abridged Report).
150. Das, B.C. (1993). *"Effectiveness of concept attainment model in terms of teaching competency of pre-service student teachers perspectives in Education."* Indian Educational Abstracts (Issue – 4) 9(1): 34-35.
151. Downe, N.M. and Health, R.W.C. (1970). Basic Statistical Methods, New York: Harper and Row.
152. Flippo, Rona F. and Carol R. Foster. *"Teacher competency Teaching and Its Impact on Educators".* Journal of Teacher Education, 35 (March – April 1984), 10-13.
153. Frank.E. (1951). *"Situational Factors in Teacher Placement and Success".* Ed.20: 121-177.
154. George. J. Mouley, (1963). *The Science of Educational Research,* Eurosia Publishing House (P) Ltd., New Delhi.
155. Ghosh S. (1975). *A study of the social maturity of Bengali children, Applied Psychology,* Calcutta University.
156. Hentry I. Garrent (1968). *General Psychology.* Eurasia Publishing House Pvt. Ltd., New Delhi, p.88.
157. John W. Best (1977). *Research in Education, Third Edition,* Prentice Hall India Pvt. Ltd., New Delhi.
158. John W. Best and James V. Khan (1989). *Research in Education, Prentice Hall* (P) Ltd., New Delhi.
159. Joki, Russell A. "Make Teacher Competency your policy". American School Board Journal 169, (November 1982): 32.
160. Kukreti (1994). *Job motivation and teacher competency. A correlation and study.* Experiments in education. Indian Educational Abstract Issue-2. 22(1):10-14.

❑❑❑